GLOBAL PERSPECTIVES ON ETHICS OF CORPORATE GOVERNANCE

GLOBAL PERSPECTIVES ON ETHICS OF CORPORATE GOVERNANCE

G.J. (Deon) Rossouw and
Alejo José G. Sison (Editors)

GLOBAL PERSPECTIVES ON ETHICS OF CORPORATE GOVERNANCE
© G.J. (Deon) Rossouw and Alejo José G. Sison (Editors), 2006.

First published in 2006 by
PALGRAVE MACMILLAN™
175 Fifth Avenue, New York, N.Y. 10010 and
Houndmills, Basingstoke, Hampshire, England RG21 6XS
Companies and representatives throughout the world.

PALGRAVE MACMILLAN is the global academic imprint of the Palgrave Macmillan division of St. Martin's Press, LLC and of Palgrave Macmillan Ltd. Macmillan® is a registered trademark in the United States, United Kingdom and other countries. Palgrave is a registered trademark in the European Union and other countries.

ISBN-13: 978–1–4039–7584–3
ISBN-10: 1–4039–7584–1

Library of Congress Cataloging-in-Publication Data
International Society for Business, Economics and Ethics. Quadrennial
    World Congress (3rd : 2004 : Melbourne, Australia)
      Global perspectives on ethics of corporate governance /
    G.J. (Deon) Rossouw & Alejo José G. Sison (Editors).
          p. cm.
      Papers presented at the 3rd Quadrennial Congress of the International Society for Business, Economics and Ethics held in Melbourne, Australia in 2004.
      Includes bibliographical references and index.
      ISBN 1–4039–7584–1
      1. Business ethics—Congresses. 2. Corporate governance—Moral and ethical aspects—Congresses. 3. Social responsibility of business—Congresses. I. Rossouw, Deon. II. Sison, Alejo. G. III. Title.
HF5387.I65 2006
174′.4—dc22   2006045304

A catalogue record for this book is available from the British Library.

Design by Newgen Imaging Systems (P) Ltd., Chennai, India.

First edition: December 2006

10 9 8 7 6 5 4 3 2 1

Printed in the United States of America.

Dedicated to
Georges Enderle
Founding Member and President of ISBEE (2001–2004)
in appreciation of his quest for global perspectives on the
Ethics of Business and Economics

CONTENTS

Part II   A Global Survey of Business Ethics and Corporate Governance

LIST OF TABLES

LIST OF FIGURES

FOREWORD

The logo of the First World Congress of the International Society of Business, Economics, and Ethics (ISBEE) 1996 in Japan was the famous woodblock print by Katsushika Hokusai (ca. 1830) "View of Fuji from beneath a Wave of the Sea at Kanagawa." It depicts huge and foaming waves, rocking boats with hard rowing oarsmen, and, in the back, the immutable Mount Fuji on solid ground. I believe it neatly captures and symbolizes the enormous challenges we face in our quest for global perspectives on the ethics of business and economics.

First of all, in the age of globalization, business and economics is not a peaceful lake but a stormy sea. The pressure, promise, and threat of global competition are stretching out to almost every corner of the world. The supply chains for goods and services are rapidly connecting countries and continents. And the international financial markets are now functioning twenty-four hours around the globe. Powerful business organizations are major drivers of globalization, and economic conflicts are at the root of countless societal problems. Indeed, business and economics from a global perspective are like stormy waters.

A second feature of the Hokusai painting shows that swimming or "bowling alone" (R. Putnam) is a recipe for drowning and destruction. We can survive the stormy sea only if we row and work together or by what the Japanese call "kyosei." The more global business and economics are becoming, the more global solidarity has to become.

Yet, as the painting also demonstrates, rowing together without a compass or point of reference like the Mount Fuji may result in going around in circles without reaching the shore and ultimately in perishing as well. What is needed is ethical guidance that makes sense and provides direction. Today the ethics of business and economics is particularly important, given their far-reaching influences on all spheres of life. This means that business and economics should not be treated as merely technical and value-neutral matters (which, by definition, cannot provide ethical guidance). Rather, overcoming ethical skepticism, we should explicitly deal with the normative-ethical dimension of economic life and engage in ethical reasoning.

This goal alone is already an enormous challenge a majority of business scholars and economists are neither prepared nor willing to address. They may deem ethics a purely private and subjective matter, abandoning the public sphere to a plain power play. And even if they talk of and deal with ethics and values, too often they do it only in a descriptive and comparative way, falling short of the normative discussion. Of course, thorough ethical reasoning is all but a simple exercise and needs acumen, sophistication, and wisdom. In fact, our view of Fuji might be hindered by the waves and obstructed by the storm. And even if we could easily perceive the mountain, could it really provide ethical guidance in other places than the sea at Kanagawa? Portraying Fuji as the lighthouse of the world, would this amount to a kind of ethical imperialism? Are not there other mountains like Everest, Kilimanjaro, Aconcagua, McKinley, or Monte Bianco that can symbolize ethical guidance as well? But then, would we glide into ethical relativism? Without pushing the symbolism of Hokusai's painting too much, it might become clear that the quest for global perspectives on the ethics of business and economics is a truly daunting challenge. Yet, to give up the quest is no option since we do live on the same planet, earth, and are being connected at a rapid pace.

Since its formation in 1989 ISBEE has pursued this quest with imagination, vigor, and perseverance, this book *Global Perspectives on the Ethics of Corporate Governance* being a recent testimony. As a group of committed people from all continents we have been trying to advance the search for global perspectives in multiple ways and may invent many more ways in the years to come, following the advice: "Ask and keep asking, and you will receive. Seek and keep seeking, and you will find." (Matthew 7,7).

Despite the fashionable talk of globalization, I think we are far less global than we believe to be. Therefore, sustained efforts are needed to develop truly global perspectives. We can do this by choosing appropriate topics such as corporate governance and fairness in international trade and investment. Instead of writing on remote countries and cultures, we can involve academics and business people from all parts of the world in order to share their thoughts and experiences with us. ISBEE did so in its world congresses and publications and certainly will continue to do so. We can ask our colleagues who teach business ethics to write case studies typical of their environments, which we may post on our websites and discuss with the authors in class through instant messengers on the internet (which, by the way, generated exciting experiences in my course on international business ethics). In order to strengthen the academic capacities of our friends in developing countries, we may promote the establishment of research centers and endowed chairs of business ethics in their own countries. Although communication, transportation, and traveling around the globe have become much easier in the past ten plus years, we still have to fight against many logistic barriers that make it hard to smoothly cross national borders. And, of course, the quest of global perspectives cannot and should not happen in the English language alone. There are more than 6,000 languages spoken in the world today, and most of us understand and speak only very few.

Georges Enderle
March 2006

BIOGRAPHICAL NOTES
ON THE AUTHORS

Heloisa B. Bedicks has been the managing director of the Brazilian Institute of Corporate Governance (IBGC) since April 2001. She holds a degree in Economics from Universidade Estadual de Campinas, in Accounting from Pontifícia Universidade Católica de Campinas and a postgraduate degree in Finance from Universidade Salesianas. She is a member of the board of directors of Mapfre Garantias e Créditos S.A. and chairperson of Tecelagem de Fitas Progresso Ltda. She also serves as a member of the advisory board of ABN AMRO Asset Management and Centro de Estudos em Sustentabilidade of Fundação Getulio Vargas—EAESP, São Paulo, Brazil.

Dr. Maria Cecilia Coutinho de Arruda is Associate Professor at the FGV-EAESP—Escola de Administração de Empresas de São Paulo da Fundação Getulio Vargas, where she teaches Business/Marketing Ethics and coordinates the Center of Studies for Ethics in Organizations. She is a founding member, the first and current president of ALENE—Latin American Business Ethics Network. Since 1997 she has served as an executive committee member of ISBEE—the International Society of Business, Economics, and Ethics.

Dr. Nobuyuki Demise is Professor of Business Philosophy at Meiji University, Tokyo, Japan. He is a member of the steering committee of Japan Corporate Governance Forum and secretary of the Japan Society of Business Administration. He authored *Corporate Governance and Accountability* (1997, in Japanese) and *Introduction to Business Ethics* (2004, in Japanese). In 2002, he gave a lecture on Corporate Governance and CSR to the Japan Association of Corporate Executives.

Dr. Wojciech W. Gasparski, Professor of Humanities, Dr. Sc., Vice Rector for Research of the Leon Kozminski Academy of Entrepreneurship and Management (LKAEM) Warsaw, director and founder of the Business

Ethics Centre. He is the Editor-in-Chief of *Praxiology*, the International Annual of Practical Philosophy and Methodology published by the Transaction Publishers (Somerset, NJ). Recently he published *French and Other Perspectives in Praxiology* (with V. Alexandre, 2005); *Lectures in Business Ethics—New Edition* (2004, in Polish).

David Kimber retired as an Associate Professor in the School of Management at RMIT University, Melbourne in 2005. He is currently a visiting Faculty member at the Indian Institute of Management—Bangalore in India and the IESEG business school in Lille, France. He has taught management, cross-cultural studies, corporate governance, international business, ethics and auditing at universities and colleges in China, Malaysia, Singapore, France, India, and Australia.

Dr. *Peter Koslowski*, Professor of Philosophy, especially Philosophy of Management and Organisations, Vrije Universiteit Amsterdam. His books include *Principles of Ethical Economy and Ethics of Capitalism* (in English and in several other languages). Personal Website: www.fiph.de/koslowski.

Dr. *David Lea* is a Professor of Philosophy in the Department of International Studies at the American University of Sharjah in the Emirate of Sharjah in the United Arab Emirates. His principal field is Applied Philosophy with central interests in the philosophical foundations of property rights and business ethics. However, he also has done research in the history of philosophy, publishing some of his work in this area in the *History of European Ideas* and *The European Legacy*. More recently he has developed interests in Islamic philosophy. He has published in the *Business Ethics Quarterly, the Journal of Applied Philosophy, Business Ethics: A European Review*, the *Pacific Economic Bulletin*, and *Middle East Policy*.

Ian B. Lee is an Assistant Professor at the University of Toronto, Faculty of Law. He holds law degrees from the University of Toronto (LL.B.) and Harvard Law School (LL.M.), and, before entering academia, practiced law with Sullivan & Cromwell LLP in Paris and New York. His research interests include corporate governance and corporate law theory.

Phillip Lipton is a Senior Lecturer in the Department of Business Law and Taxation, Monash University, Melbourne, Australia. He is a coauthor of the leading Australian company law text *Understanding Company Law* now in its thirteenth edition (2006). He is also a coproducer of a corporate law website www.lipton-herzberg.com.au and corporate governance website www.australian-corporate-governance.com.au.

John Little is the Director of CREDO (the newly established Centre for Research into Ethics and Decision-Making in Organisations) at the Australian Catholic University. He has been, for the most part of his career, a self-employed management consultant in strategic planning, leadership, and organizational change and an Associate Program Director with Mt. Eliza Centre for Executive Education of the Melbourne Business School at the University of Melbourne.

Dr. Doreen McBarnet is Professor of Socio-Legal Studies at Oxford University. She graduated from Glasgow University with an MA honors in History and Sociology, and PhD in the Sociology of Law. Her research has addressed various areas of law, including the criminal justice process. However, her main interest for many years now has been business and the law, particularly in the context of corporate finance, tax avoidance, creative accounting, and corporate responsibility. She teaches Corporate Responsibility for the MBA at Oxford's Said Business School. Her publications include the books *Conviction* (1981, 1983), *Creative Accounting and the Cross-Eyed Javelin Thrower* (with C. Whelan, and Wiley 1999), and *Crime, Compliance and Control* (2004).

Dr. G.J. (Deon) Rossouw is Professor and Head of the Philosophy Department at the University of Pretoria in South Africa. He was the founding president of the Business Ethics Network of Africa (BEN-Africa) and is the current president of the International Society for Business Economics and Ethics (ISBEE). He wrote four books on Business Ethics: *Business Ethics: A Southern African Perspective* (1994) and *Business Ethics in Africa* (2002), *Developing Business Ethics as an Academic Field* (2004) and *Business Ethics* (2004).

Dr. Lori Verstegen Ryan is Associate Professor of Management and Research Director of the Corporate Governance Institute at San Diego State University in California. She received her PhD in Management and MA in Philosophy from the University of Washington. She is an active member of the Academy of Management and Society for Business Ethics, and is Program-Chair Elect for the International Association for Business and Society.

Dr. Alejo José G. Sison teaches Philosophy and is the Rafael Escolá Chair of Professional Ethics at the School of Engineering (TECNUN) of the University of Navarre. Previously, he had worked at IESE (Barcelona) and at the University of Asia & the Pacific (Manila). His research deals with the issues at the juncture of Ethics with Economics and Politics. His book *The Moral Capital of Leaders: Why Virtue Matters* (2003) has been translated into Spanish

(2004) and Chinese (2005). He is currently working on a volume that brings Aristotle's ideas in the politics to bear on issues of corporate governance.

Dr. Josef Wieland is Professor of Business Administration and Economics with emphasis on Business Ethics at the University of Applied Sciences, Konstanz since 1995. He is director of the Konstanz Institut fur WerteManagement (KleM) and director of the Zentrum fur Wirtschaftsethik (Center for Business Ethics). His main fields of work are: Business Ethics; New Organizational Economics / Institutional Economics; Empirical research on equitableness and justice; and History of Economic Theory.

INTRODUCTION

G.J. (Deon) Rossouw and Alejo José G. Sison

Corporate governance has gained unprecedented prominence in recent years. The failures and successes of modern corporations are equally responsible for this. Modern corporations are not innocent victims of external conditions; rather, they created the very circumstances that made corporate governance so prominent. It cannot be denied that spectacular corporate failures, the abuse of managerial power, and the phenomenal growth in social power and influence of corporations contributed significantly to the prominence of corporate governance issues.

Corporate governance is geared toward ensuring that companies take responsibility for directing and controlling their affairs in a manner that is fair to stakeholders. This responsibility can be taken either voluntarily by the boards of directors of companies or imposed upon them by regulatory authorities. Also, the scope of stakeholders toward whom the company should be responsible is a contested issue, as some corporate governance regimes restrict these stakeholders almost exclusively to shareholders, whilst others are much more inclusive.

Irrespective of how corporate governance is conceived, it still has a distinct ethical character. This ethical character is reflected in that corporate governance requires companies to take responsibility for their impact on societies and on stakeholders. It therefore comes as no surprise that the prominence of corporate governance coincides with a rise in interest in business ethics.

This ethical nature of corporate governance is evident in the typical requirements of a corporate governance system, such as board composition and functioning, risk management and auditing, and reporting and disclosure requirements. All these requirements serve to ensure that the corporation will act in a manner that is fair, accountable, responsible, and transparent. Corporate governance on both regulatory and enterprise levels intends that a sound balance be struck between the interests of the company and those of its stakeholders. This gives rise to the hope that corporate governance will restore trust in business. This intrinsic ethical nature of corporate governance can be referred to as the ethics of governance.

It is useful to distinguish between the ethics of governance and the governance of ethics (Rossouw and Van Vuuren 2004, 197). The latter refers to how companies govern their ethical performance. It is manifested in how the board or executive management directs and controls the company in a way that the company as a whole acts with integrity. Members of the board and managers determine the ethical standards of the company on the strategic, systems, and operational levels and ensure that the company abides by them.

This book brings together perspectives from all continents on the ethics of governance and the governance of ethics. All contributions were originally presented at the Third Quadrennial World Congress of the International Society for Business, Economics and Ethics (ISBEE) held in Melbourne, Australia in 2004. The book consists of two parts. The first part of the book provides theoretical perspectives on the ethical dimension of corporate governance, while the second part is devoted to an empirical survey of the relation between business ethics and corporate governance in various regions of the world. This combination of perspectives ties in well with two of ISBEE's main objectives: (1) to enagage theoretically with the ethical dimension of business and economics, and (2) to generate perspectives from all parts of the world in order to develop global perspectives on the ethics of business and economics.

Part I. Theoretical Perspectives on the Ethics of Corporate Governance

The chapters in the first part of the book intends, to borrow a phrase from management guru Henry Mintzberg, to take a "hard look at the soft practice" of corporate governance (Mintzberg 2004). After all, corporate governance is nothing else but management at the topmost level of corporations. And as a "practice" it is certainly fraught with its share of ethical challenges and dilemmas.

In discussing the "practice" of management, Mintzberg takes pains in establishing that it is, above all, neither a "pure science" nor a "pure art." This insight also holds true for corporate governance. Good corporate governance is neither just a matter of rigid analysis and strict rule-following nor one of inspired and creative interventions exclusively. Rather, it relies heavily on a kind of knowledge that can be gained only through experience.

Such knowledge on good governance is thus hardly codifiable or trans-ferrable. However, this peculiar trait should not be an excuse for not sub-jecting the theory behind the ethics of corporate governance to a thorough examination, albeit from multiple interlocking perspectives as the following chapters purport to do.

One of the main approaches to the ethics of corporate governance adopts the viewpoint of rules and regulations. It focuses on laws that demarcate the regulatory environment in which corporations function, on the codes of conduct that apply to specific sectors of the economy or to individual firms, and on codes of best practice that certain boards of direc-tors voluntarily assume. Ian B. Lee of the University of Toronto explains in "Ethical Investing: Implications for Corporate Governance and Corporate Social Responsibility" (chapter 1) how the "nexus of contracts" theory of firms in fact supports ethical investing. There is nothing in this contractar-ian conception of the corporation that requires investment decisions to be based solely on the pursuit of profit or other self-interest. In "Toward Ethical Compliance: Lessons from Enron" (chapter 2) Doreen McBarnet of Oxford University enjoins us to look beyond outright fraud to the practice of "creative compliance". She forewarns us against pinning our hopes on law alone to improve corporate behavior; it is imperative that ethics inform the way business executives and their legal advisers take action. In the same vein David Lea of the American University of Sharjah underscores in "Stakeholder Theory and Imperfect Duties" (chapter 3) the priority of obligations over rights. Likewise, he clarifies the distinction between imperfect and perfect duties as well as the relation between imperfect duties and the virtues, drawing inspiration from the work of the British philosopher Onora O'Neill for this purpose.

Laws, regulations, and norms are absolutely necessary for good corporate governance. At the very least, they serve as safeguards against arbitrariness in practice. Yet, by themselves, they are clearly insufficient and require the complement of substantive goods and values. This is precisely what John Little of the Australian Catholic University explains in "Trust in the Mind and Heart of Corporate Governance" (chapter 4). With the help of some ideas from the Canadian thinker Bernard Lonergan he fashions a com-pelling account of how basic human goods, particular goods, and sustain-able goods should lay at the heart of decision making and action among the different corporate stakeholders. Regarding the all-but-forgotten notion of common good, Peter Koslowski of the Free University of Amsterdam insists that it is not only a political concept but also a managerial one. The common good is therefore totally germane to the practice of corporate governance, as the title of the piece "The Common Good of the Firm as the Fiduciary Duty of the Manager" (chapter 5) suggests. Management—a fortiori, corporate directors—is not only obliged to fulfill its fiduciary duty toward shareholders but is also bound to realize the common good of all the members of the firm.

Insofar as the work of a manager or corporate director on behalf of the common good defines the task or "office" of governance, we are reminded of the need for virtues, another traditional element in ethics. Virtues allow us to go beyond rules without breaking them and show us how to put goods into practice. To this end Alejo José G. Sison of the University of Navarra draws our attention in "Governance and Goverment from an Aristotelian Perspective" (chapter 6) to the blatant neglect of the virtues in the education and selection of corporate executives. This attitude is often accompanied by excessive dependence on rules, processes, and structures. Following Aristotle he develops the analogy between the tasks of a corporate director and a politician, and he presents a case in favor of the superiority of virtues (habits and customs) over laws and norms. Barring coercion, it is from habit and custom that laws draw strength. Continuing with this theme Wojciech Gasparski of the Kozminski Academy of Mangement and Entrepreneurship explores in "Corporate Governance and Management Science Theories" (chapter 7) the issue of legitimacy in corporate governance with the government of states as background.

By bringing together these different approaches based on norms, goods, and virtues we hope to have covered the three major theoretical pillars on which the ethics of corporate governance rests.

Part II. A Global Survey of Business Ethics and Corporate Governance

The chapters in the second part of the book are the outcome of a research project that was launched to gauge what the impacts of recent corporate governance reforms are on the role and prominence of business ethics in diverse regions of the world. For the purpose of this project the world was divided into six regions, namely, Africa, Asia–Pacific, Japan, Europe, Latin-America, and North America. Researchers from each of these regions investigated corporate governance regimes and recent corporate governance reforms in their respective regions to determine the impact thereof on business ethics. Amongst others they identified the different models of corporate governance in their regions, the nature and extent of stakeholder engagement, the role of business ethics within corporate governance as well as how business ethics is managed and reported.

In his report on Africa (chapter 8), Deon Rossouw from the University of Pretoria in South Africa examines the codes of corporate governance of the 14 African countries that already published national codes of corporate governance. He indicates that corporate governance reform in Africa is to a large extent driven from the bottom up. He also found that with the exception of one country all the others follow an inclusive corporate governance model that emphasizes stakeholder engagement.

David Kimber from RMIT University in Melbourne, Australia, joined forces with Phillip Lipton from Monash University in the same city to produce the Asia-Pacific report (chapter 9). In their survey they opted to study four countries in their region: Australia, China, Singapore, and India. They show how differrence with regared to historical development, cultural and social factors, legal system, political system, and economic development have a profound impact on the corporate governance models of these countries. This in turn influences the way business ethics is perceived and practiced.

In Japan, Nobuyuki Demise from Meiji University, Tokio (chapter 10), found that Japanese companies find themselves caught in a transition between two very different systems of board governance. Despite this uneasy transition, many Japanese companies have started institutionalizing business ethics in their organizations. He found that a number of prominent ethical issues dominate business ethics in Japan such as death from overwork (*karoshi*), harassment at work, illegal collusion (*dangou*), and defrauding consumers and governments.

The report on Europe was compiled by Josef Wieland from the University of Applied Sciences, in Konstanz, Germany (chapter 11). In his empiric study of Corporate Governance Codes from 22 countries in Western, Central, and Eastern Europe he shows that the predominant majority of European corporate governance codes orientate themselves to stakeholders and the company. They do not follow the maximizing model but the cooperation model of the company. Shareholders' interests are thus accepted as important, not as dominant.

Maria Cecilia Coutinho de Arruda from Escola de Administração de Empresas de São Paulo da Fundação Getulio Vargas, and her compatriot Heloisa B. Bedicks who is the managing director of the Brazilian Institute of Corporate Governance studied corporate governance developments in Argentina, Brazil, Chile, Colombia, Mexico, Peru, and Venezuela (chapter 12). They found a general incline in corporate governance awareness in these countries, which leads to a similar incline in awareness of the role and importance of business ethics as an integral part of good corporate governance.

Lori Verstegen Ryan from San Diego State University in California, United States, took charge of the North American survey, focusing on Mexico, United States and Canada (chapter 13). She found that differences between these countries in terms of ownership dispersion, level of corruption, and legislative intervention have a marked impact on how corporate governance and business ethics is perceived and practiced. Despite these differences all three countries currently share a common focus on fundamental corporate governance reform that has profound implications for business ethics.

The Challenge

The increasing mobility of capital and the emergence of a truly global market make interaction between different models of corporate governance and their respective ethical requirements inevitable. The global perspectives on corporate governance and business ethics that are introduced in this book can facilitate the comparative corporate governance discourse that follows in the wake of interaction between different models of governance. They can make a meaningful contribution in the search for a global convergence in corporate governance standards, whilst avoiding the rash imperialistic imposition of the standards and style of governance of one region of the world upon the rest of the globe. What needs to be avoided at all cost is that standards of governance and ethics that originated within a specific cultural and regional context be allowed to masquerade as global standards.

References

Rossouw, D., and Van Vuuren, L. 2004. *Business Ethics (3rd Ed.)*. Cape Town: Oxford University Press.

Mintzberg, H. (2004). *Managers Not MBAs: A Hard Look at the Soft Practice of Managing and Management Development*. San Francisco: Berret-Koehler.

PART I

THEORETICAL PERSPECTIVES ON THE ETHICS OF CORPORATE GOVERNANCE

CHAPTER 1

ETHICAL INVESTING: IMPLICATIONS FOR CORPORATE LAW AND CORPORATE SOCIAL RESPONSIBILITY

Ian B. Lee

Introduction

This chapter explores the implications of ethical investing—the making of investment decisions at least partly on the basis of considerations other than profit or self-interest—for the debate about corporate social responsibility and for certain related questions of corporate law. In particular, I address three topics. First, I argue that, contrary to popular belief, corporate law does not mandate "shareholder primacy," by which I mean that it does not obligate managers to disregard the interests of nonshareholders or to treat them as merely instrumental considerations in the service of shareholder wealth maximization. My argument highlights the importance of ethical investing for scholars interested in corporate social responsibility, since it turns out to be the preferences and behaviour of stockholders, to a greater extent than corporate law, that constrain managers' freedom to exercise their powers responsibly. The second topic I address concerns the conflict between the concept of ethical investing and the behavioural assumptions that underlie the standard line of argument in defense of shareholder primacy. Many corporate law theorists who endorse shareholder primacy respond to this conflict by characterizing ethical investing as either

irrational and aberrant, or else rational and potentially pernicious. I argue
that both of these responses are misguided.

Third and finally, I discuss the implications of the foregoing for two
concrete questions of corporate governance that arise in connection with
ethical investing, specifically the appropriateness of shareholders' use of the
proxy system to communicate with one another on matters of social
responsibility and the debate about whether corporate disclosure to
investors on matters of social responsibility should be mandatory. I argue in
support of the shareholder social proposal mechanism, but I express mis-
givings about mandatory social disclosure.

Is Corporate Social Responsibility Legal?

The Persistently Ambiguous State of the Law

The dominant view among U.S. legal academics is that managers' fiduciary
duty obligates them to maximize profits and requires all other considerations
to be instrumentally related to the primary goal of profit maximization.
One sign of the dominance of the shareholder primacy view is that even its
critics acknowledge its status as orthodoxy (Elhauge 2005; Blair and Stout
1999; Bakan 2004). However, the fact that a view is dominant does not
mean that it is correct. Indeed, no less an authority than the respected
former chief justice of Delaware's specialized corporate law court—
Chancellor William Allen—has described the law as "schizophrenic"
(1992). Upon close examination, it is apparent that the law is persistently
ambiguous as to the existence of a managerial duty to maximize shareholder wealth.

The high-water mark for shareholder primacy is the 1919 decision of
the Michigan Supreme Court in *Dodge v. Ford Motor Co.* Henry Ford had
proclaimed far and wide that the Ford Motor Co. had accumulated enough
wealth and that the focus of the business should thenceforth be to reduce
car prices, democratize car ownership, and create employment. In the face
of these statements, the court said:

> There should be no confusion (of which there is evidence) of the duties
> which Mr. Ford conceives that he and the stockholders owe to the general
> public and the duties which in law he and his co-directors owe to protesting,
> minority stockholders. A business corporation is organized and carried on
> primarily for the profit of the stockholders. (*Dodge*, 684)

The foregoing statement has led many people to believe that corporate law
obligates management to act exclusively with a view to the maximization

of the stockholders' profit (Bakan 2004, 36–37). However, subsequent cases have been much more nuanced. Indeed, many of them are sufficiently ambiguous that both commentators who believe that there is a duty under corporate law to maximize profits, and those who dispute this view, claim that the same cases are supportive of, or at least consistent with, their contradictory positions.[1]

Consider, for example, the well-known case of *Theodora v. Henderson* (1969), in which the court held that corporate management may make reasonable charitable donations. The court's opinion opens with the observation that it is per se appropriate for managers to make such donations, in light of corporations' social responsibilities (*Theodora*, 404). But the court also observes that the shareholders benefited from the particular donation, in the long run (*Theodora*, 405). The opinion is drafted in such a way that one cannot tell from reading it whether the decision rests on the first, the second, or both of these elements. Moreover, if shareholder benefit was a necessary condition of the donation's legality, the court paid no more than lip service to it, since the benefit identified by the court could not have been more tenuous. According to the Court, the charitable donation benefited the shareholders by helping to legitimate the institution of private property (*Theodora*, 405).

Two reasons explain why the courts have been able to preserve ambiguity on the question of shareholder primacy. The first is that there is almost always a plausible profit-oriented rationalization for an act of corporate social responsibility. It is not difficult to defend as a profitable business strategy a policy of dealing generously with customers and employees. Acting with sensitivity to broader social and environmental concerns may with similar ease be rationalized by citing their importance to the corporation's customers or regulators. The second reason for the persistence of ambiguity is that courts are loath to second-guess, in hindsight, the merits of management's business judgments.[2] As the court in *Dodge v. Ford* said, "judges are not business experts" (*Dodge*, 684). Together, as *Theodora* demonstrates, these two facts make it virtually impossible for a dissenting shareholder to challenge an act of corporate social responsibility in court. It is sometimes forgotten that even in *Dodge v. Ford* itself, the court ultimately refused to interfere with management's plan to reduce prices because the judges were not certain that the plan would not ultimately result in greater profits (*Dodge*, 684).

The takeover context is sometimes cited by defenders of shareholder primacy as a situation in which the case law endorses their view. However, the takeover context is distinguished by the fact that the bidder is making an offer to the shareholders to buy their shares, with the consequence that management's defensive tactics could be seen as an intrusion into the shareholders' freedom to dispose of their shares. Yet, even here, one finds that the courts stop short of imposing shareholder primacy (all that is needed is "rationally related benefits" to shareholders) (*Revlon* 1986, 182) unless a change of control or break-up of the corporation is inevitable (*Paramount* 1990, 1994). And, outside of this special situation in which the directors try to stand between the shareholders and their sovereign right to dispose of their shares, the case law nurtures both sides of the shareholder primacy debate.

Market Constraints versus Legal Constraints

The argument that managers have a fiduciary duty to focus exclusively on the maximization of shareholder value is to be distinguished from a different and stronger argument, namely that structural features of corporate law—especially the market for corporate control—provide managers with incentives to do so (Manne 1965, 112–113; Mitchell 2001, 99–108). However, the essential point is that corporate law does not impose profit maximization on corporations or on managers. It simply subjects management's determination of the "best interests of the corporation" to discipline by market forces, especially the stock market. Managing a corporation in a way that is congenial to current and potential shareholders will be rewarded with a higher stock price. By contrast, if management departs from what shareholders want, the stock price will suffer and management will be punished either through the operation of equity-based compensation or, in more extreme cases, because a depressed stock price makes the corporation a takeover target. Thus, to a degree of approximation, it is the aggregated preferences of stockholders that ultimately determine management's freedom to act responsibly, just as the aggregated preferences of consumers ultimately determine whether cosmetics are "cruelty-free" and whether the tuna fishery is "dolphin-safe."

The latter point highlights the relationship between ethical investing and corporate social responsibility. Ethical investors—investors for whom ethical considerations are relevant, in addition to the financial considerations of risk and expected return—are significant because with them, and not managers alone, lies any hope one might have for greater corporate social responsibility.

Ethical Investing and the Theoretical Underpinnings of Shareholder Primacy

Most corporate law academics in the United States believe not only that the law endorses shareholder primacy as a descriptive matter, but also that shareholder primacy is normatively desirable. In this part, I discuss the conventional argument in support of shareholder primacy and identify the conflict that exists between the behavioural assumptions underlying that argument and the concept of ethical investing. I warn against responding to this conflict by disparaging ethical investing, as some prominent theorists have done.

Ethical Investing and the Nexus of Contracts

There was a time when the conventional argument for shareholder primacy rested on the notion that the shareholders are the owners of the corporation and, on its corollary, that the directors and managers ought to be viewed as, in essence, the shareholders' employees. This view rested on an analogy between corporations and partnerships, and predominated in the mid- to late-nineteenth century, when the analogy corresponded more closely to economic reality than it does now (Allen 1992, 266).[3] The idea of shareholders as owners remains a popular metaphor (Friedman 1970). However, it has fallen by the wayside within the legal academy as corporations have grown in size and as their shareholders, more numerous and less active, have come to seem less like owners and more like suppliers of passive capital.[4] In addition, with the rise of pragmatic approaches to law in the mid-twentieth century (Cohen 1935), scholars have turned away from legal constructs such as "ownership" as sources of justification.

The theoretical model of the corporation that now prevails in the corporate law academy rests on two pillars. One pillar of the model is the "nexus of contracts," or contractarian conception of the corporation (Jensen and Meckling 1976; Easterbrook and Fischel 1989). According to this conception, what is most significant about the corporation is that shareholders, management, workers, and creditors all agree voluntarily to the terms of their participation in the corporation. No one forces them to join the corporation. As a result, the corporation should be viewed as a kind of bargain. The bargain, whatever its terms, should be upheld by the courts, just as they would enforce any other contract.

A second pillar of the model introduces the concept of presumed contractual terms. If for any reason the parties to the corporate bargain have not agreed explicitly as to how a particular matter would be dealt with, the law should impute to them the terms that reasonable people would have settled upon had they turned their minds to it. Thus, although the parties to the corporate bargain virtually never agree explicitly that the management shall be guided exclusively by the maximization of the stockholders' profits, the dominant view holds that there is a reason to presume such a term. The reason has to do with "agency costs," the costs associated with the imperfect diligence and loyalty of managers, including the costs involved in monitoring the latter's performance. Defenders of shareholder primacy suggest that the parties should be imagined to want to reduce "agency costs" by giving management a crisp command to maximize profits rather than a vaguely specified mandate that would involve the balancing of the disparate interests of more than one constituency (Easterbrook and Fischel 1989, 1446). They conclude that reasonable, self-interested participants in the corporation would agree at the outset that management should focus exclusively on the maximization of corporate profits. It is, therefore, appropriate that corporate law should presume such a term.[5]

Ethical investors are the fly in the ointment of this elegant argument. From the standpoint of the first pillar—the nexus of contracts—there is, of course, no conflict between ethical investing and the idea of the corporation as a bargain. Ethical investing is simply an exercise of the investor's freedom of contract. On the other hand, the practice of ethical investing is inconsistent with an additional behavioural assumption needed to support exclusive shareholder wealth maximization. Specifically, it is inconsistent with the implicit assumption that shareholders are interested only in keeping agency costs to a minimum and have no concern about the ethical conduct of the business or the impact of corporate activity on third parties.

Conceptualizations of Ethical Investing

We have seen that the concept of ethical investing is awkward for corporate law theorists who are committed to shareholder primacy, because of the conflict between ethical investing and the behavioral assumptions underlying shareholder primacy. At the same time, it is difficult for contractarians to attack ethical investing directly, because of their commitment to freedom of contract. When the defenders of shareholder primacy do not ignore ethical investing entirely, they typically respond to the conflict in one of two ways. They either exceptionalize it by dismissing ethical concerns as intrinsically irrelevant to investment or incorporate the concerns within an egoistic framework, raising the spectre of rent-seeking.

Are ethical considerations extraneous to investing?

Exemplary of the first response is a comment by Henry Manne, a pioneer in the economic analysis of corporate law. In response to an author who argued that investors were interested in both profit and social justice, Manne wrote:

> It is difficult to reconcile [that author's] two statements about shareholder motivation. . . . When he refers to shareholders wanting to make money, he

is probably referring to the mass of true investors . . . . When he refers to shareholders who want to make social policy, he is then talking about himself and company. (1972, 492)

To Manne, "true investors" are interested only in profits.

In my view, Manne's response may be faulted for mistaking a model for reality.[6] Economists conventionally model the capital markets as populated by investors interested only in wealth and the avoidance of risk. However, if one's preferred model assumes universal investor selfishness, and it turns out that some investors are not selfish, this deviation reflects on the validity and robustness of the model, and not on whether the people are "true investors."

Indeed, even people whose main goal is to profit financially from their investment will, one would expect, at least sometimes be influenced in their decisions by nonfinancial aspects of their investment. To draw an analogy, the fact that the main purpose of a car is to provide transportation does not mean that when purchasing a car, suitability for transportation is the sole criterion. Also, in operating a car—in deciding whether to accelerate, brake, or turn—the sole consideration need not be that the passengers and cargo are brought more quickly to their destination. Car buyers may care about creating jobs domestically or rewarding a local dealership's sponsorship of an amateur sports team. A driver may swerve to avoid a pedestrian or prevent a collision. Similarly, even individuals whose main purpose in investing in shares is to provide for their retirement may be influenced by the knowledge that that the issuer of the shares earns some portion of its profits from, say, the sale of tobacco to children, and such investors may rationally be influenced by this factor in their investment decision.

To be sure, just as behavioural economists have emphasized that individuals exhibit "bounded rationality" (Jolls, Sunstein, and Thaler 1998, 1477–78), so too do they exhibit what I have termed "bounded empathy" (Lee 2005a, 19–21). The fact that individuals' empathy is bounded is no threat to the relevance of ethical deliberation for human behaviour, any more than evidence of bounded rationality justifies the abandonment of rational choice theory. Nevertheless, at least three factors limit our conscientiousness as shareholders. First, the victims of corporate irresponsibility are often far away and their suffering unseen, which may dull our empathy. As Adam Smith famously observed, even catastrophic harm to "a hundred millions" of people far away moves any of us far less than a "paltry misfortune" to ourselves (1976, 136–37). Second, the opacity of the corporate world may deceive us into overlooking the fact that corporate activities are undertaken for our benefit as shareholders. Many are the critics of corporate irresponsibility who blame "psychopathic corporations" without recalling that shareholders are the beneficiaries of corporate conduct and that it is ultimately the shareholders' preferences that determine the extent of managers' freedom to deviate from profit maximization.[7] Third, shareholders may feel that they are not responsible for corporate conduct over which, as individuals, they have no practical influence. We may not always be mindful of Louis Brandeis' suggestion that it is sufficient to engage our responsibility as shareholders for corporate behaviour that we "accept the benefits of the system" (1965, 75).

I do not deny, therefore, that investors will often ignore or overlook ethical considerations, or that such considerations will often be overshadowed by narrower financial motivations. I merely suggest that it is a mistake to suggest, as some theorists have done, that ethical conscientiousness is intrinsically alien to investing.

Is the ethical investor a rent-seeker? The theorists' second response to ethical investing is to expand the notion of self-interest to accommodate a "taste for social responsibility." On this approach, "socially responsible" portfolio selection is unobjectionable as it amounts to a consumption decision, by which those investors who are so inclined willingly sacrifice financial returns to obtain some other desired benefit, such as the promotion of a particular social cause (Langbein and Posner 1980, 74–75).[8]

However, theorists who adopt this approach tend to be hostile to investor activism, which they regard as rent-seeking behavior. For example, Daniel Fischel, another law professor known for his contributions to the economic analysis of corporate law, wrote:

> [L]et us assume a corporation decides to modify its behavior . . . in direct response to [socially motivated shareholder advocacy]. While reformers would no doubt be ecstatic about this result, shareholders as a class have little to be excited about. What has occurred is that a tiny minority . . . has caused the corporation to abandon a wealth-maximizing strategy favored by the majority of shareholders. (1982, 1279)

This hostility is, in my view, misplaced. In the first place, it rests upon a questionable philosophical premise, namely the denial of any distinction between serving one's own interest and trying to do the right thing.[9] Here again, I would warn against our becoming so committed to the egoistic assumption underlying the conventional defense of shareholder primacy that we cannot understand the exercise by individuals of their ethical faculties, when it occurs.

I would also suggest that shareholders' vulnerability to rent-seeking is exaggerated. A defining characteristic of share ownership in a widely held corporation is liquidity. Shareholders unhappy with excessively responsible corporate policies, or with the particular social causes whose proponents succeed in capturing management's attention, have available to them the same "Wall Street Rule" that some defenders of shareholder primacy have historically urged socially conscious shareholders to use,[10] and they are, of course, also protected by the market for corporate control.

For these reasons, I conclude that the conceptualization of ethical investing by defenders of shareholder primacy, either as aberrant or as potentially pernicious rent-seeking, is misguided.

Concrete Questions

Ethical investing is rarely discussed in corporate law literature, with the exception of two specific issues. The first is whether corporate law should filter out socially motivated shareholder proposals; the second, whether corporate disclosure of "social information" should be mandatory.

Shareholder Proposals

Rule 14a-8 under the U.S. Securities Exchange Act of 1934 permits a shareholder to submit a proposed resolution and a short supporting statement, which corporate management must include in the annual proxy circular sent to all shareholders. These resolutions sometimes relate to social responsibility matters.

Many economic theorists of corporate law are critical of shareholder social responsibility proposals. For instance, Roberta Romano has described such proposals as hostile to the "objective of U.S. corporate law," that is, the maximization of corporate profits (2001, 186 n. 30). Manne and Fischel have criticized social proposals as an attempt by activists to obtain publicity at the expense of shareholders generally (Manne 1972, 491; Fischel 1982, 1279; Liebeler 1984, 425).

For many opponents the shareholder proposal mechanism itself (never mind proposals directed at social responsibility) is of dubious utility. Rational shareholders are not interested in being involved (even through voting) in questions relating to the management of the corporation: rational shareholders invest in widely held corporations *because of* and not despite the separation of ownership and control. Moreover, shareholders have no reason to vote on a shareholder proposal or on any other matter submitted to shareholders, since they rationally have no expectation that their vote will make a difference to the outcome. For both of these reasons, economic theorists of the corporation typically have difficulty reconciling their model with the shareholder proposal mechanism.

The debate about shareholder social responsibility proposals raises two subquestions. First, are matters of corporate social responsibility any business of the shareholders? Second, if the answer to the first question is affirmative, should the proxy mechanism be available for communication on such matters?

In answer to the first question, it appears to me that corporate social responsibility *is* the shareholders' business. Shareholders have an ethical stake in the conduct of the business, as they occupy voluntarily the position of ultimate beneficiaries of that conduct. To be sure, the expectation of nonpivotality creates a disincentive to vote. However, some individuals will still cast votes, as many do in political elections, out of a desire to express their values or to participate in or dissociate themselves from a collective activity.

The answer to the second question turns on whether the dissemination of the relevant communications is beneficial to the shareholders as a whole or only to the proposing shareholder. If the former, then the costs should be subsidized by the corporation; if the latter, the costs should not be subsidized. Arguments against shareholder social proposals tend to presuppose that the communications are of no benefit to shareholders as a whole, but this assumption may be unwarranted. By enabling informed shareholders to alert others to possible sources of ethical concern in relation to their investment, the mechanism reduces the costs of gathering and analyzing this information for all shareholders.

Two additional considerations militate for the availability of the proxy mechanism for shareholder social proposals. First, the costs are modest: Alan Palmiter estimated in 1994 that corporations spent an aggregate of $15-million in circulating shareholder proposals (1994, 883).

Second, although Rule 14a-8 is formulated as mandatory, it explicitly permits corporations to exclude proposals that are inadmissible under state law (Rule 14a-8(i)(1)). In consequence, if enough shareholders believed that no communication from other shareholders on social responsibility matters would ever be of interest to them, one would expect to see some states amending their corporate law to exclude such resolutions. A prominent opponent of shareholder proposals has written in a different context that "states . . . have incentives to adopt efficient rules of corporate law to attract incorporations. . . . [State] rules that have survived over time, therefore, are entitled to at least a weak presumption of efficiency" (Fischel 1984, 135). By the same token, if states have not seen fit to rule out shareholder social resolutions and spare corporations the expense of circulating them, it casts doubt on the proposition that investors are ill-served by the status quo.

Mandatory Social Disclosure

Some "progressive" corporate law scholars, most notably Cynthia Williams (1999), have argued that the Securities and Exchange Commission should adopt rules requiring certain categories of "social disclosure" by public corporations. She argues that the information is relevant both to the purely economic aspect of an investment decision and to investors' social concerns.

I agree with an important premise of Williams' argument, namely, the rejection of a strict compartmentalization of human values that would categorically deny the relevance of ethical and social considerations to investment decisions. However, the burden upon the proponents of mandatory social disclosure is not to demonstrate the relevance of social information; they must explain why a disclosure regime for such information should be mandatory.

More specifically, the question arises as to why an SEC regulation should displace the existing market in social information. People who are interested in social information can obtain it from commercial information providers or can invest in mutual funds that add value in part by obtaining and analyzing information about corporations' social practices and impact. The argument for mandatory social diclosure presumes that investors are interested in social information, whereas opponents of mandatory social disclosure assert that they are not. The truth, as usual, is probably in-between: some investors want social information and some do not, and those who do vary in the type of information they want and in the value they attach to it. In the presence of such diversity, it is not clear why we should not rely on the market to determine the amount, type, and quality of social information rather than imposing a one-size-fits-all disclosure rule drawn up by the SEC.

Is there a market failure that would justify regulatory interference with the market outcome? The most commonly invoked market failure in the context of information markets concerns the so-called public goods character of information. The argument proceeds along the following lines: collective action problems deprive shareholders of information that they all want because none of them is willing to bear, alone, the costs of obtaining information that can then be used, for free, by everyone (Mendelson 1978, 53–54; Blair 1992). However, if social information were being underproduced for this reason, we would expect to observe free-riding by shareholders who would otherwise purchase social information. I doubt that the reason that commercial providers of social information to investors do not have more customers is that potential customers are obtaining the information elsewhere for free.

An influential argument against mandatory disclosure in general is that if enough investors are interested in a particular type of information and their willingness to pay is sufficient to justify the cost of producing the information, corporations will make it available voluntarily. Thus, for instance, even unregulated institutional and offshore offerings not subject to the mandatory disclosure regime are accompanied by extensive voluntary disclosures. Critics of this argument have tended to raise two objections to it. First, they argue that even if corporations have incentives to make voluntary disclosures, a mandatory regime will supply standards that ensure that the information is comparable across firms (Williams 1999, 1293). Second, mandatory disclosure may be needed to overcome a "first-mover" problem: no corporation will want to move first in disclosing information about the social impact of its activities because it is likely to face criticism even if it is no less "socially responsible" than its nondisclosing rivals (*Anon.* 2002, 1452; Mehri, Giampetro-Meyer, and Runnels 2004, 444).

In relation to the first objection, diversity in social disclosure may admittedly impede interfirm comparisons, but it may also be the result of variations in the demand for social information across investors and in the type of information that is appropriate and cost-effective to provide in different business settings. In other words, there is a trade-off between desirable standardization and desirable responsiveness to diverse individual wants. In any event, even on the assumption that the desirability of standardization justifies public investment in the development of disclosure templates, it falls short of providing a reason for the disclosure itself to be mandatory.

As for the second objection, it may insufficiently credit the ability of firms with especially strong social responsibility records to find ways of communicating to investors (and consumers) their advantages over their rivals. Moreover, where voluntary disclosure by corporations fails to provide information desired by investors, third-party providers of information will often be more than happy to do so, if the investors' willingness to pay justifies the cost of producing the information.

The substitution of a regulatory regime for the current market in social information would also pose two major problems. First, how would a regulator determine what information to require? There is, in my view, a real risk that an SEC social disclosure regulation would resemble a laundry-list of the causes that happen to be fashionable at the time the regulation is written.

Second, the compliance costs of a mandatory social disclosure regime, unlike those of the shareholder proposal mechanism, are likely to be considerable. Total compliance costs associated with the general mandatory disclosure regime were estimated at $1 billion in 1980 (*Anon.* 2002, 1451). Those associated with the new requirements imposed by the Sarbanes-Oxley Act (2002) have been estimated at $12 billion per year (Cunningham 2004, 280, n. 41). Without a widespread belief on the part of investors that the information is useful to them, I fear that the result is likely to be perfunctory compliance by management and resentment on the part of the majority of investors.

Conclusion

Corporate law does not obligate managers to maximize profits: the letter of the law is ambiguous, and in practice the courts will not interfere. Structural features of corporate law, especially the market for corporate control, tend to align managers' incentives with the interests of shareholders. In consequence, it is the aggregated preferences of shareholders as revealed in the stock market that largely determine the extent of managers' freedom to exercise their powers responsibly.

We need not be hopelessly idealistic to believe that shareholders have, and are capable of recognizing, ethical responsibilities in relation to their investment decisions. Corporate law is largely accommodating of these responsibilities, as it should be. On the other hand, there is a tension between the concept of ethical investing and the behavioral assumptions that underlie the arguments for shareholder primacy that are widely accepted within the corporate law academy. Many prominent defenders of shareholder primacy have responded to this tension by disparaging ethical investing, conceptualizing it as aberrant or irrational, or as potentially pernicious rent-seeking. The main argument of this chapter has been to counsel against this approach. If the behavior of ethical investors deviates from the assumptions that underlie conventional understandings of the corporation, it is a reflection, not of the irrelevance of ethical and social responsibility to the shareholder's decision, but of the limitations of the dominant theoretical framework.

Notes

This chapter is based on remarks presented at the World Congress of the International Society for Business, Economics, and Ethics, held in Melbourne in July 14–17, 2004. The themes dealt with in this chapter are explored at greater

length in an article published in the Stanford Journal of Law, Business and Finance
(Lee 2005a). Thanks to Heidi Libesman for comments on a draft and to Huw Evans
for research assistance.

1. See *e.g. Shlensky v. Wrigley*, 237 N.E.2d 776 (Ill. App. Ct. 1968), cited
   both by Blair and Stout, 303, n. 141 (arguing against the existence of a
   shareholder wealth maximization rule) and by Stephen M. Bainbridge,
   "Director Primacy: The Means and Ends of Corporate Governance,"
   Northwestern University Law Review 97 (2003): 547, at p. 601, n. 266 (argu-
   ing for the existence of such a rule); and *Credit Lyonnais Bank Nederland
   N.V. v. Pathé Communications Corp.*, No. 12150, 1991 Del. Ch. LEXIS
   215 (Dec.30, 1991) cited both by Blair and Stout, 295–96, and by Jeffrey
   G. MacIntosh, "The End of Corporate Existence: Should Boards Act as
   Mediating Hierarchs?: A Comment on Yalden" in Anita I. Anand and
   William H. Flanagan, eds., *The Corporation in the 21st Century: Ninth
   Annual Queen's Business Law Symposium* (Kingston: Queen's University,
   Faculty of Law, 2003) at 56 (arguing that the case confirms that when the
   corporation is solvent directors must maximize profits).
2. See *e.g. Aronson v. Lewis*, 473 A.2d 805 (Del. 1984); *Kamin v. American
   Express*, 383 NYS 2d 807 (Sup. Ct. 1976), aff'd 387 NYS 2d 993
   (App. Div. 1976); *Smith v. Van Gorkom*, 488 A.2d 858 (Del. 1985).
3. Among other things, the theory spawned the U.S. Supreme Court's
   famous holding in 1886 that the Fourteenth Amendment applies to corporations: corporate property was protected because, it was in essence, the
   shareholders' property. See Horwitz (1985, 181–182).
4. Horwitz 1986, 223 (discussing the displacement of the so-called aggregate
   theory in the early 20th century as the more passive role of shareholders
   reduced the theory's "evocative power").
5. For most of these theorists, shareholder primacy is only a presumption
   and, therefore, may be overridden if there is evidence of a different actual
   bargain. As examples, these theorists point to companies such as the
   New York Times, in which the priority of journalistic objectives over
   profits is written into the corporation's charter (see Easterbrook and
   Fischel 1989, 1427).
6. See, for example, David Wishart (2003, 546) (warning against "recon-
   structing the world to fit the theory").
7. I have argued elsewhere that Joel Bakan (2004) commits this error in his
   diagnosis of corporations as "psychopaths." See Lee (2005b).
8. Under this approach, the practice becomes diversion when it is done by
   intermediaries, such as pension funds, without the consent of the principals
   or beneficiaries (Langbein and Posner 1980).
9. For discussion of the related debate about psychological egoism, see, for
   example, Feinberg (1978); LaFollette (1989); Sober (2000).
10. See Fischel (1982, 1278) ("[t]he ability freely to sell one's shares, . . . the so-
    called 'Wall Street Rule,' is without question the single most important
    safeguard to all shareholders that managers will act in their best interests").

References

Allen, William T. 1992. Our Schizophrenic Conception of the Corporation. *Cardozo Law Review* 14: 261–281.

Anon. 2002. Should the SEC Expand Nonfinancial Disclosure Requirements? *Harvard Law Review* 115: 1433–1455.

Aronson v. Lewis, 473 A.2d 805 (Del. Ch. 1984).

Bainbridge, Stephen M. 2003. Director Primacy: The Means and Ends of Corporate Governance. *Northwestern University Law Review* 97: 547–606.

Bakan, Joel. 2004. *The Corporation: The Pathological Pursuit of Profit and Power.* Toronto: Penguin Group.

Blair, Mark. 1992. The Debate over Mandatory Corporate Disclosure Rules. *University of New South Wales Law Journal* 15: 177–195.

Blair, Margaret M., and Lynn A. Stout. 1999. A Team Production Theory of Corporate Law. *Virginia Law Review* 85: 247–328.

Brandeis, Louis D. 1965. On Industrial Relations. In *The Curse of Bigness: Miscellaneous Papers of Louis D. Brandeis*, ed. O.K. Fraenkel. Port Washington, NY: Kennikat Press, pp. 70–95.

Cohen, Felix S. 1935. Transcendental Nonsense and the Functional Approach. *Columbia Law Review* 35: 809–849.

Credit Lyonnais Bank Nederland N.V. v. Pathé Communications Corp., No. 12150, 1991 Del. Ch. LEXIS 215 (Dec. 30, 1991).

Cunningham, Lawrence A. 2004. The Appeal and Limits of Internal Controls to Fight Fraud, Terrorism, Other Ills. *Journal of Corporation Law* 29: 267–336.

Dodge v. Ford Motor Co., 170 N.W. 668 (Mich. 1919).

Easterbrook, Frank H., and Daniel R. Fischel. 1989. The Corporate Contract. *Columbia Law Review* 89: 1416–1448.

——. 1991. *The Economic Structure of Corporate Law.* Cambridge: Harvard University Press.

Elhauge, Einer. 2005. Sacrificing Corporate Profits in the Public Interest. *New York University Law Review* 80: 733–869.

Feinberg, Joel. 1978. Psychological Egoism. In *Reason and Responsibility: Readings in Some Basic Problems of Philosophy*, ed. J. Feinberg. Encino: Dickenson Publishing Company, 529–539.

Fischel, Daniel R. 1982. The Corporate Governance Movement. *Vanderbilt Law Review* 35: 1259–1292.

——. 1984. Insider Trading and Investment Analysis: An Economic Analysis of *Dirks v. Securities and Exchange Commission. Hofstra Law Review* 13: 127–146.

Friedman, Milton. 1970. The Social Responsibility of Business Is to Increase Its Profits. *The New York Times Magazine*, September 13, p. 6.

Jensen, Michael C., and William H. Meckling. 1976. Theory of the Firm: Managerial Behavior, Agency Cost, and Ownership Structure. *Journal of Financial Economics* 3: 305–360.

Jolls, Christine, Cass Sunstein, and Richard Thaler. 1998. A Behavioral Approach to Law and Economics. *Stanford Law Review* 50: 1471–1550.

Kamin v. American Express, 86 Misc. 2d 809 (N.Y. 1976).

LaFollette, Hugh. 1989. The Truth in Psychological Egoism. In *Reason and Responsibility: Readings in Some Basic Problems of Philosophy*, ed. J. Feinberg. Belmont: Wadsworth Publishing Company, pp. 500–507.

Langbein, John H., and Richard A. Posner. 1980. Social Investing and the Law of Trusts. *Michigan Law Review* 79: 72–112.

Lee, Ian B. 2005a. Corporate Law, Profit Maximization and the "Responsible" Shareholder. *Stanford Journal of Law, Business and Finance* 10: 31–72.

———. 2005b. Is There a Cure for Corporate "Psychopathy"? *American Business Law Journal* 42: 65–90.

Liebeler, Susan W. 1984. A Proposal to Rescind the Shareholder Proposal Rule. *Georgia Law Review* 18: 425–468.

MacIntosh, Jeffrey G. 2003. The End of Corporate Existence: Should Boards Act as Mediating Hierarchs?: A Comment on Yalden. In *The Corporation in the 21st Century: The Ninth Annual Queen's Business Law Symposium*, ed. A.I. Anand and W.F. Flanagan. Kingston: Queen's University (Canada), Faculty of Law, pp. 37–75.

Manne, Henry G. 1965. Mergers and the Market for Corporate Control. *Journal of Political Economy* 73: 110–120.

———. Shareholder Social Proposals Viewed by an Opponent. *Stanford Law Review* 24: 481–506.

Mehri, Cyrus, A., Giampetro-Meyer, and M.B. Runnels. 2004. One Nation, Indivisible: The Use of Diversity Report Cards to Promote Transparency, Accountability, and Workplace Fairness. *Fordham Journal of Corporate and Financial Law* 9: 395–448.

Mendelson, Morris. 1978. Economics and the Assessment of Disclosure Requirements. *Journal of Comparative Corporate Law and Securities Regulation* 1: 49–68.

———. 2001. *Corporate Irresponsibility: America's Newest Export*. New Haven, CT: Yale University Press.

Palmiter, Alan R. 1994. The Shareholder Proposal Rule: A Failed Experiment in Merit Regulation. *Alabama Law Review* 45: 879–926.

Paramount Communications, Inc. v. QVC, 637 A.2d 34 (Del. 1994).

Paramount Communications, Inc. v. Time Inc., 571 A.2d 1140 (Del. 1990).

Posner, Richard A. 1998. Rational Choice, Behavioral Economics, and the Law. *Stanford Law Review* 50: 1551–1575.

Revlon, Inc. v. MacAndrews and Forbes Holdings, Inc., 506 A.2d 173 (Del. 1986).

Romano, Roberta. 2001. Less is More: Making Institutional Investor Activism a Valuable Mechanism of Corporate Governance. *Yale Journal on Regulation* 18: 174–251.

Sarbanes-Oxley Act of 2002, Pub. L. No. 107–204, 116 Stat. 745.

Shlensky v. Wrigley, 237 N.E.2d 776 (Ill. App. Ct. 1968).

Smith, Adam. 1976. *The Theory of Moral Sentiments*, ed. D.D. Raphael and A.L. Macfie. Oxford: Oxford University Press.

Smith v. Van Gorkom, 488 A.2d 858 (Del. 1985).

Sober, Elliott. 2000. Psychological Egoism. In *The Blackwell Guide to Ethical Theory*, ed. H. LaFollette. Oxford: Blackwell Publishers Ltd., 129–148.

Theodora Holding Corp. v. Henderson, 257 A.2d 298 (Del. Ch. 1969).

U.S. Securities Exchange Act of 1934, 17 C.F.R. §240.14a-8 (2004).

Vermont Business Corporations Law, Vt. Stat. Ann. tit. 11A, §8.30 (2004).

Williams, Cynthia A. 1999. The Securities and Exchange Commission and Corporate Social Transparency. *Harvard Law Review* 112: 1197–1311.

Wishart, David. 2003. Arguing against the Economics of (Say) Corporations Law. *University of New South Wales Law Journal* 26: 540–566.

CHAPTER 2

TOWARD ETHICAL COMPLIANCE: LESSONS FROM ENRON

Doreen McBarnet

Introduction

In any contemporary discussion of corporate governance and the erosion of trust in business, one name is unavoidable: Enron. Enron has become an icon for corporate fraud on a massive scale with, to date, 30 indictments, going to the top of the corporate hierarchy. There has also been an extensive legislative response. In any attempt to restore trust, however, two points will have to be acknowledged. First, Enron has exposed to a wider public not just vast fraud, but the pervasive practice of "creative compliance" (McBarnet and Whelan 1997; McBarnet 2003). The irony is that much of Enron's misleading accounting was based on "perfectly legal" devices that constitute normal business practice in the United States and beyond. Second, we need to take care in pinning our hopes on change only through law. Legal regulation of business cannot succeed without a new focus on business ethics—not ethics as ancillary to law, but ethics as intrinsic to the way business executives and their advisers view law and define their responsibilities under it. This chapter draws on empirical research to demonstrate the limits of law and the need for a shift in the ethics of compliance.

Many of Enron's practices involved outright breach of law, but they also demonstrate creative accounting. Its core technique was the use of "special purpose vehicles" (SPVs) that were structured with a close eye on the rules of law, such that they fell outside the technical definitions of subsidiaries and did not have to be included in Enron's accounts. It could be argued from SEC guidelines (Partnoy 2003) that if just 3 percent of SPV capital came from an independent outside body that bore the risk on it, and controlled the SPV, then the vehicle could be treated as "off balance sheet" (OBS). Huge debts and losses could therefore be omitted from Enron's own books, boosting its performance and enhancing its value. Complex deals, largely using derivatives, were then done between the SPVs and Enron itself, both to formally manage risk and to further enhance reportable financial performance. Some 4300 SPVs were in play by the time of Enron's demise.

These transactions were astonishingly complex and the indictments involve clear allegations of fraud in the construction of the deals. Enron's core SPVs did not always comply with the rules that allow such entities to remain off the balance sheet. There were instances in which the 3 percent rule was invoked to justify an accounting treatment, but not actually adhered to (Powers 2002). Yet, even if Enron had only engaged in off balance sheet structuring *within* the rules, it could still have kept significant debts and losses out of its own accounts. Indeed it is arguable that much of Enron's off balance sheet activity did not breach the rules. Rather it creatively exploited the rules or utilised regulatory gaps, including the "regulatory black hole" of derivatives (Partnoy 2002, 2). Certainly, Enron's OBS vehicles were not, as has sometimes been said, "secret" partnerships. Their existence was disclosed in the notes to the accounts as is required by the rules. They may have been disclosed in ways that were economic with the truth, or via other forms of "non-disclosing disclosure" (McBarnet 1991, 2004) but they were disclosed. Enron demonstrates not just fraud but creative compliance at work—but the effect is the same. Corporate governance is undermined, false images of financial performance are projected, shareholders and wider stakeholders are deceived.

Enron: The Tip of the Iceberg

Enron is far from alone in setting up OBS SPVs to hide liabilities and create paper profits, and this practice has a long history. My own research in the UK in the late 1980s and 1990s demonstrated the widespread use of SPVs and other OBS techniques to manipulate accounts. Creative accounting, generally, was rife in the UK in this period (Griffiths 1986). Similar practices were in use in the United States. Partnoy, for example, notes that "accounting subterfuge using derivatives is widespread" (Partnoy 2002). Nor is creative accounting an Anglo-Saxon phenomenon. One Enron indictment concerns abuse of reserves but our research demonstrated use of reserves to be common practice in Germany as a way of manipulating accounts.

OBS SPVs were routinely used in the UK in the 1980s, by household name companies, to manipulate accounts. "Nonsubsidiary subsidiaries" were set up, companies that were in economic substance subsidiaries, but carefully structured in their legal form to fall outside the rules defining a subsidiary (subsidiaries' finances having to be included in group accounts). Debts or losses could then be tidied away in them, off the balance sheet of the company setting them up.

As company law rules defining subsidiaries stood, it was far from difficult to keep bad financial news hidden in a way that could claim to be not breaking the rules but complying with them and therefore "perfectly legal." True, company law also contained the overriding principle that accounts should give a true and fair view, and the accounts produced after the set-up of such SPVs, it could be, and was, argued, did not do that, but accountants and lawyers looked to the detail of the law, to specific definitions and precedents, queried the meaning of "true and fair" and its capacity to override specific rules, and endorsed the practice. Companies could properly claim they had the approval of their advisers. Just like Enron.

Also like Enron they sometimes had to shop around to get accountants and lawyers who would say that some of their more exotic structures and accounting innovations were perfectly legal. But there was and is no requirement to disclose just how much opinion shopping had gone on until an endorsement was achieved. So long as one legal or accountancy firm was prepared to take a "bullish" interpretation of the law, that was all that was needed in practice to claim reporting treatments were perfectly legal.

OBS SPVs were used for all sorts of things including manufacturing paper profits. A property development company, for example, would set up an SPV for its development. It then lent it money for the purpose and charged interest. The SPV did not pay the interest but since the interest was *payable*, the company could add it to its books to enhance its profits (by many millions of pounds at a time). Meantime the SPV used another creative accounting technique, defining the interest as capital expenditure so the cost did not appear on its own profit and loss account (as a loss). Magic. Profits from nowhere and vanishing expenses. Just like Enron. Property development company, Rosehaugh, for example, had 16 SPVs. Just like Enron their existence was disclosed in the notes to the accounts, at length indeed—seven pages of detail—also, just like Enron's "impenetrable footnote disclosure" (Partnoy 2002) or "obtuse" provision of information (Powers 2002, 17), disclosure was opaque. Such "non-disclosing disclosure" is a recurrent theme in both creative accounting and tax avoidance (McBarnet 1991).

Unlike Enron most companies did not collapse, but they were still misleading the market. And keeping debts off the balance sheet and profits up had a number of valuable consequences, indeed purposes. Performance related pay and bonuses for senior executives could boom. Just like Enron. Huge debts could be taken out that would not have been possible if they had to go on the balance sheet—or at least would not have been possible without upsetting the debt/equity ratio. This ratio is key in corporate finance and corporate governance. It is used most obviously for assessing good/bad buys in the stock market. But it is also used as a trigger in loan covenants for calling in loans if banks think the company's debt is getting out of hand, and is also frequently used in a company's memorandum and articles of association, as a trigger requiring shareholder consultation before, for example, directors may make a highly leveraged acquisition. Artificially protecting the debt/equity ratio, then, meant basic corporate governance controls could be bypassed.

This was exemplified in the case of Beazer, a UK housebuilding company. It acquired, through an SPV, the U.S. corporation, Koppers, worth twice Beazer's own value, in a deal described as "impossible" and "sheer magic" (Angus Phaure of County NatWest, quoted in *Accountancy*, April 1988, 9). Just as in Enron, derivatives formally shifted the risk, which, however, ultimately fell on Beazer, not the SPV, and indeed came back to haunt it within a few years (McBarnet and Whelan 1997; McBarnet 2004).

And some companies did collapse. When property development company Rush and Tomkins went bust in 1991, an estimated £700 million pounds worth of hitherto unreported debts suddenly emerged from associated but OBS joint ventures (*Times*, April 30, 1990). Sometimes the scope to take on more debt than could really be sustained itself led to collapse— or fraud to try to hide it. Maxwell Corporation is best remembered for raiding pensions, but one of the reasons it did so was because it had overextended itself by buying MacMillan via huge debts. The purchase was made via an OBS SPV. It could not have been done without it, there being too much debt already. But in practice, as is often ultimately the case, the risk came back to Maxwell.

In short, Enron's manipulation of its accounts and other regulations needs to be understood in this wider context of normal business practice, normal, and arguably "perfectly legal" legal practice—"creative" rather than fraudulent accounting—yet nonetheless routinely frustrating the whole idea of true and fair accounts, routinely distorting market information, and undermining corporate governance.

Creative Compliance and the Limits of Law

The immediate reaction to a scandal such as Enron is a demand for legal change, and the United States quickly produced the Sarbanes-Oxley Act. But law is not always the panacea hoped for. Such problems as compromises built into new law, inadequate sanctions, and inadequate resources for policing, can all be listed as potential factors in law's failure to offer effective control. It is also increasingly recognized that new rules, even if they are fully resourced and uncompromised, can themselves prove inadequate simply because of the ability of the regulated to adapt to them. A new rule may stop today's objectionable creative accounting device, but leave the way open for the new device ingeniously constructed tomorrow to thwart the new rule. The more specific and prescriptive the rule is the clearer the criteria the new structure has to meet or circumvent.

In post–Enron, U.S. proposals have therefore been put forward not just for a tightening of regulations and strengthening of sanctions but for a change of regulatory style. The suggestion is that there should be less emphasis on specific rules and more on principles. Harvey Pitt, for example, SEC chairman at the time, argued to the House of Representatives: "Present day accounting standards are cumbersome and offer far too detailed prescriptive requirements for companies and their accountants to follow. We seek to move toward a principles-based set of accounting standards, where mere compliance with technical prescriptions is nether sufficient nor the objective." (Pitt 2002). This is exactly the strategy adopted by the UK in the 1990s in a bid to constrain creative accounting and specifically off balance sheet financing.

Enron's SPVs were built on rules and guidelines that determined whether or not an entity should be consolidated into a group's accounts partly on the basis of specific thresholds of equity ownership. This was also the case in 1980s company law in the UK. The rules on consolidation (the requirement for a holding company to include all its subsidiaries in its group accounts) at that time involved two questions for determining whether company B was a subsidiary of company A, and therefore had to have its financial accounts included in A's. First, does A own more than 50 percent in nominal value of B's equity share capital? Second, is A a member of B and does it control the composition of B's board of directors?

There were simple and complicated ways to ensure B fell outside these criteria and therefore could stay off A's balance sheet. It would be a "nonsubsidiary subsidiary," a subsidiary in substance but not in form. One way was to set up a "diamond structure," in which A set up 2 subsidiaries B and C, owning 100 percent of B and 50 percent of C. B and C then owned

50 percent each of D. A in effect owned 75 percent of D but D fell outside
the definitions of a subsidiary. Another route was for A to get a friendly
bank, B, to hold 50 percent of the SPV, C, in the form of preference shares.
C had a board of four directors, two from A and two from the Bank, but
A's directors had more voting rights and A therefore controlled the vote of
the board without controlling, as the statute phrased it, its composition.
Though such practices might have been constrained by concerns over challenge under the purportedly "overriding" principle that accounts give "a
true and fair view," the *Argyll* case (Ashton 1986; McBarnet and Whelan
1999), and wider legal discussions of the exact nature and status of the
"override" provided ammunition to counter any such challenge and
indeed, encouraged the spread of the practice.

Creative accounting using OBS techniques was rife, but there also
followed scandals, collapses, review committees, a campaign to clean up
accounting, and significant changes in law and in accounting regulation.
The story, and the changes made, are complex and are detailed elsewhere
(McBarnet and Whelan 1999), but for the purposes of this chapter the
point is that radical changes in the law were made, with the express purpose of controlling creative accounting, and specifically the abuse of OBS
financing and SPVs. What were these changes and how has the new regime
fared?

At the core of the new regime was the view that law was failing to
control creative accounting because of weak enforcement, inadequate
regulation, and too much emphasis on rules. Precise rules and thresholds
were too easy to circumvent; creative accounting thrived on repackaging
transactions and structures to fall just outside them. They provided too
clear a recipe for avoidance. Changing from one precise rule to another to
catch the latest device simply stimulated the creation of yet another new
device designed to escape the latest legal criteria. A new approach had to be
adopted. Lord Strathclyde, for example, in the House of Lords, stated:
"Our intention is to curb the use of off balance sheet financing schemes
through controlled non-subsidiary undertakings. Any definition of the
term will encourage attempts to avoid the provision by artificial constructions with the intention of escaping from the letter of the definition"
(Strathclyde, HL Deb vol. 03, col. 1018).

In essence, therefore, the new regime adopted a philosophy of shifting
regulatory style from detailed prescriptive rules to broader purposive principles, from narrow criteria to broader catch-all ones in the drafting of
definitions, and from an emphasis on legal form as the criterion for deciding
on appropriate accounting treatments to an emphasis on economic substance. There was also a revision of the law on the "true and fair override"

to make it more accessible. The stated mission was that there be a shift of focus in financial reporting, and by implication in auditing, from the letter of the law to its spirit (e.g., Dearing *The Times*, January 24, 1991). A new standard setting body was set up under creative accounting's arch enemy, David Tweedie, and a new agency, the Financial Reporting Review Panel, was set up to investigate accounts, policing no longer being left entirely to auditors. New sanctions were introduced for directors found in breach of regulations.

The off balance sheet SPVs of the 1980s, and the rules that were interpreted as permitting them, were clearly targeted. So in the 1989 Companies Act (itself implementing European company law's Seventh Directive), the definitions of a subsidiary included a "catch-all" definition that avoided mention of 50 percent thresholds or precise forms of control and instead required consolidation in broader terms. B would have to be included in A's consolidated accounts, in the event of A having "a participating interest" in B (which might take forms other than equity ownership), and "exercising an actual dominant influence" ("actual" rather than in any particular legal form). A lynchpin of the new regime was Financial Reporting Standard 5 (FRS5, ASB 1994). This stated categorically that transactions should be reported according to their economic substance, putting economic reality before formal legal structuring. It also specifically tackled "quasi-subsidiaries," entities that fulfilled the functions of a subsidiary despite falling outside the statutory definitions of one, and required their inclusion in the "quasi-holding company's" accounts.

Great hope has been attached by opponents of creative accounting to the potential of a principle based regime for avoiding the limitations of rule based regulation and providing a more effective means of controlling creative accounting. Tweedie noted, for example: "We believe this is the surest means of forming standards that will remain relevant to innovations in business and finance and which are most likely to discourage ingenious standards avoidance practices" (FRC, 1991, para. 5.5). Close analysis of the new regime, however, and of other jurisdictions following similar strategies, suggests even a shift to principles poses problems for effective legal control. Again this is detailed elsewhere (McBarnet and Whelan 1999; McBarnet 2003, 2004) and here I simply note some of the main problem areas.

First there is a problem with sustaining principles as principles. There are too many factors that can produce a drift from principles to rules, clarifying and narrowing the ambit of their control, and providing more recipes for creative accountants to work on. Lobbying, demand for guidelines, court cases, and just the build-up of informal precedents on what is allowed in practice and what is not are examples of the factors that eat away at principles and can convert them in effect back to rules.

Second, our empirical research suggests enforcers face problems in putting principles and indeed stronger powers in general into practice. There is too much room for contestability over what is true and fair, what is substance. There is concern about losing in court. Indeed, there is concern about winning in court if the win would nonetheless lead to tighter definitions of what is not allowable and by implication what is. There is concern about losing control to the judges.

The strength of a principle based regime as a means of control also lies in the uncertainty it generates. Hence David Tweedie's response, when asked early in the new regime how it would fare is this:

> We're like the cross-eyed javelin thrower at the Olympic Games. We may not win but we'll keep the crowd on the edge of its seats. (McBarnet and Whelan 1999)

Not knowing where the regulatory javelin will fall may make for greater caution among would-be creative accountants. It also encourages settling with enforcers rather than contesting them; there is reluctance to be the company that puts its head on the block to test the legal interpretation of the new regime. On the other hand if uncertainty is strength, the last thing the regime wants is to have its limits clarified, and regulators too may be too wary of a court case to flex their muscles too much. Yet there is a paradox here, because if the javelin is never wielded it will cease to deter.

What is more, the strength provided by uncertainty is also a potential weakness in terms of issues of legitimacy. Principle based regimes can be readily open to criticism as too uncertain, as open to retrospectivity, as giving regulators too much power, as opening the way to arbitrary decision making. The strategic response to creative accounting is itself susceptible to critique as "creative control," and as an unacceptable violation of the rule of law. One empirical consequence of this is a tendency on the part of enforcers to limit themselves in how they use their powers. In turn the consequence of that is to limit in practice the theoretical scope of the principle based regime for control.

Finally, even principle based systems can fall prey to creative accounting. Regulations, even regulations based on principles, have to be based on words, and even abstract words can be scrutinized for creative interpretations or uses. Alternatively coexisting rules or even other principles can be brought in to limit the reach of the principles in question.

The 1989 Companies Act, we saw, introduced the "catchall" phrase "actual dominant influence" in an effort to stop novel methods of control slipping through the net of more specific definitions. Yet that phrase then spawned "deadlocked joint ventures" where A and B set up a partnership, C, in which the equity was held 50–50 and the power of each was "deadlocked": neither A nor B exercised "actual control" and C remained off the balance sheets of both. Rush and Tomkins' unknown debt-laden partnerships were deadlocked joint ventures of this kind. Though further regulations, especially FRS5, might be thought to catch this now, accountancy firms have suggested there could still be ways of constructing entities to keep them, arguably, off balance sheet, for example by using "revolving chairs," with A and B appointing a chairman for C with a casting vote each alternate year. Other sections of company law, and Generally Accepted Accounting Principles on consistency, could then be invoked to keep C out of the accounts of both (Ernst & Young 1997). Even the idea of "substance over form" itself has been used creatively and counterpurposively, for example, through exploitation of "in-substance defeasance" (McBarnet and Whelan 1999).

Whether rule based or principle based, there are then problems in controlling creative accounting through law. Yet one could argue that ultimately creative accounting is only a problem because of another issue, and that is not just the law itself but the attitude taken toward law by those allegedly subject to it, and those policing it. Turning to that takes us from issues of law to issues of ethics.

Creative Compliance and Ethics

Whatever law, and whatever kind of law, is put in place as a mechanism for controlling business, it is mined for opportunities for circumvention. That is the reality of business regulation in action, whether in the arena of corporate governance or elsewhere. Law is seen as entailing no ethical obligation but as a material to be worked on to one's own advantage.

Routine techniques are to search out gaps in the law—"where does it say I can't?"; to scrutinize the "ex-files" of law—exemptions, exclusions, exceptions—to see whether transactions or structures can be repackaged to fit within them, whether they naturally do so or not; to find or press for specific definitions and thresholds as guidance then "work to rule"; to construct completely innovative techniques that the law has not yet regulated and avoid control that way.

What this underlines is not just the nature and inherent limitations of law, but the fact that limitations of law are also a product of the way law is received and acted upon. Creative accounting is in fact the product of two factors. Limitations inherent in the nature, substance, and enforcement of law provide the opportunity, but that opportunity also has to be actively taken up by those subject to the law and by those charged with guiding and policing them, in this case, corporate management, their professional advisers, and their auditors. It is not just how law is constructed and enforced that determines its impact but how it is received. If change is to come, therefore, it is not just the law we need to address but the attitude toward law assumed by those subject to it. We need to recognize that how businesses choose to comply with law involves judgment. It is not just a technical matter but an ethical matter.

It may be time to put the spotlight on the corporate and professional culture that sees as acceptable indeed applauds as smart, the manipulation of law and defeat of legal control. It may be time to question the ethics of this attitude to law, and to ask *why* creative compliance is deemed legitimate when fraud is not. The intention, to defeat legal control, and the consequences, in terms of the frustration of legal policy and the impact on victims, are, after all, the same. What is clear is that changes in the law alone will not lead to a change in practice unless this culture is addressed, and a new, more ethical, attitude to law and compliance is adopted by business and auditors alike.

Many companies in their codes of conduct have made a point of declaring their commitment to compliance with the law. Indeed Enron did just that, stating in its last social and environmental report that "We are dedicated to conducting business according to all applicable local and international laws and regulations (Enron 2001, 8)." Given the fraud that was going on as this code was published, there was not much to foster confidence in codes of conduct. Even if Enron had complied totally with its code, it would have done nothing to constrain creative as opposed to fraudulent accounting. Although Enron's Code committed it to compliance with the law, it did not spell out *how* the company would comply. A commitment only to minimalist, literal, and creative compliance would foster, not prevent, creative accounting.

That point is, however, beginning, implicitly, to be acknowledged. We are already seeing a handful of companies expressly committing themselves in their codes of business ethics, not just to compliance with the law, but to compliance with the *spirit* of the law. Not all commitments in corporate codes of conduct can be taken at face value, as Enron amply demonstrates (though even commitments undertaken lightly may rebound when they are used to hold their instigators to account). And commitment to the spirit of the law could yet raise all kinds of legal controversies. However, the move suggests some acknowledgment, at least at the level of rhetoric, that it is not just breaking the letter of the law, but breaking the spirit of the law, that raises ethical questions. What is more, this commitment occurs not just in companies' voluntary corporate codes but in the Ethical Codes for Chief Executive Officers and Chief Financial Officers required of companies trading on the US Stock Exchange by the Sarbanes-Oxley Act. In short some companies are going so far as to make a commitment to ethical compliance in an overtly legal context.

Enron has put the spotlight not just on fraud but on creative compliance in corporate governance and has made transparent to a wider public the esoteric practices of corporate finance. It has also exposed the corporate culture in which law is simply a material to be worked on to one's own advantage, and in which it is considered, to cite from my research interviews with corporate lawyers and accountants, perfectly legitimate to take a "bullish interpretation" or "sail close to the wind" in the legal construction of creative devices, devices constructed specifically for the purpose of undermining the objectives of corporate governance. The debates sparked by Enron and other accounting scandals may provide an ideal moment for that culture to be questioned, and for an expectation to be fostered that *ethical* compliance means compliance with the spirit, not just the letter of the law. The experience of Enron may also begin to drive home the message that ethics cannot simply be seen as separate from legal control, but as necessary for legal control to be effective.

Note

This chapter is based on research funded by the ESRC's Professorial Fellowship Scheme, as well as earlier work on "creative compliance" including work with Chris Whelan. A version of this chapter, focussing on auditors, was presented at the CAPPE workshop on Auditing and Ethics (electronically published, ANU, McBarnet 2005b). An extended version, presented at the 2004 colloquium on *Governing the Corporation*, Queen's University, Belfast, goes further to explore the culture of creative compliance, and the potential role of Corporate Social Responsibility. Sections of that chapter are drawn on and reproduced here with kind permission of the publisher (McBarnet 2005a, © John Wiley & Sons Limited).

References

Accounting Standards Board (ASB). 1994. *FRS5 Reporting the substance of transactions*. London: ASB.

Ashton, Raymond K. 1986. The Argyll Foods case: A legal analysis. *Accounting and Business Research*, 16 (65): 3–12.

Ernst and Young. 1997. *UK GAAP*. Basingstoke: MacMillan.

Enron, 2001. Corporate Responsibility Annual Report.

Financial Reporting Council (FRC). 1991. *The State of Financial Reporting: A Review*. London: FRC.

Griffiths, Ian. 1986. *Creative Accounting*. London: Sidgwick & Jackson.

McBarnet, Doreen. 1991. Whiter than white collar crime: Tax, fraud insurance and the management of stigma. *British Journal of Sociology* 42: 323–344.

———. 2003. When compliance is not the solution but the problem: From changes in law to changes in attitude. Braithwaite (ed.), *Taxing Democracy*. Ashgate and McBarnet 2004.

———. 2004. *Crime, compliance and control*, Collected Essays in Law: Ashgate.

———. 2005a. After Enron: Corporate governance, creative compliance and the uses of Corporate Social Responsibility. J O'Brien (ed.), *Governing the Corporation*. Chichester: John Wiley.

———. 2005b. "Perfectly legal": A sociological approach to auditing. T. Campbell and K. Houghton (eds.), *Ethics and Auditing*, ANU Press, pp. 25–43.

McBarnet, Doreen, and Chris Whelan. 1997. Creative compliance and the defeat of legal control: The magic of the orphan subsidiary. K. Hawkins (ed.), *The human face of law*, OUP and McBarnet 2004.

McBarnet, Doreen, and Whelan C. 1999. *Creative Accounting and the Cross-Eyed Javelin Thrower*. Chichester: John Wiley & Sons.

Partnoy, Frank. 2002. Testimony concerning the unregulated status of derivatives and Enron, testimony at hearings before the United States Senate Committee on Governmental affairs January 24, 2002.

Partnoy, Frank. 2003. *Infectious Greed*. London: Profile Books.

Pitt, Harvey L. 2002. Testimony Concerning the Corporate and Auditing Accountability, Responsibility, and Transparence Act. Before the Committee of Financial Services United States House of Representatives. Washington, DC, March 20, 2002.

Powers, William. C., Troubh, Raymond S., and Winokur, Herbert S. 2002. Report of Investigation by the Special Investigative Committee of the Board of Directors of Enron Corp, February 1, 2002. <http//fl1.findlaw.com/news.findlaw.com/hdocs/docs/enron/sicreport/sicreprt020102.pdf.>

CHAPTER 3

STAKEHOLDER THEORY AND IMPERFECT DUTIES

David Lea

Toward a General Reconciliation of Virtue
Ethics and Universal Principles

O'Neill (1996), in her work, begins with the distinction between universalist and particularist approaches to ethical theory. The universalist approach is one that focuses on certain universal principles that serve as guides to ethical behavior most perspicuously advanced by Kantian deontologists and utilitarians. The general universalist approach, as is well known, came under criticism from virtue ethicists who hold that moral or virtuous action must be grasped in terms of culturally and socially specific descriptions. O'Neill points out that what is at issue is the abstract character of act descriptions that universalists identify as the proper content of universal principles, and the virtue ethicist's insistence that we cannot guide or judge action by using abstract descriptions or principles that incorporate them. Action, they say, must be grasped in terms of culturally and socially specific descriptions and thereby intelligible and accessible to particular audiences. Robert Solomon (1993; see also Mintz 1996; Hartman 1998) has probably been the most ambitious in taking efforts to apply virtue ethics to business practice.

Accordingly, O'Neill presents what she calls a constructivist approach to justice and morality that strives to integrate the insights of both schools of thought. One notes that recent work by Kantian and contractarian business ethicists, whose theories incorporate universal principles, has been receptive to the idea of integrating the universalist and particularistic accounts

(Bowie 1999; Donaldson and Dunfee 1999). Where O'Neill's work proves to be most interesting is in her endeavor to integrate both the universalist and particularist accounts through an analysis of obligations.

Whereas deontologists, both Kantian (Bowie 1998; 1999) and contractarian (Donaldson and Dunfee 1994; 1995; 1999) have frequently distinguished themselves from utilitarians by attributing deontic priority to rights, O'Neill gives primacy to obligations. This allows her to extend the range of moral responsibility and to draw important distinctions within this range of responsibility by reference to Kant's conception of perfect and imperfect duties. These distinctions then become the key to understanding how virtue and character become operative within a given set of general and special responsibilities.

Obligations and Rights

With respect to normative stakeholder theory, one notes that many business ethicists, in their endeavor to give content to principles enjoining certain general responsibilities toward stakeholders, have also frequently postulated some set, or list of rights that should command corporate loyalty. For example, Evan and Freeman (1993, 82), in their groundbreaking essay promoting the interests of all company stakeholders, argue that the corporation should be managed for the benefit of stakeholders and the "rights of these groups . . . assured." Not only this but the groups must have the right to participate, in some sense, in decisions that substantially affect their welfare. Bowie (1998, 47) argues that recognition of stakeholder interests should involve "getting input from all affected stakeholders." McCall (2001) goes further and has recently argued that employees as nonowner stakeholders have a moral right to codetermine corporate policy. Some, for example, argue that employees in accordance with stakeholder theory should have the right to purchase the firm in the event of bankruptcy, while others believe there should be a right to secure employment and immunity from employment at will, and so forth (Millon 1995).

Given that moral action that would accord with stakeholder theory and greater public responsibilities is often fleshed out by attributing rights to the various stakeholder groups, the worrying aspect is that there is no unanimity concerning these rights. One also needs to notice that rights invested in important stakeholders are often in the nature of welfare rather than liberty rights. Companies are not simply obliged to refrain from harming these groups, that is, violating liberty rights—which should apply regardless of stakeholder theory—but moreover are expected to provide some positive good in accordance with a given welfare right. Evan and Freeman (1993), for example, mention better parks and day care facilities in discussing the stakeholder claims of the local community.

O'Neill points out that responsibility for enhancing the welfare of others may be easily avoided if we give rights rather than obligations deontic primacy. She argues that many welfare rights become vacuous where rights rather than obligations that are left unspecified are emphasized. Familiar welfare rights in the UN Universal Declaration of Human Rights or Donaldson and Dunfee's (1999, 75) right to basic economic opportunity for both genders become vacuous, if there exists no institutional context that identifies those invested with the responsibility to ensure fulfillment. On this point O'Neill (1996, 134) observes that welfare rights are different from liberty rights in that to institutionalize the former is not just to secure the backing of the law and the courts but also to define and allocate obligations to contribute and provide the relevant goods and services. The failure to assign obligations and responsibilities to individuals who would be responsible for ensuring these rights means that the right is virtually undefined and unspecified. In these circumstances the welfare right holder is, in effect, without a definable right capable of being asserted.

With respect to stakeholder rights, the corporation is much like a nation state that has assented to certain welfare rights. These rights remain meaningless unless the collective entity creates an appropriate organizational mechanism for adjudication and management of resources to address these putative rights. This involves the creation of a complex organizational structure that includes the designation of trained individuals to adjudicate issues involving the identity and claims of the right holders as well as others who are responsible for committing and ensuring that resources are applied to meet the varied claims these rights represent.

Conversely, O'Neill points out that obligations without corresponding rights are far from meaningless, and they indeed form the basis for the cultivation of the social virtues. O'Neill argues that making obligations primary entails responsibility for a given situation, even if the institutionalized setting does not obtain. If, on the other hand, one remains content with attributing rights without specifying obligations, there is an unavoidable tendency to feel that moral constraints really extend only to liberty rights that clearly instantiate specific obligations requiring noninterference.

Thus, if we regard stakeholder claims as obligations rather than simply rights, firms do not necessarily escape their responsibility to promote the welfare of a given stakeholder group. This would be so even if there exists no institutionalized organization that defines these claims in the language of stakeholder rights and commits resources to satisfy them.

Imperfect and Perfect Duties

Given these reasons for promoting obligations, rather than rights, as the primary deontic category, O'Neill (1996, 140) observes that obligations, framed in universal principles, provide a moral grounding for the virtues that we ought to cultivate. An account of virtues that are duties provides a framework for an account of certain social virtues, which are duties as well as virtues. Many important virtues like honesty, fairness, beneficence, and courage have been held to span across many roles and activities although lacking counterpart rights. Many important virtues have been construed in this way, she says. Thus, although individuals may, for example, feel obligated to cultivate the virtue of beneficence, no one possesses a counterpart right that requires that he/she be treated beneficently. Likewise, no one possesses a right that requires that others exercise courage on their behalf, although all are under a duty to act courageously when the occasion arises.

O'Neill's constructivist account of ethics emphasizes the importance of distinguishing between *imperfect* and *perfect duties*, and identifying the social virtues with the former. *Imperfect* duties, as we know, are generally indeterminate. The person subject to these duties is free to exercise judgment in determining the content of the duty, what exactly is to be done, and free to determine the object or the beneficiary. Additionally, the agent is free to choose the occasions on which to perform the duty. An appropriate example is the Christian duty of charity, which is extremely open ended. The obligation itself does not indicate what exactly is to be done, the individuals or groups to be benefited, or the frequency of performance. In contrast, *perfect* duties indicate unambiguously exactly what is to be done, the individual or group that is responsible for the duty, and frequency of performance. A good example would be the obligations undertaken under contract in a hire purchase agreement or the duties the company owes to its shareholders according to specific contractual obligation, for instance, the duty to hold an AGM (Annual General Meeting) with shareholder voting rights.

The characterization of responsibilities to stakeholders as being special imperfect duties allows us to distinguish them conceptually from other duties owed to stakeholders that are not based on stakeholder status. There exist also *universal perfect duties* whose counterpart liberty rights are possessed by all (not just stakeholders) and often protected by law, for example, environmental legislation that prohibits the dumping of toxic effluent that is a general danger to health. Similarly, regardless of the so-called stakeholder duties, the company already owes many of the stakeholders *special perfect duties* arising from contractual relationships, for example, the duty to pay wages, or satisfy creditors, and so forth. It is obvious that stakeholder theory goes beyond these commonly recognized obligations to refrain from injury (*universal perfect duties*) and acknowledge contractual constraints (*special perfect duties*), and imposes certain unspecified duties that require the bestowing of some positive benefit not dissimilar to the positive benefits bestowed upon shareholders. Because these duties involve only special groups affected by the operations of the firm, the duty cannot be universal. Moreover, because the duties are largely unspecified and dependent on the judgment and cultural contingencies, these responsibilities closely resemble imperfect duties. We will define these as *special imperfect duties*.

For our purposes, duties owed to nonshareholder stakeholders—all those directly affected by the operations of the firm—would be examples of *special imperfect duties*. These imperfect duties are created through particular relationships in which certain groups are directly affected by the firm's activities. However, although there are no counterpart rights attached to these duties, firms are still obligated to act in the interests of these groups. How would these rights differ from universal imperfect duties, which also require us to promote the interests of the universalized other? Essentially a universal imperfect duty would resemble Locke's famous universal obligation, to preserve the rest of mankind, as much as one can, which is interpreted as a command of God. In contrast, special imperfect duties arise from a special relationship as in the case of parenthood, for example. In the latter, obligations are much stronger and exercise greater moral force and are more specific but do not necessarily invest a set of rights in the infant or child. Parents are obligated to do the best for the child but this does not necessarily mean the child has an enforceable right against the parent to provide a college education. Likewise local stakeholders impose an obligation on the firm to act in their interests but this does not mean they have an enforceable right to a public park to be provided by the local firm. Ultimately, giving obligations primacy and identifying stakeholder obligations with imperfect duties allows for the exercise of judgment and recognition of the particular context that determines the appropriate response.

Objections to the Deontic Primacy of Obligations over Rights

However, some might favor rights over obligations on the grounds that an individual who lacks a specific right to some form of welfare but remains the holder of certain related duties has limited choices. Rights give one the option to actively assert or waive the right. In other words, one without rights is reduced to an object of patronage and paternalism, dependent on the beneficence of the benefactor, rather than an engaged autonomous agent.

There is certainly a degree of truth to this argument, but my position is that giving obligations deontic priority does not obviate the possibility of creating an organizational framework that invests specific rights in stake-holders. Buchanan (1996, 33), for example, suggests that competitors might get together to perfect imperfect duties through an arrangement that included the coercive power of contract law to achieve mutual self-binding. This might mean allowing representatives from the local community the right to participate in board meetings, especially on issues that affect their welfare. Creating such rights would not deny that obligations had deontic priority. For example, Locke's famous natural rights are derived from a duty to preserve ourselves and to the best of our ability the rest of mankind. "Every one is bound to preserve himself and not to quit his sta-tion wilfully; so by the like reason when his own Preservation comes not in competition, ought he, as much as he can, to preserve the rest of mankind" *Two Treatises* II: 6).

However, supporters of the rights might also argue that emphasis on rights gives us a better opportunity to transform responsibilities to stake-holders into legal obligations. Giving deontic primacy to rights may be a better way to ensure that these moral rights are transformed into legal rights, and so to ensure stakeholder protection. But I argue that to attempt to define and fix these responsibilities by attributing specific rights to the beneficiaries and *perfect* duties to companies actually undermines the moral character of these responsibilities. Moreover, it may well rebound to the disadvantage of the intended beneficiaries.

Although many would persist and demand that rules be changed so that firms are legally required to undertake certain explicit policies and actions that promote the interests of these stakeholders, the implementation of these changes in the law may rob widely accepted normative stakeholder theory of its moral aspect. If we become overly legalistic about these responsibilities we may restrict moral choice, which is essential to the attri-bution of moral value. H.L.A. Hart (1961) in writing on the distinction between law and morality argued that if all morality became identical with the criminal law, then the idea of morality might well die out rather than be preserved. In some sense, the point of being moral is that you have free-dom to choose to be that way, not that you are forced to act that way and have no choice.

Despite assertions about the value of unconstrained decision making and moral autonomy, some may assert an overriding utilitarian advantage. Many might persist and insist upon enforcing duties to stakeholders through the law or structural changes to the corporation on the grounds that overall benefits to a wide range of stakeholders outweigh considerations of freedom, individual autonomy, or the value of moral choice. Moreover, insisting on these sorts of changes may defeat the realization of the intended benefits and even effect a situation in which all parties are made worse off.

The awareness of possible disutilities begins with the recognition that capitalism succeeds where voluntary choice is a reality. Francis Fukuyama (1995) has argued that one finds a high correlation between the presence of voluntary associations and societies that have generated significant economic wealth. He affirms that "most serious social observers have noted in the past that the United States historically has possessed many strong and important communal structures that give its civil society dynamism and resilience" (Fukuyama 1995, 50).

In addition, the most important vehicle for the production and distribution of wealth in Western society for almost 300 years has been the corporation. The modern corporation and its predecessor, the joint stock venture, have historically been organizations whose membership is voluntary.

But if one persists and forces the issue and demands that these stakeholder rights be institutionalized, the result may be far from happy. Essentially, as we said, the corporation is a voluntary association maintained through contractual arrangements. If the law required that investors take on increased liabilities with respect to employees, for example, forgoing employment at will or giving the employees the right to buy the business at less than market value, any benefit to employees might well be short lived (Maitland 2001). Investors cannot be compelled to supply capital to businesses. Greater risk and lower returns might well move investors to demand a premium. On the other hand, Maitland points out, investors may divert funds to other forms of enterprise or invest in real estate, gold, treasury bonds, or foreign corporations such as the Japanese firm. The result might well be that the Western form of the corporation, as an organization for the generation of wealth, might cease to exist, thus negating all the efforts at reforms that were initially intended to adjust inequities.

One might accuse us of having shifted focus from a deontological analysis of stakeholder responsibilities based on the primacy of obligation to one based on utilitarian concerns. However, we might also reject the institutionalization of stakeholder responsibilities on Kantian grounds that proscribe action based on self-defeating maxims.

Kant's great insight was that morality and rationality possess an intimate affinity such that the moral is what can be generally practiced without contradicting a generalized purpose. The categorical imperative tells us to "Act only with the maxim through which you at the same time can will that it become a universal law" (Kant 2002, 421). We might do well to restate

Bowie's (1999, 15) explanation. Bowie quotes Korsgaard, "A practice has a standard purpose and if its rules are universally violated it ceases to be efficacious for this person, and so ceases to exist." Bowie (1999, 27) following Korsgaard calls this a "pragmatic contradiction" (Korsgaard 1996). To avoid a pragmatic contradiction, one should not act on a maxim that, if universalized, would defeat the purpose behind the maxim. In universalizing stakeholder responsibilities through legislation, we may well create a situation in which people are no longer interested in voluntarily joining a corporation, in so far as universalizing the responsibilities in this way may no longer be efficacious for the people who would join. In effect, the institution itself may cease to exist. In this way, we contradict the purposes of responsibilities to stakeholders, that is, promoting their interests.

The conclusion reached is that responsibilities to stakeholders are morally required, but the policy of enforcing them through the law may well fail as an ethically sound principle, if following such a principle defeats or contradicts the purpose, that is, promoting the interests of the stakeholders.

In characterizing stakeholder duty as imperfect, we also recognize that the degree of responsibility is variable and dependent on particularities and circumstance. Although all Christians have the responsibility of charity toward the poor, the strength of the obligation is certainly dependent on financial well being. Those who are well endowed financially are under greater obligation to use their resources to alleviate the sufferings of the impoverished, and those with less, less obligated. For example, an individual with barely sufficient means to ensure the well being of his/her family would hardly be expected to contribute significant sums to the Saint Vincent DePaul Society or the Salvation Army.

The same argument applies within the commercial world with respect to stakeholder theory. Business ethicists, in offering generalities about what stakeholder theory entails, seldom seem to acknowledge diversity in commercial enterprises. Some corporate entities are immensely wealthy and successful like Coca Cola or Microsoft, while others may be small, struggling corporate organizations with less than a hundred members, not to mention the variety of smaller partnerships and sole proprietorship firms. In these circumstances we cannot really demand that the struggling firm make significant contributions to the creation of parks and day care centers for the local community, for example.

Finally, the reification of imperfect stakeholder responsibilities that renders a determinate list of rights and of so-called perfect duties that legally expand corporate responsibility poses a real danger in that stakeholder theory may be used to reassign responsibilities to private and public sectors. Stakeholder theory, which seeks to impose on business a self-regulatory responsibility for providing benefits while constraining profit maximizing, may be used as an excuse for government to abdicate both its supervisory role and the responsibility for necessary collective goods. Expansion of corporate responsibility may lead governments to constrict and restrict their own activities with respect to the defense of both essential rights, and welfare services (Lea 1998). This can have infelicitous social and economic implications.

Conclusion

We have argued that an appropriate approach to business ethics is one that integrates both universalist principles and particularist accounts based on virtue ethics, as exemplified in the constructivist ethics of Onora O'Neill (1996). We applied this approach to stakeholder theory and issues of corporate governance, and argued that too often these normative models are fleshed out through a rights based approach. Following O'Neill we argue that liberal philosophy generally and stakeholder theory in particular would be better served through prioritizing duties rather than rights. We argue that rights, especially welfare rights, are vacuous without specifying, identifying, and legally institutionalizing specific obligations and responsibilities. Prioritising duties, on the other hand, ensures that there is no escape from responsibility. Imperfect duties imply the development of certain virtues because virtues are really obligations for which there are no corresponding rights (O'Neill 1996, 157). We go on to argue that many responsibilities to stakeholders are of this imperfect nature. Informal imperfect duties are preferred to legalized stakeholder rights on the following grounds. First, legal proscription would rob normative stakeholder theory of its ethical character; it would seriously undermine both the moral autonomy and freedom of choice of the agents. Second, the consequence may well be serious disutilities effected by undermining freedom of association and freedom of contract, not to mention the contradictions that arise when we attempt to enforce these moral obligations through the law. The maxim that would universalize these duties through the machinery of the law may well contradict its purposes if the corporation becomes unviable as investors desert the corporate structure to seek other forms of wealth generation. Finally we argued that there is also a danger that institutionalizing and legally formalizing stakeholder duties may result in the reassignment of responsibilities belonging to private and public sectors. Ultimately, the position argued for is that responsibilities to all stakeholder groups should remain as uniformalized imperfect duties that the firm is free to perfect in ways appropriate to cultural and societal settings, and in accordance with its capacity.

References

Bowie, Norman. 1998. A Kantian Theory of Capitalism. *Business Ethics Quarterly*, Ruffin Series: Special Issue 1: 37–61.

——. 1999. *Business Ethics: A Kantian Perspective*. Malden, MA: Blackwell Publishers.

Buchanan, Allen. 1996. Perfecting Imperfect Duties. *Business Ethics Quarterly* 6, No. 1: 28–41.

Donaldson, Thomas, and Thomas W. Dunfee. 1994. Toward a Unified Conception of Business Ethics: Integrative Social Contracts Theory. *Academy of Management Review* 19: 157–69.

——. 1995. Integrative Social Contracts Theory: A Communitarian Conception of Economic Ethics. *Economics and Philosophy* 11: 85–112.

——. 1999. *Ties that Bind: A Social Contracts Approach to Business Ethics*. Cambridge, MA: Harvard Business School Press.

Evan, William M., and R. Edward Freeman. 1993. Stakeholder Theory of Modern Corporation: Kantian Capitalism. In *Ethical Theory and Business*. 4th ed. Tom Beauchamp and Norman Bowie, eds. Englewood Cliffs, NJ: Prentice Hall, pp. 97–106.

Fukuyama, Francis. 1995. *Trust: The Social Virtues and the Creation of Prosperity*. London: Penguin Books.

Hart, Herbert L.A. 1961. *The Concept of Law*. Oxford: Clarendon Press.

Hartman, Edwin M. 1998. The Role of Character in Business Ethics. *Business Ethics Quarterly* 8, No. 3: 547–59.

Kant, Immanuel. 2002. Groundwork of the Metaphysics of Morals. New Haven: Yale University Press.

Korsgaard, Christine. 1996. *Creating a Kingdom of Ends*. New York: Cambridge University Press.

Lea, David. 1998. Corporate and Public Responsibility, Stakeholder Theory and the Developing World. *Business Ethics: A European Review* 8, No. 3: 151–63.

Maitland, Ian. 2001. Distributive Justice in Firms: Do the Rules of Corporate Governance Matter? *Business Ethics Quarterly* 11, No. 1:129–45.

McCall, John J. 2001. Employee Voice in Corporate Governance: A Defense of Strong Participatory Rights. *Business Ethics Quarterly* 11, No. l: 195–215.

Millon, David. 1995. Communitarianism in Corporate Law: Foundations and Law Reform Strategies. In *Progressive Corporate Law*. L.E. Mitchell, ed. Boulder, CO: Westview Press, pp. 16–22.

Mintz, Steven M. 1996. Aristotelian Virtue and Business Ethics Education. *Journal of Business Ethics* 15: 827–838.

O'Neill, Onora. 1996. *Towards Justice and Virtue: A Constructive Account of Practical Reasoning*. Cambridge: Cambridge University Press.

Solomon, Robert. 1993. *Ethics and Excellence: Cooperation and Integrity in Business*. Oxford: University Press.

CHAPTER 4

TRUST IN THE MIND AND HEART OF CORPORATE GOVERNANCE

John Little

Introduction

The collapse of Enron is not atypical of what can happen when a large organization is discovered to be less than open about "high risk" activities. In particular, it demonstrates that the actions of a few can bring havoc to the whole, and much besides. Countless innocent and trusting individuals lost their life savings when Enron fell and Arthur Andersen ceased to exist when its role as Enron's sole auditor became known.

In the wake of such events, a group of business people and academics have been meeting at CREDO, the Centre for Research into Ethics and Decision-Making in Organisations, at the Australian Catholic University, to discuss ethics and business. Drawing on the ideas of Canadian philosopher, Bernard Lonergan, we have explored questions about responsibility, trust, and the relationship between the individual and the corporate entity in governance and decision making.

In our discussions we have sought to lay bare the foundations of the corporation. We started with the human capacity to ask questions and find answers. By examining what we were doing ourselves, we developed, under Lonergan's influence, a structure of decision and control (Lonergan 1985, 1974; Daly 1993). We then applied this structure to corporate governance and identified eight value-adding process outcomes requiring the exercise of five core competencies or quality criteria for successful corporate development. If any competency is neglected or suppressed at whatever level or function within the corporation, stagnation, decline, or collapse will likely follow.

What follows is the broad outline of our discussions and how we developed our foundational model for corporate governance. References are made to the case study of the Penrith Lakes Development Corporation's highly acclaimed reclamation of a mining quarry near Sydney to illustrate the model's applicability.

This chapter is divided into three sections:

1. The foundational structure of mind and heart: What I am doing when deciding and acting.
2. The structure of governance: What the corporation is doing when deciding and acting.
3. A strategy for corporate renewal.

In the first section, the reader, by observing and reflecting on his own data of thinking, can verify the structure of decision and control we put forward. This structure, based on the mental acts or operations we perform in making a decision, also reveals parallel infrastructures of mind and consciousness. The five core competencies or capabilities we identify for effective decision and control—being open and persistent, attentive, intelligent, reasonable, and responsible—are, in our view, primary quality criteria for good governance.

The most startling feature of the live structure of the mind is its capacity to freely direct and manage itself. The five core capabilities act together in harmony as a metastructure controlling the performance of any one capability and of the whole in its relational performance. We have called this metastructure "the minder." It is not an extra structure but one that is integral both to the mind and to oneself as a set of consciously appropriated powers. Lonergan maintains its appropriation as the foundation of self-knowledge. This notion of self-knowledge, extended to the organization, provides the foundational base for corporate governance, progress, and renewal.

In the second section, we show how this structure of decision and control, extended to the organization, reveals eight clearly distinguished attributes of the corporate process. Together, these attributes provide a powerful template of the dynamic, relational nature of the corporate entity. As the patterns embedded in this map correspond to those embedded within ourselves, we can confidently and seamlessly apply the five quality norms of personal "minding" to corporate "minding." Furthermore, within the multiplicity of relationships and their associated schemes, a central "minding" function of trust confers upon them a foundational orientation to openness, possibility, and control.

In the third section, we put forward a strategy for corporate renewal, based on the application of the five quality criteria or core competencies of the mind.

The Foundational Structure of Mind and Heart: What Am I Doing When Deciding?

Decisions have their origin in questions, and questions in wonder. Questions, pivotal in changing the world, provide the key to our structure of decision making and control and, at the corporate level, to the structure of governance.

Questioning is a commonplace human activity. Questions seek to penetrate darkness, discover and extend knowledge, and provide direction for action. We seldom wonder about this power, and tend to use it automatically.

The corporate world is a world of questions: How do we sell this product? Where is our market? Whom will we consult? What kinds of skills do we need to implement this program? The answers sought will play some part in contributing ultimately to the delivery of valued goods or services.

Corporate failure or collapse can often be traced back to the failure of appropriate people to ask relevant questions at appropriate times (Victoria Royal Commission 1992). An investigation into corporate collapse is called an "inquiry," implying appropriate questions will be asked. Good journalists and lawyers are skilled in asking questions. The art and science of decision making include the art and science of questioning. Questions seek answers, and answers often raise more questions.

But questions can be endless. If questions lie behind decision making, then to gain some control over their structure could enhance our skill and effectiveness. How might we view questions as a structure?

Prior to questions there is wonder. We represent this in figure 4.1. Wondering (W) arises within the person (circle) in response to some stimulus (X).

Figure 4.1   Stimulus Invites Wonder

From wondering (W), questions (Q) arise about the stimulus (X). These questions seek answers (A) for the stimulus (X). A is represented outside the circle, as an answer that can be shared with others. The bidirectional arrow indicates that an equivalence is sought between A and X, for answers may be wrong. This is represented in figure 4.2. The arrow linking Q and A lies both within and outside the circle. Thus figure 4.2 represents the most basic structure of the mind and, being a closed loop of arrows, it also represents the most basic structure of control.

Lonergan wondered about wondering. He examined the operations that occurred between stimulus X and answer A-represented by the arrows-and identified the key place and role of insight (Lonergan 1957). We represent this in figure 4.3, with both question "Q" and insight "I" occurring "privately" within the mind of the person, and "A" being the public answer.

Lonergan distinguished four distinct powers of the mind activated by the power of wonder or inquiry, thus providing four value-adding levels of an answer. They are the powers of:

1. Attentiveness
2. Intelligence
3. Reason
4. Responsibility

Daly (2000) provides a quick way to access our experience in each of these four levels through a system of classifying questions. He arranges questions

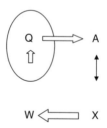

Figure 4.2 Wonder Gives Rise to Questions to Find Answers

Figure 4.3 Insight Lies between Questions and Answers

on the basis of the kinds of answers they seek. He identifies four categories into which all answers fall. Those are:

1. Gained through pointing
2. Long
3. Exceedingly short
4. Actions.

To establish the truth of this schema, we need only to examine ourselves or to wonder about our own wondering and the answers we get.

Questions and answers are specific, but the operations (including wondering) that provide them are general and recurrent, a kind of process infrastructure behind the content. Behind the answers we discover the underlying infrastructure, comprising general, recurring operations, and their quality criteria, equivalent to Lonergan's four levels:

Level 1: attentiveness / answers gained by "pointing"

- In more general terms, these answers would include things, events, persons, places, and times. They would be "data," what is "given" (Latin) to which we attend and "get in touch." We give "names" to things to which we point or refer. In decision making we need to be in touch with the data.
- Typical questions that lead to our "pointing" answers are: "when?" "where?" "who?" and "which?"
- Our "operations" on this level include sensing, experiencing, imagining, perceiving, and remembering. The quality criterion is being attentive.

Level 2: intelligence / long answers:

- These may be very, very long and specialized. They are explanations that include theories, postulates, formulae, novels, concepts, coherent accounts of "things", and meanings. If insight does not inform the long answer, it will be incoherent and confused. This second level of the mind draws on the first: "understanding" adds value to "data". In decision making, we need to have clear ideas about what the data mean.
- Typical questions for understanding are: "what is it?" "how?" and "why?"
- Operations include understanding, formulating, and conceiving. The quality criterion is being intelligent.

Level 3: reason / very short answers. The shortest answers is a "yes" or a "no."

- These are definite answers, the result of careful deliberation and reasoning by which we judge data. If unable to say either "yes" or "no"
  with any definiteness, I may hedge by saying "maybe", "perhaps", "all
  things being equal", and so on. We also assess risk and probability.
  Judgment adds value to "understanding" by testing and confirming its
  robustness. In judgment, we seek to find truth and avoid error.
  Decisions made on bedrock of fact and reality are sustainable; those
  based on fiction and illusion are not.
- The question for judgment is: "Is it so?"
- Operations at this level include judging, reasoning, reflecting, assenting, dissenting, agreeing, and disagreeing. The quality criterion is
  being reasonable.

Level 4: responsibility/answers that are actions:

- Answers, as actions, are unique to the person, reflecting choice of values in decisions. When "walk" and "talk" are aligned, actions and
  words correspond. This reflects personal integrity. When words and
  deeds are not aligned, there is dishonesty and hypocrisy, politely
  referred to as "spin".
- The primary question for personal responsibility is: "Will I?"
- Our operations on this level are evaluating, deciding, choosing, acting,
  performing, and behaving. The quality criterion "being responsible"
  applies.

This schema, which Lonergan developed in depth, can facilitate our insight
into the powerful recurring system of value-adding mental operations as a
structure within oneself. It is a pattern driven by enquiry, moving from
experiencing through understanding, formulating, judging, assenting,
deciding, and acting to return to experiencing again. By attending to our
experience of these operations, we can grasp their unity as a structure and
test its robustness. In this we can establish virtual certainty about the
structure of our own selves.

Figure 4.4 represents this structure in three columns. The two left-hand
columns are "internal" and private to the person; the right-hand column
refers to public answers or to what is visible to others. The matrix is
primarily relational, linking "me" to the "world".

In this model, one moves up the four levels from "experience" at level 1
to "decide" at level 4.

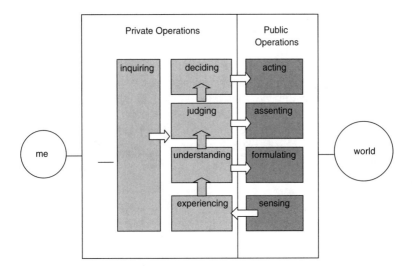

Figure 4.4   The Structure of Control

Experience includes everything that the senses deliver as data to the mind, including pain and pleasure. It also includes our memory, dreams, imagination, and perceptions; the "taste" of "self" and experience of one's operations at all levels, and the feelings or emotions of awe, joy, humility and courage that may accompany these operations. Experience includes everything that is conscious.

Decision as Seeking to Implement the Good
The fourth level of decision is the focus of our interest in decision and governance. In addition to being based on fact, decision also draws on values. Values are preknown or embedded in memory and understood to be relevant; they are judged to be "good" on the basis of direct experience or trust and are thus desired. Values give strength to decision and reflect what is good in it. Decision seeks to make the "good" concrete.

We can distinguish three types of goods in any decision: particular, sustainable, and basic. We can illustrate these by reference to a glass of water, given that we only have words, images, or concepts with which to point or allude to a reality.

If I am thirsty, a glass of water is a particular "good"; it is potentially "good" when I desire it and concretely "good" when I have it to drink. The storage and distribution system I use when I need the water is a sustainable "good" insofar as it is operational.

But I drink not only to satisfy thirst, but also to preserve life, in the final analysis. From this perspective, life itself is a basic good, common to all. In this mode of thinking, Finnis (1991) has proposed a set of seven basic human goods that lie behind particular and sustainable goods: life itself, knowledge, aesthetic experience, excellence in work and play, inner peace, and harmony with a higher source of meaning. He defines basic goods as those reasons that lie at the end of the personal "audit" trail of any decision we make; we can uncover them by persisting to ask ourselves, "why did I do/want that?" until we can go no further. A basic good is the final and sufficient answer to such a question.

The Structure of Control

The recurring nature of this four level structure is evident. When we act, we experience our own action. This may give rise to further questions, insights, judgments, decisions, and so on.

It also represents our own structure of control or feedback loop. We start with our capacity to experience our own acts then continue with our ability to understand this experience. Afterward, we judge our understanding if it is in accordance with our intention and then decide what to do, maintaining or adjusting our acts accordingly. Finally, we experience this very adjustment.

My mind finds itself thus constituted. It has the complexity of diverse levels and the simplicity in seeking its own unity and cohesion. It is also mine. This unity of mind and me lends further depth to this wondering about wonder.

As we examine ourselves, we find it difficult to perform a pure operation at any level. It may be easier to discern a whole group of operations working together in support of one, as "minding" it. For example, in reading this text, one will be attentive to the patterns of print on the page, thus exercising the core competence of level 1, being attentive. But one will also be able to identify many other operations supporting one's attention: one will understand the words one reads (level 2), check out whether one has understood the emerging sense correctly (level 3) and control one's eyes (level 4) to read on or to go back. The support of the other levels is rapid and seamless, resembling computer multitasking. One may also be listening for a knock at the door, wondering what to say to whoever comes or resisting distraction while planning for an event. This is represented in figure 4.5 in which all the acts and the minder can be focussed on performing any one activity of the mind.

We can thus distinguish competencies within the mind and the minder. The minder contains the full set of competencies acting in harmony to

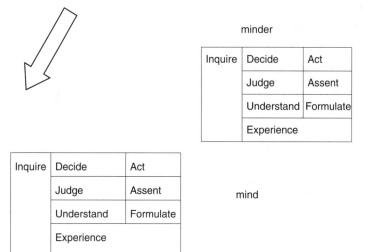

minder		
Inquire	Decide	Act
	Judge	Assent
	Understand	Formulate
	Experience	

Inquire	Decide	Act
	Judge	Assent
	Understand	Formulate
	Experience	

mind

Figure 4.5   The Mind and Its "Minder"

support the performance of any one competency. The minder operates in two modes, one for self-management and another for managing one's relationship with others in the world. In the latter, a central place is reserved for judgments of trust and decisions made on these judgments.

The minder can be visualized as a kind of helicopter, moving freely around all levels of the mind. Its "sensing" refers to all the data in the mind, the deposits in one's memory, and experience. One could say that it transcends time and place for, it can access data from other times and places instantly. The minder accesses data about "the good" stored within. Our inner voice belongs to the minder (Daly 2000). We have also called the minder the "heart of mind."

In our model, actions are right or wrong to the extent that they implement or suppress appropriate and legitimate "good." A disquiet of the "minder" may indicate that more attention needs to be given to "the good" at stake in a decision. Business people often refer to the "sleep" test, the "daylight" test, or the "golden rule" as quick ways to test the quality of their decisions. In the first, they test whether they are at peace with their decision; in the second, whether they would not worry if their actions were scrutinized by the media; and in the third, whether they have treated others as they would themselves.

The Structure of Governance: What Is The Corporation Doing When Deciding?

The corporation is an entity of human cooperation and can be viewed through the lens of question and answer. From the perspective of answers, we can identify eight categories in the corporate process. Lonergan developed a similar schema for the study of theology, in which he identified eight functional specialities (Lonergan 1972).

In the decision structure, as we ascend through the four levels from experience to decision, each new level adds value to the one below. In the corporate model, we can, in addition, move down the structure, from decision to "valued outcomes on the ground", identifying four products of implementation. Eight products are now described: four in the ascent, four in the descent, two for each level. A circular movement around inquiry gives the model its dynamic property as a recurring scheme open to possibilities of emergent development.

The "minder" can be discerned in the cooperative effort required to produce an outcome at any level. Thus the pattern of the whole structure can be found in any part. The five quality criteria of "being open, attentive, intelligent, reasonable, and responsible" guide being attentive, for example, in gathering data for research in stage 1.

Figure 4.6 shows these eight value-adding products of the corporate process. For purposes of illustration, let us take a mining company. There are four stages in the ascent, each expressing a distinct quality criterion:

1. Be attentive: Research is the cooperative activity involved in "getting data". This may involve sophisticated technology and aerial mapping of a new mining territory. Corporate data collection can be highly professional and dedicated work, yet it still requires further development if it is to yield something more than mere data, for data is not fact.
2. Be intelligent: Interpretation, possibilities, and opportunities are the products of the corporate understanding of what research data reveal. A new copper deposit is signified by the data. This is corporate intelligence in relation to ore deposits, but it still needs to be validated.
3. Be reasonable: Fact, probability, risk. Validation is undertaken; further assays of the ore body made; cores extracted; tests undertaken; assessments of purity conducted; calculations made about the costs of mining, transport, and processing; market assessed; competition

evaluated; and future needs projected. It entails a whole series of cooperative efforts requiring corporate judgment.

4. Be responsible: Positions taken up by different stakeholders in relation to the opportunity. They represent the range of expectations, needs, and desires that could be met by the opportunity.

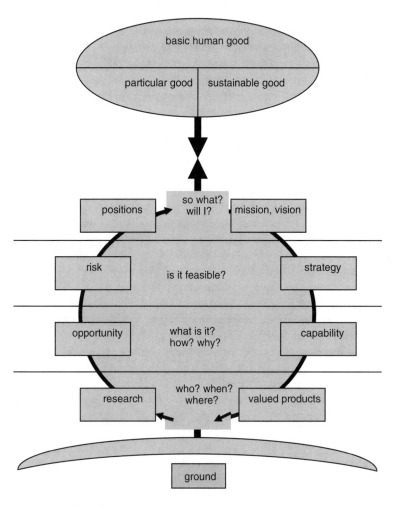

Figure 4.6   The Structure of Governance

Then, prior to descent, a critical element is introduced: the corporate decision based on a particular set of values. This is the core responsibility of decision making in governance that gives rise to corporate commitments. The four quality criteria define each stage in reverse direction.

In the descent, the following products are evident:

5. Be responsible: Mission, vision, and value. This is the core statement of corporate purpose, commitment, and promise that draws on the corporate "good". It is forever enlarging and developing with time and experience. It may articulate particular values of growth, diversity, excellence, sustainability, environmental responsibility, employment opportunities, and being a key player in national and international development. With respect to a particular position, a vision is most appropriate.

6. Be reasonable: Strategy and policy. Here corporate judgment establishes the boundaries, constraints, resources, and directions required to implement corporate mission, vision, and purpose. It establishes that such strategy and policy be realistic, not illusory; that they be feasible and that good outcomes be delivered if adopted. It provides a framework that is robust, yet revisable in light of new circumstances. Strategies may be developed for production, marketing, finance, and so on.

7. Be intelligent: Plan and capability. The "how" question (for level 2) generates possibilities (a "how might we" answer) for immediate outcomes. They are intelligent adaptations, inventions, and adjustments that define the "how to": roles and skills, structures, systems, infrastructure, and budgets. They refer to specifications for capability building, to corporate formulations of the intelligent way to proceed within the guiding framework of strategy and policy.

8. Be attentive: Action delivering valued outcomes. Here the corporate product is produced and exchanged with full attention to the customer. Value-adding is complete. The process can start again, leading through linkage and monitoring to a new "ascent": continuing research, data gathering, and monitoring of effectiveness, relevance and environmental change.

Although these eight products imply a continuing clockwise movement, the practice is more haphazard, with movement to and fro.

The critical juncture in this model lies in the event that links stage No 4 to 5, the definitive choice of values derived from "the corporate good". This choice is potentially transformative, involving a deliberate calculus of the "good" involved that may expand it.

Table 4.1   Stakeholder Good

Stakeholder	Particular Good	Sustainable Good
Owner	Return on investment	Growth
Customer	Quality product	Service
Employee	Just wage	Job opportunity, safety
Supplier	Fair dealings	Continuity
Community	Compliance to law	Social responsibility

Using stakeholder interest to extend the notion of "personal good" to "corporate good", we can identify a range of particular and sustainable goods. These are set out in the table 4.1 and we maintain that they should influence this calculus.

The relationship between a stakeholder and the corporation is based on mutual trust, judgments, and decisions each makes. Both parties have specific and different interests in mind—based on the particular and sustainable goods each is seeking—that influence their commitment to cooperate with the other, in the expectation that each will honor the trust given the other. For some, the terms of this trust are made explicit in legal contracts or written agreements with shareholders, for example. In our view, apart from their relationship with shareholders, directors are also custodians, for the most part, of an implicit trust between the corporation and its stakeholders, and they have the responsibility that this trust is not betrayed and that "goods are delivered". Should the corporation fail, aggrieved stakeholders will rightly seek redress. Trust and stewardship go together and underpin the corporate's willingness and commitment at stage 5.

Melchin (1994) approaches this notion of mutually bestowed trust in his account of a particular subset of corporate processes as a typical commercial transaction. He identifies four clear stages that underpin the confidence of both buyer and seller in their particular and potentially recurring commercial transaction. The four stages he identifies—expectations and first encounter, understandings, agreements, and commitments—correspond, in structural terms, to the heuristic, or emerging, developmental nature of Lonergan's four levels of cognition outlined earlier. Each party in the transaction undertakes and completes these four levels in order for the scheme to operate. The replication of this pattern in time reveals a particular recurring scheme that unfolds and develops under the influence of appropriate innovation and adaptation.

The pattern of these four stages also informs all other negotiations through which the organization conducts its business, and thus provides a fresh way to view its nature. But not all relationships are so established. Some are implicit, such as the relationship of the organization with the community in which it operates. But the same issues of trust, entrustment, and confidence will follow.

At the governance level, directors have in their relationships with stakeholders an implicit "minding" obligation to understand what "goods" each stakeholder entrusts to the corporation and what responsibilities and commitments follow for the corporate entity. And each stakeholder has a legitimate expectation that directors have understood, are committed to, and will give due recognition of and account for the practical outcomes of this trust. Of course, some directors may be "out of touch" with the implicit obligations, preferring to focus simply on the owner. In our view, the neglect of any legitimate stakeholder good will eventually damage the corporation. In practice, directors depend on those engaged in day-to-day transactions with stakeholders to honor this trust, such as a sales manager with a customer, a purchasing officer with a supplier, or a manager with a member of staff. In foundational terms, this entrustment of stakeholder "good" to the corporation in its directors and staff provides the cornerstone of corporate ethics. From this perspective, ethics lies not in laws, principles, or codes, but in the daily "minding" function of each person representing the corporation, at whatever level.

The corporation can thus be defined in terms of the "good" entrusted to it and of the "goods" it actually delivers. Some contemporary corporate instruments attempt to define performance in these terms and assist corporations in their measurement (Caux Round Table 2003). The corporation, operating from a clear notion of "the corporate good," will seek to maximize the benefit for all stakeholders. This notion of abundance can liberate powers of optimism, trust, and confidence amongst those leading corporate decisions and establish a vital climate of trust with all stakeholders. This was, in our view, the key to the successful Penrith Lakes Development Project, achieved through the "minding" influence of its Chief Executive Officer over multiple stakeholder relationships.

The calculus of the "good" to be achieved, the weighing up of the relative merits of all stakeholder expectations, is the work of the governing board. Each director will have his own particular answer to this calculation, not necessarily easy to articulate or explain, but one that guides his "gut" instinct. Answers will reflect each director's personal history, education, and formation.

A CEO may have a larger view than the Board and persuade the Board to adopt it. Or a single Board member may have such a vision and persuade others of its merits. Personal influence, charisma, power, and authority derive from a more deeply held notion of the "good".

In obtaining the goods they desire, stakeholders will remain loyal to the corporation. If the goods are not delivered, they will lose trust and go elsewhere. The contagious nature of distrust can precipitate rapid crisis within a corporation.

Sustainable goods create conditions for a longer wave of innovation and development. The presence of a sustainable good shapes expectations that particular goods will persist. The quality movement, for example, is a sustainable good. It has heightened consumers' expectations and established conditions for continuing innovation in computers, telephones, vehicles, aircraft, and consumer products. All these have high performance criteria and consumer confidence benchmarks. Competitive forces head for constant improvement, driven by the inquiry "how do we make it not only good, but better, or even best?"

A Strategy for Corporate Renewal

The corporate mind has four levels of value-adding that reflect the structure of decision and control. There are some critical observations we can make about this structure and its application in governance:

- "Inquiry" underpins its dynamic nature
- Mistakes can be made in "understanding". Insights can be inappropriate.
- Judgments can be premature and false.
- Decisions can be made arbitrarily, without proper concern for the genuine good.
- The structure cannot be revised, for one would be forced to use this structure to argue for an alternative structure or to dispute its validity.
- We are not obliged to use the structure, but the structure's quality criteria lessen the chances of error and build authenticity in decisions.

These observations apply individually and corporately: questions are not asked, data are ignored, errors occur, silly judgments are made and inauthentic, self-seeking decisions are taken. The solution is to establish a practice of applying the five quality criteria of thinking. The eight process outcomes in the delivery of "goods" depend on corporate "minding" or the application of a good method for thinking. The personal appropriation across the corporation of the five quality criteria for thinking—being open and persistent, being attentive, being intelligent, being reasonable, being responsible—can provide the foundation for corporate renewal.

These criteria also point to a more substantial understanding of compliance, the inbuilt law of mind and heart that one obeys to avoid decline.

1. Be open and driving: This criterion is about the basic disposition to wonder, ask questions, and persist with them until one reaches satisfactory answers. An organization that encourages questions and demonstrates openness will promote this fundamental value. Willingness to share information will build trust among stakeholders.

2. Be attentive: This is the basic disposition to get in touch with the world. Combined with the first criterion, it seeks to enlarge one's horizon, explore new experiences, notice new things, and "read" accurately what is happening around one. As a "minder" skill, it means attentiveness to one's own consciousness, feelings, and emotions. At the corporate level, it is about attention to detail, changes in environment, and in stakeholder needs and expectations.

3. Be intelligent: This is the drive to make sense of one's world. Combined with the first two criteria, it is the structure of creativity, entrepreneurship, and enthusiasm. It also makes sense of one's own "inner state"; of one's discomfort, fear, optimism, and other emotions. It is open to "other explanations" aside from those from a familiar paradigm.

4. Be reasonable: Combined with the previous criteria, this criterion gives us the structure of knowing. It is the critical and reflective ability to challenge conventional wisdom; to draw out reasons in support of or against new ideas; to protect the corporation from self-deception and illusion. Its development is recognized in wisdom and depth of experience.

5. Be responsible: The high point of corporate achievement raises the question of responsibility. Drawing on the previous four criteria, it refers to the adoption of a position and the willingness, courage, persistence, patience, and commitment to deliver this position. It entails a clear idea of the good.

Those who appropriate these criteria will deepen and enhance their leadership, management, and interpersonal skills and thus stimulate a corporate culture immersed in these values. Education and training reinforce these value.

Relationships with stakeholders based on these criteria will generate open exchange, insights, and a greater capacity to take up and respond to their interests and demands. Trust will be upheld.

Corporate instruments that encourage questions and discussion inevitably develop these criteria. SAIP (Self Assessment Improvement Process), an instrument from the Caux Round Table, is one example. It provides three levels of questions for the Board and the members of the executive and management teams to explore stakeholder issues and improve the firm's index of corporate social responsibility.

The implementation of these quality criteria, however, begins with oneself. Thus, we are back to our observation about corporate collapse: that the actions of one or a few can damage the whole. The obverse is also true. The actions of one or a few can contribute to prosperity and progress of the whole world.

Note

The author wishes to acknowledge the help of Stephen Ames, Tom Daly, Rick Hayes, Sean McNelis, Jamie Pearce and Ian Stainton in developing these ideas for a presentation at the ISBEE Third World Congress. An earlier version of this work appeared in the *GGU Journal of Business* I, 1, 2005 (Guru Ghasidas University, India).

References

Caux Round Table. 2003. *Self Assessment Improvement Process (SAIP)*. <http://www.cauxroundtable.org/resources.html> (accessed January 17, 2006).

Daly, Tom V. 1993. *In Learning Levels. The Australian Lonergan Workshop*. Lanham: United Press of America.

———. 2000. *Conscience and Responsibility in the Unity and Complexity of the Human Person*. Paper delivered at the annual conference of the Catholic Moral Theology Association of Australia and New Zealand, July 14, Campion Hall, Kew, Australia.

Finnis, John. 1991. *Moral Absolutes*. Washington: Catholic University of America Press.

Lonergan, Bernard. 1957. *Insight: A study of human understanding*. London: Longmans, Green and Co.

———. 1972. *Method in Theology*. London: Longman & Todd.

———. 1985. Dialectic of Authority. In *A Third Collection*. Ed. Frederick E. Crowe. New York: Paulist Press, pp. 5–12.

Melchin, Ken. 1994. Economies, Ethics and the Structure of Social Living. *Humanomics* 10: 21–57.

Victoria Royal Commission. 1992. First Report of the Royal Commission into the Tricontinental Group of Companies. July 30. <http://www.liv.asn.au/library/cat/3802.html> (accessed January 17, 2006).

CHAPTER 5

THE COMMON GOOD OF THE FIRM AS THE FIDUCIARY DUTY OF THE MANAGER

Peter Koslowski

Introduction

Working toward the common good is usually seen as the task of government and an obligation for politicians, not for managers of large corporations. The common good is a concept that is talked about constantly, made concrete rarely, and viewed as an empty promise ever so often. It seems to be a difficult obligation to work for the common good and to consider the effects of one's own action on the public good if, as occurs in a market society, every one has the right to follow his self-interest or private good.

Nevertheless, the concept of public interest is indispensable, particularly for politics. No one defends the right of a politician to follow his private interest and that of his immediate clients in his office. The role description of a politician establishes that he work for the common good and not for his party's good. Here, the demand to work for the public interest is not an empty concept but something like a general clause that applies to all actions of politicians.

Politicians can consider their self-interest and strive for fame and prestige in their career as a side effect of their intention to realize the public good, but they should not view the common good as a side effect of the realization of their self-interest.

It is often said that in a market society the reverse is true. The shareholder and the manager of a corporation realize the common good of public efficiency as a side effect of the pursuit of their self-interest and profit. Thus, in a market society, the demand to realize the common good does not hold.

Mainstream economic theory teaches that the common good is not realized in the market by intending it, but by the working of the invisible hand that turns selfish interests into efficiency and wealth-creation. The core of the invisible hand theory is that the common good of efficiency and wealth-creation is realized in a market society as a side effect of the pursuit of self-interest. It is not clear, however, to what extent Adam Smith proposes this theorem as a description of fact or as a normative statement.

The Common Good of States and the Common Good of Other Social Groups and Business Corporations

Characteristic of the common good theory is that it does not confine the realization of the common good to the State. Every community or organization has its common good and the duty to realize it (Gundlach 1959, 738). The idea of the common good of groups shows that the common good is not only for the totality of the common good of the whole of State and society but also for the internally structured totality of totalities. Every community or organization, be it a business corporation, a university, or a school, is not only characterized by the private interest of each individual working in them but also by the general interest of all those working in these institutions. All are interested in that their institution prosper and that this prosperity continue, since the continuation of the whole institution and its constituent groups is endangered if certain individuals or groups suffer damage in their good. The solidarity of interests and of the common good of the groups or stakeholders in an organization makes it impossible to define the good of an organization only in terms of the good of a single group or of some individuals.

However, the connectedness or solidarity of groups and individuals in an institution not only holds for their institution. It also holds, although to a lesser degree, for the different individuals or institutions working in the same field, insofar as they participate in a shared profession or industry.

Recent research in business ethics shows that there is a common good of an industry and of a profession besides the corporate good of the corporation. The corporations of an industry or the individuals of a profession are connected in their prosperity and share a common interest in the well-being of the industry or profession. If, for example, certain firms do consumers harm, they damage the reputation of the whole industry. A member of a profession—for instance, a medical doctor—damages the reputation of the whole profession by doing harm to a patient. A person, by his "unprofessional" behavior, not only harms the consumer or client but also the other members of an industry or a profession.

A similar connectedness of the common goods holds true on higher levels of the economy, from that of a region or continent to that of the whole world. Economies are connected in their common good even if this is ever less so, depending on the remoteness of groups from each other. No part of humanity can prosper in the long run if another part of humanity is in desperate need.

The structure and sequence of communities results in a structure and sequence of the common goods of groups. These common goods of groups, in turn, correspond to the specific connectedness of their members. Their common good and joint interest are caused by the closeness of the human beings in their respective groups and by the subsidiarity among groups and organizations in performing their tasks. The public interest of smaller groups and institutions is the subsidiary condition for the common good of the whole of society and vice versa. The political union or State can only prosper if the intermediate social institutions such as families and corporations prosper.

Is Modernity the Emancipation of Self-Interest?

Modernity is often seen as the era of the emancipation of self-interest, such that the demand for a consideration of the common good in the pursuit of individual interest has become obsolete. Modernity seems to have no need for the intent to realize the common good. Some thinkers who belong to the school of Public Choice and espouse its model of democracy go as far as saying that even the political order of the democratic state cannot be understood in terms of the common good. It must be seen as the mere result of the composition of individual self-interested votes and of self-interested politicians. Public Choice theory is an important innovation if understood as a theory critical of the actual motivation of politicians and of the naive idea that politicians have different and per se better motives than private sector decision makers. However, Public Choice theory becomes problematic if it excludes a priori the possibility that politicians try to find out and to realize the common good. James Buchanan, does not, in fact, discard the common good principle completely, but retains it as a regulative principle. He contends that by imposing the contraint of the nondiscrimination principle on all political decisions, politicians would be forced to think about "approaches which truly consider the common good interest" (Buchanan 2004, 13).

Adam Smith—considered by some social scientists to be the founder of modernity—only stated as a fact, not as a norm, that it is not from the benevolence, but from the self-interest of the butcher, brewer, or baker that we expect to get what we need for food (Smith 1963, 21). This statement by Adam Smith seems to be interpreted by some of today's economists as a normative statement describing how things *ought* to be. They contend that it is not only a matter of fact that we depend on the producer's self-interest but that it is normatively demanded that we depend only on the producer's self-interest to be provided with goods.

On the basis of the text and the synopsis of his two works, *The Theory of Moral Sentiments* and *The Wealth of Nations*, we must conclude that Adam Smith took this only as a statement of fact and not as a norm. The butcher is free, of course, to provide his services also for the common good, even for philanthropic or altruistic reasons. The market cannot rely on these higher motives but it does not exclude them. There is no norm that these higher motives ought not to be realized. The transformation of the self-interest theorem to a normative principle would make the "Adam Smith Problem" of compatibilizing ethical and economic theory unsolvable. Since Smith wrote both treatises, they must be reconcilable in his mind. The market coordinates self-interested action. The content of the motives of self-interest is left open by the pricing system. A common good orientation is as possible as one of narrow self-interest; just as mixed motives and an over-determination of human action by various self-interested and common good motives are also possible.

The Public Interest of Institutions and the Increased Responsibility of Those Managing the Institutions, Depending on Their Power, toward the Public Interest

Every organization and institution possesses its specific common interest or common good. It bears the task of realizing the interest of the organization as a whole. The obligation toward the public interest increases with the increasing impact of decisions and of the decision maker's power over the side effects, positive or negative, of his action. Acting persons are obliged to consider the public interest in those actions that are relevant for the public interest. That the decision problem becomes more difficult and complex because of the duty to consider the public interest should not free the decision maker from considering an action's side effects on the public interest. The increasing complexity of decision making only implies that its difficulty has to be taken into account in judging the success of a decision in itself and in considering the public good.

The obligation to include the side effects of one's decision making on the public good increases with power. This increasing obligation to consider the public good indicates that power itself is a moral phenomenon. The more power a person possesses, the more the person must consider the side effects of his decision making. The idea of the public interest points out to this relationship between power and the duty to consider the public good.

As Roman Herzog has demonstrated, Thomas Aquinas introduced two important insights on political philosophy through his idea of the common good: first, that sovereignty and the exercise of political power do not have their criterion of action in themselves but refer to a higher authority and are therefore constrained in their freedom, and second, that the state *and* the individual are bound by the common good (Herzog 1974, 256). In his theory of the common good Thomas Aquinas starts from monarchy and binds the ruler to an authority outside of the ruler's own will and self-interest. The ruler should not only follow his free and sovereign will. He is not only directed by his own interest but also by the higher authority of the common good that constrains his will and sovereignty. His office or duty is to further the common good. Government does not exist to further the self-interest of those governing.

The idea of the common good leads to the development of the modern idea of office. The political office is obliged to realize the common good; it is not there to increase the power or advantage of the office-holder and his self-interest. It is not only the self-interest of the state, the raison d'état, the sovereignty of the prince, or king and his self-interest that matters. The office, particularly the political office, bears in itself the obligation to good governance and is bound by the effect of its decisions on the common good.

The idea of office that derives from the concept that power is bound by the public good constrains not only political power, but also the economic, cultural, and religious ones. The idea of office shows that power is a moral phenomenon and therefore always related to the common good. Political power is an office defined not only by the sovereign will of the one in power; it is also subject to what is demanded by the realization of the common good. The same holds true for those who possess economic, religious, and cultural offices and their concomitant powers.

The obligation to include the idea of the common good in individual decision making and in the use of economic, religious, cultural, and political powers follows from the fact that individualist decision making processes in the market and in a democracy cannot function without such a consideration of the public good. Frictions in the economic and political realms arise if decisions are based on self-interest only.

The need to consider the common good in the market and in democracy arises, in first place, from the aggregation or composition problem of individual decisions determined by self-interest concerning market prices and political decisions. The phenomena of market failure and the failure of democracy describe such frictions of coordination. On the other hand, the need to consider the common good also arises from the fact that holders of economic and political responsibility are not only agents of the principals who give them agency power but also, albeit of a lesser degree, of those whose lives are deeply influenced by their decisions. The holders of an office must consider the common good of the institutions beyond their mere agency duties to those who gave them the power to manage or to govern, that is, their principals. Fiduciary duty entails something more than agency, something more than merely acting in the interest of one's principal. It is the duty to act for the good of the whole institution, the entity for which one has been authorized to act by the principals.

The Obligation of Managers to Realize the Common Good of Their Corporations

The obligation to consider the common good is not only valid for the politician. The politician is the agent not only of his constituency and party but is also the representative of those who did not vote for him. Likewise, the manager of a large firm is the agent not only of those who employed him—the shareholders or owners of a firm—but also the fiduciary of those who work under his leadership by virtue of his being the fiduciary of the whole firm. The obligation to realize the common good of the institution is, therefore, also valid for the manager of the large firm (Alford and Naughton 2002). It is the fiduciary duty of the manager toward the firm.

The fiduciary duty defines the duties of the manager as the duty to good faith, the duty to loyalty toward the firm, the duty of care and prudence, and the duty of disclosure (Johnston 2005). The manager is not free to follow his own interest or the shareholder's interest at the cost of neglecting his fiduciary duties toward the firm. Rather, shareholders invest managers with their office to further the good of the whole corporation, and not only their—that is, the shareholders'—own good. The fiduciary duty instituted by the law goes beyond mere shareholder and manager interests.

Among fiduciary duties, the duty of loyalty obliges the manager to an undivided and unselfish loyalty to the corporation, not to shareholders. It is more than a mere contract. Rather, it is an obligation toward the firm as a whole. The duty to care and prudence obliges managers to act in the interest of their corporation, not in the interest of themselves or of the firm's shareholders.

The duty of disclosure obliges managers not to take advantage of knowledge confidentially acquired in the course of their work for the firm or of knowledge given to them by shareholders about the firm. Their fiduciary duty of disclosure excludes the use of this knowledge for making insider deals as managers of the firm or as a private party. The prohibition of making use of insider knowledge or the duty to disclosure follows from the fiduciary duty of managers toward the firm and the shareholders, not to the shareholders only.

The manager is not only the agent of his principals, be they shareholders or single owners. He has duties beyond that of realizing the interest of the shareholder group in profit maximization. The manager must consider the interest of the whole firm that includes the interests of other stakeholders when he seeks the legitimate shareholder interest in return on investment. In maximizing shareholder value, the manager must at the same time realize the common good of the entire firm. The manager's task to realize the maximum productivity of the firm cannot be secured by the market, competition, and the price system alone. The manager must realize productivity even where the power of competition does not force him to do so, for example, in imperfect markets or in developing nations. This indicates that the productivity of the firm is a kind of common good of the firm beyond mere profit maximization (Tavis 1997).

The decision maker of an institution cannot dispense himself from the responsibility for the common good of the institution by pointing to the duty toward the shareholders alone. Referring to a narrow principal-agent relationship instead of the full fiduciary duty toward the whole firm may be an act of shirking from responsibility. Every kind of principal-agent relationship or acting for the sake of someone else and his goals leads to a reduced moral obligation since, by virtue of the agency relationship, responsibility is divided between the principal and the agent and can be shifted forward and backward between them.

The danger of a reduced responsibility of management for the common good of a firm is the exaggeration of shareholder value as the only goal of the firm. The theory that the only task of the firm is to increase the value of its shares for the owners and that management success is measured only by the attainment of this goal reduces the complexity of management's obligation toward the common good of the firm (Koslowski 2002). The goals of other groups of firm members are rendered solely as means for the final end of return on the owner's investment. The effect is that management can exculpate itself from the responsibility toward the other groups of the firm.

The manager is not only the agent of the owners but is, at the same time, the steward of all groups in the firm and the fiduciary of the firm as a whole. The distinction between agency and fiduciary duties, between being an agent and being a fiduciary, holds true even more for the politician with a democratic mandate. The politician cannot be seen as the agent of his immediate constituency only. He must accept that he has the duty of office or the fiduciary duty toward the common good, the duty to represent all voters. Politics and management are fiduciary offices that include not only the duty toward furthering the interests of the principals, be they shareholders or voters, but also the fiduciary duty and duty of stewardship toward the common good. The interest of the principal, voter or shareholder, and the interest of all people concerned, the total voting population, or all employees of the firm must be considered at the same time. There is no unlimited autonomy of the voter or shareholder as principals to define the duties of their agents, the politician, or manager. The manager's fiduciary duty is not only an obligation toward shareholders. Even if it is primarily so, it is also a duty toward the corporation as a whole.

By giving agency power to a member of parliament, a minister, or a manager, the person invested with this power, the politician or the manager, cannot be obliged to neglect the common interest and only realize the interest of his immediate principals. In the market, the consumer, the shareholder, and the manager representing them must understand their right to decide to be in office and the fiduciary duty that aims at the common good of their institutions. The same holds in politics for the voter and the member of parliament representing the voter. The politician or the manager cannot understand themselves as autonomous lobbyists or agents of that segment of the constituency or the firm that voted for them or employed them only.

The idea of the common good and of the obligation of decision makers in government and in economic institutions toward the good of their institutions by their fiduciary duty is not an idea imposed from the outside in a normativist way on the principals' and the agents' individual self-interest, be they voters and politicians in the political arena or shareholders and managers in the market. The idea of the common good does not impose a situation of heteronomy on them. Rather, the idea of the common good demands the inclusion of the public interest in the enlightened self-interest of those who have power to decide. Powerful decision makers can only realize their own and their principals' self-interest if the institutions they direct are flourishing. Decision makers cannot reply to the objection that the common good of their institutions is not realized by saying that they only acted as agents of their principals. The politician cannot exculpate himself in cases of government failure by answering that he only acted in the interest of those who gave him their vote. The manager whose firm shrinks while paying high dividends to shareholders cannot justify his action by pointing to the fact that the interest of the shareholders has been realized. Fiduciary duty is more than mere agency for someone else.

The idea of the common good implies that the general, entire, or total interest of an institution is fulfilled. The total interest of an institution is to be derived from the nature or task of the institution. The neglect of the common good leads to a violation of the total good of an institution. It leads therefore to functional friction and to the incomplete fulfillment of the task of the institution.

The idea of the common good of an institution shows that institutions cannot reach their optimal performance and due diligence without anticipating their common good in the self-interested decisions of the people acting in them. The interest on the realization of optimal performance and due diligence leads to acknowledging as inevitable the task of considering also the common good as the self-interest of its members in the governance of institutions, be they political or economic (Koslowski 2004). The purely individualistic pursuit of goals in the market or in a democracy without consideration of the common good of the polity or the firm in the individual interests of those who have to make far-reaching decisions causes a suboptimal performance of the institution in question, be it the firm or the polity.

Note

A first version of this chapter has been published in Capaldi, Nicholas, ed. 2005. *Business and Religion: A Clash of Civilizations.* Salem, MA: Scrivener. Permission to republish this is gratefully acknowledged.

References

Alford, Helen, and Michael Naughton. 2002. Working the Common Good: The Purpose of the Firm. In *Rethinking the Purpose of Business: Interdisciplinary Essays from the Catholic Social Tradition.* Stephen A. Cortright and Michael J. Naughton, eds. Notre Dame, IN: University of Notre Dame Press, pp. 27–47.

Gundlach, Gustav. 1959. Gemeinwohl. In *Staatslexikon der Görres-Gesellschaft.* 6th ed. Freiburg i. Br.: Herder, pp. 737–740.

Herzog, Roman. 1974. Gemeinwohl II. In *Historisches Wörterbuch der Philosophie.* Joachim Ritter, ed. Darmstadt: Wissenschaftliche Buchgesellschaft.

Koslowski, Peter. 2002. Shareholder Value and the Purpose of the Firm. In *Rethinking the Purpose of Business. Interdisciplinary Essays from the Catholic Social*

   Tradition. Stephen A. Cortright and Michael J. Naughton, eds. Notre Dame,
   IN: University of Notre Dame Press, pp. 102–130.

———. 2004. Public Interest and Self-Interest in the Market and the Democratic
   Process. In *The Invisible Hand and the Common Good*. Bernard Hodgson, ed.
   Berlin, NY and Tokyo: Springer-Verlag, pp. 13–37.

Smith, Adam. 1963. The Wealth of Nations. In *The Works of Adam Smith*. Vol. 2,
   Aalen: Otto Zeller [1776, Reprint: 1811–1812].

Tavis, Lee A. 1997. *Power and Responsibility: Multinational Managers and Developing
   Country Concerns*. Notre Dame, IN: University of Notre Dame Press.

CHAPTER 6

GOVERNANCE AND GOVERNMENT FROM AN ARISTOTELIAN PERSPECTIVE

Alejo José G. Sison

Governance and Government

Zingales (1998, 498) defines corporate governance as "the complex set of constraints that shape the *ex post* bargaining over the quasi-rents generated by a firm." Shleifer and Vishny (1997, 737) state that it "deals with the ways in which suppliers of finance to corporations assure themselves of getting a return on their investment." In effect, "the fundamental concern of corporate governance is to ensure the means by which a firm's managers are held accountable to capital providers for the use of assets" (Gregory 2001, 438). Corporate governance becomes a particular case of the problems related with "agency theory." Agency theory deals with issues arising from the fact that although one party, the agent (managers), agrees to act for the benefit of another, the principal (capital providers), the principal cannot always monitor the agent's performance (Boatright 1999, 46–53).

From a wider perspective, corporate governance is the relationship among shareholders, management, and board as it determines the direction and performance of corporations (Monks and Minow 2001, 1). It refers to the processes as the election of board members, their compensation and evaluation. Although this outlines the board's major functions, it obscures other dimensions of governance. As Koehn observes, "corporate governance is better understood as the art of governing—in a principled fashion—so as to maximize the welfare of the company and of its relevant stakeholders" (Koehn 1999, 1). Perhaps agency problems are better addressed not with legal safeguards and economic incentives alone, but also with trust-building institutional practices (Koehn 1999, 13).

Corporate governance, more comprehensively, relates to how power and authority are exercised in a firm. Power refers to the capacity to effect change, authority, the validity of the motive for change. Change would be "authorized" only if it furthers the common good, not when due to force or to an agent's exclusive self-interest. Corporate governance means properly governing the firm as a social institution.

Aristotle's *Politics* is an obligatory reference for the government of states (Politics, henceforth Pltcs 1288b). Given that corporate governance, too, is some form of government, what guidance could Aristotle's *Politics* offer?

Analogy between Aristotelian City-States and Firms

First, we have to develop an analogy between city-states and firms. Corporations have evolved into economic entities possessing limited liability for investors, transferability of investor interests, legal personality, and a professionalized management (Monks and Minow 2001, 8–10). For historical reasons Aristotle could not have imagined such an independent economic institution. On the other hand, Greek city-states have metamorphosed into nation-states (Krasner 1999, 20–25). They are self-contained territories inhabited by people related by blood, sharing the same birthplace and culture. Would it still be possible to find fundamental similarities between city-states and corporations?

Yes, inasmuch as both city-states and firms are social institutions. They are composed of different groups of people organized in a manner that best pursues their common purpose: one of a political nature for the city-state, and one of an economic nature for the firm.

"First among the materials required" for a city-state is population, "the number and character of the citizens" (Pltcs 1326a). The state cannot be "a mere aggregate of persons," but rather "a union of them sufficing for the purposes of life" (Pltcs 1328b). Numbers are not enough and there has to be men of different kinds (Pltcs 1261a). It is also necessary that people "have a common place" and "share in that one city" (Pltcs 1261a). Unlike alliances for mutual protection or commercial exchange, citizens live together to achieve their purpose of "excellence" (Pltcs 1280b).

Similarly, we find herein the fundamental differences between city-states and firms. With respect to the "different groups of people", city-states are primarily divided into citizens and noncitizens; corporations, into either shareholders and nonshareholders or stakeholders and nonstakeholders, depending on the theory of the firm used.

Citizens, Shareholders and Stakeholders

A citizen is he who "shares in the administration of justice, and in offices" (Pltcs 1257a). By "administration of justice" we mean taking part in the deliberative or judicial administration of the state (Pltcs 1257b), and by "sharing in offices," holding some kind of rule (Pltcs 1276a). In essence, "a citizen is one who shares in governing and being governed" (Pltcs 1283b). For Aristotle, other groups aside from citizens are necessary for the state: children, the artisan class, and laborers. For citizenship, it is not enough to be a free man, one also has to be freed from necessary services.

An important feature of Aristotle's teachings on citizenship is its relativeness to government (Pltcs 1278b). Citizenship implies a hierarchy (Pltcs 1254a). Only citizens qualify to rule the state.

There are two possible analogues to citizens in the corporation: shareholders or stakeholders. They establish the dividing line between the classes of people in the firm.

It is erroneous to think of shareholders as "owners" of the company, when they only own shares (Clarkson and Deck 1998, 608). Share certificates entitle holders to the firm's "residual equity." Shareholders enjoy limited liability and reap profits through dividends or increases in share price. Other shareholder rights include choosing board members, participating in meetings and voting on changes in capital structure. According to the shareholder theory as explained by Milton Friedman in the *New York Times* article "The Social Responsibility of Business Is to Increase Its Profits," (September 13, 1970) board members (and by extension, managers, and employees) behave as "agents" and have a fiduciary duty to maximize the wealth of shareholders, their "principals."

The term "stakeholder" was first coined in a Stanford Research Institute document in 1963, designating "those groups without whose support the organization would cease to exist" (Freeman 1998, 602). The intention was to widen the group of people to whom management is responsible. A stakeholder refers to "any group or individual which can affect or is affected by an organization" (Freeman 1998, 602). We count shareholders, suppliers, customers, employees, competitors, communities, governments, and so forth among stakeholder groups. Each is characterized by "legitimate interests in procedural and/or substantive aspects of corporate activity" (Donaldson and Preston 1995, 67). Stakeholder theory purports that managers pay attention to all stakeholders and not to shareholders alone. The demands to maximize shareholder wealth ought to be tempered by the concern for the welfare of other stakeholders.

The protection of stakeholder interests clashes with certain legal traditions, as that of the United States for example (Boatright 1999, 172). However, granting priority to the financial interests of shareholders does not mean granting them exclusivity, for these could best be served—arguably—when framed in the long-term. A long-term perspective necessarily includes inputs from other stakeholder groups. As the American Bar Association Committee on Corporate Laws clarifies, "directors have fiduciary responsibilities to shareholders which, while allowing directors to give consideration to the interests of others, could compel them to find reasonable relationship to the long-term interests of shareholders" (Monks and Minow 2001, 37).

If citizenship includes participation in government, what is its equivalent in the firm? It is the condition that allows one to take active part in governance. Our first candidates are managers, who exercise power and authority in the firm. The problem is that they are "agents," and their work serves the interests of others, the "principals." Remember that for Aristotle, citizens perform the task of government not for any group other than themselves. Managers, aside from "agents," would also have to be "principals" to fulfill analogously in the firm the requirements for state citizenship. This only occurs with manager-shareholders.

Shareholder status is not enough to qualify for corporate "citizenship." It guarantees legal rights, but does not imply involvement in management. One thing is to possess a right and another to exercise it. Corporate "citizenship" requires the latter.

How are stakeholders compared to citizens? We identified as "stakeholders" those with "legitimate interests" (Donaldson and Preston 1995, 67) in a firm. This does not mean that those interests warrant legal protection, although jurisprudence sometimes accords them recognition. The legitimacy of stakeholder interests could come from social awareness or ethical appreciation. *Not all stakeholders* have to participate in *all corporate decisions*. It would suffice that those with legitimate interests do so in the issues that concern them.

Whether stakeholders are to corporations what citizens are to states demands a different answer for each stakeholder group. The mere possession of "legitimate interests" seems weak when compared to citizenship, which entails "sharing in the administration of justice, and in offices" (Pltcs 1257a). Nonshareholding employees are in the firm like slaves and foreigners in the state: without them, the company ceases to exist, yet they are not "citizens" because their tasks are done for others. Customers, suppliers, and competitors are, through contracts and agreements, like people who enjoy rights under trade treaties or military alliances. Although they are not citizens they share in the state's life. The most problematic case is that of government: its authority and power extend over the corporation, but it has to respect the freedom of enterprise. Shareholder-managers form the only stakeholder group that clearly passes the muster of corporate "citizenship."

Corporate Despots and Corporate Constitutional Rulers

The second element of our analogy between the state and the firm refers to *organization*. Both require a governing body, a rule, or constitution. The major difference is that state government is sovereign, while corporate governance is not. Firms are always subject to the state.

In the *Politics*, Aristotle explores a plurality of regimes, depending on the number of those who govern and for whom. The main division is between a "despotic" and a "constitutional" rule. Despotic rule is exercised over subjects who are "by nature slaves," constitutional rule over those "by nature free" (Pltcs 1255b). Although slave and master may have coincident interests, a slave is ruled primarily for the master and only accidentally for himself (Pltcs 1278b). Compare this with a father's government of wife and children—constitutional rule—in which the good of the governed or common good comes first (Pltcs 1278b). Aristotle states, "there is one rule which is for the sake of rulers and another rule which is for the sake of the ruled; the former is despotic, the latter a free [constitutional] government" (Pltcs 1333a). Since a despotic regime regards only the interests of rulers, it is "perverted", whereas a constitutional rule that looks after the common interest is a "true" regime (Pltcs 1279a).

Both "true" or "perverted" regimes are subject to further divisions, depending on the number of rulers. Among the true forms of government we have "kingships", when there is one ruler, "aristocracies", when the best men—who are few—rule, and "constitutional rules", when many rule (Pltcs 1279a–b). Among the perverted forms are "tyrannies", when the ruler is one, "oligarchies", when the ruler is more than one, and "democracies", when the rulers are many (Pltcs 1279a–b).

How relevant are these classifications to firms? The division into despotic and constitutional rules are applicable, because some firms are run for private interests, others for the common good. Some companies are governed justly, with everyone receiving his due, others unjustly, with parties short-changed. Some corporations may be despotically run, when the governed are treated as slaves, others constitutionally, when they are regarded as freemen.

Next come the distinctions among corporate "monarchies", "aristocracies", and "constitutional regimes", on the one hand, and corporate "tyrannies", "oligarchies", and "democracies", on the other. A corporate "monarchy" is a firm whose shareholding-CEO is chairman of the board, the "imperial CEO/Chairman". Such concentration is not by itself wrong, for it could bring heightened effectiveness, although the danger of abuse is undeniable. The "imperial CEO/Chairman" would be a tyrant if he put private interests before the common good.

A corporate "aristocracy" is found when governance is in the hands of a few who are the "best". In the Anglo-Saxon tradition, that is a perfectly "balanced" unitary board, with power shared among a handful of shareholding executive directors and nonexecutive directors; or in the Central European tradition, the dual boards, in which supervisory and management board members hold shares and exercise executive functions. The issue of being the "best" is not easy. At least we know that it refers to people whose claim to governance does not rest on their wealth and property alone—a corporate "oligarchy"—but on a concern for the good of the governed.

Hardest to find is an equivalent to a corporate "constitutional rule". This requires that "the many" participate in governance and seek the good of all. We probably have to look among cooperatives, in which workers own stakes and share in profits. However, the requisite that "owner-workers" participate in governance still stands.

It is really difficult for a corporate "democracy" to flourish. First, because "the many" who are poor would not have capital for a business. Second, that each member pursue his private good is a recipe for disaster. Finally, we should not confuse corporate "democracy" with "shareholder activism", when small shareholders come together to exercise rights, challenging managers and majority shareholders.

States and Firms, Ends and Means

The third basis of our analogy between city-states and firms alludes to *purpose*: a political one in the former, an economic one in the latter. Due to their purpose, city-states are considered "natural" and "perfect" societies, corporations, "artificial" and "imperfect" associations.

The state, like the family and the village, is a "natural" society, stemming from an innate tendency in human beings (Pltcs 1252b). However, unlike the family and the village, only the state is "perfect" because it alone is "self-sufficing". In the state men's everyday needs are satisfied, such that efforts are directed toward "living a good life". The state represents the "end" or "final cause", the fully developed stage of human life (Pltcs 1252b).

What does a "good," "perfect and self-sufficing", and "happy and honorable life" (Pltcs 1280b) consist in? Aristotle offers several accounts in the *Politics*. One lists its basic ingredients, conditions met only in the state: food, arts, arms, revenue, religion, and a power of deciding the public interest and what is just (Pltcs 1328b). Another enumerates the necessary elements for a flourishing life: external goods, goods of the body, and goods of the soul (Pltcs 1323a). And a third establishes a hierarchy among them, such that external and the material goods are conditions for excellent actions, the goods of the soul (Pltcs 1324a).

The firm is an "artificial" society, because it arises neither directly nor organically from human nature. It is "imperfect" because it is not self-sufficing; it is an "intermediate association" between the family and the state.

Although Aristotle does not mention the corporation in the *Politics*, we find allusions in the "family connections, brotherhoods, common sacrifices, and amusements" (Pltcs 1280b) that draw men together. The economy was born within the family, as "household management". The first corporations arose from the family's struggle to cope with basic needs through the division of labor and specialization. Only later, when those needs became more complex did larger corporations appear. But even then, the family remained as the basis of "economic friendships" (Pltcs 1280b).

Despite the importance that Aristotle granted to the economy, he firmly thought that it functioned exclusively in the realm of means. Because "the end of the state is the good life, and these [i.e., family connections, brotherhoods, common sacrifices and amusements, and by extension, firms] are the means towards it" (Pltcs 1280b). The economic ends that corporations seek are *means* to the political end of city-states. The production of goods and services which is the purpose of firms is not self-justifying; it is desirable insofar as it contributes to an excellent life in the state.

Aristotelian Orientations for Corporate Governance

In his inquiry on the best regime, Aristotle distinguishes between the best in abstract, absolute terms, that which is "most in accordance with our aspirations, if there were no external impediment", and the best "relatively to circumstances", that which is "adapted to particular states" (Pltcs 1288b). This caveat is fully applicable in our search for the "best regime" for corporations.

Aristotle advocates polity or constitutional government—a fusion of oligarchy and democracy—as the best attainable regime (Pltcs 1293b). So, too, for corporations.

This mixed regime is not free from difficulties. First, both oligarchy and democracy are despotic forms of government. Second, there is a contradiction in entrusting government to the few and the many. How could Aristotle's position be reconciled?

The mark of an oligarchy is that rulers possess property, of a democracy, that they have freedom (Pltcs 1279b–1280a). That the wealthy be few and the free many is accidental. It is possible to have a regime in which the many who rule are free and wealthy. Also, a combination between oligarchy and democracy could be obtained through an interplay of written law and customs (Pltcs 1292b).

In this mixed regime, the defects of oligarchy and democracy are tempered and their strengths enhanced. A polity boasts of a dominant middle class. This makes the polity secure, because the middle class, having sufficient goods, does not covet those of others; the extremes are also prevented from tipping the scales of justice (Pltcs 1295b).

The corporate equivalent of a polity is where government is deposited in shareholding executives with relative wealth and freedom. They belong to an egalitarian "middle class." This corporate "middle class" should be dominant, to avoid the interests of extremes from prevailing. Having a minimum of property, rulers do not fall to envy, but neither do they have too much as to neglect the administration of justice. This corporate mixed regime is the most stable and secure form of government.

Aristotle teaches that only in the best state will the excellence of the "good man" be identical to the excellence of the "good citizen" (Pltcs 1288a, 1293b). By extension, only in the best corporation will the excellence of the "good man" be identical to that of the "good shareholder-executive." This is true partly because in a polity—as in a corporation—rulers who initially may already be "good and wise" only learn to rule by first learning to obey well. It is not possible, therefore, in the best state, to separate the excellence of the ruler from that of the citizen or from that of the good man. Neither is this possible in the best corporation, with regard to the virtue of the shareholder-executive and the virtue of the shareholder-executive as a human being.

If the best state is the one that affords the best life for its citizens, then the best corporation, similarly, is the one that bestows the best life upon its shareholder-executives. Happiness or "the best life" consists in acting rightly; and in order to perform right actions, one needs the excellences or virtues. However, virtues by themselves are insufficient, because "the best life, both for individuals and states, is the life of excellence, *when excellence has external goods enough* for the performance of goods actions" (Pltcs 1324a, emphasis added). Therefore, external goods together with virtuous actions are indispensable for happiness or "the best life". Finally, Aristotle sets as a stringent final condition for a happy life in the best state: that all citizens be excellent and that they all have a share in government (Pltcs 1332a).

Among the institutional practices of corporate governance is the enactment of codes. Codes apply to a firm, an economic sector, or to organizations in general. They have varying degrees of obligatoriness and sanctionability. Common to all is a two-part structure: the first delves into the nature of corporate boards and the second, into the functions of its committees.

Mission, Composition, and Structure of Corporate Boards

The board's mission is the supervision of management, approving strategies and appointing top executives. Implicit is the search for the "common interest" or "justice" (Pltcs 1253a), balancing the interests of stakeholders.

Boards often ponder whether it is beneficial to have a written code. Aristotle argues for the supremacy of law, insisting that magistrates only regulate matters on which the law cannot decide. Not that written law is unalterable or superior to custom; Aristotle opines that "in politics it is impossible that all things should precisely be set down in writing" (Pltcs 1269a). But since laws are universal, and actions particular, it is sometimes necessary to change laws. Nonetheless, alterations should not be taken lightly, "for the law has no power to command obedience except that of habit, which can only be given by time, so that a readiness to change from old to new law enfeebles the power of the law" (Pltcs 1269a). So habit, custom, or education is superior to written law: "the best laws . . . will be of no avail unless the young are trained by habit and education in the spirit of the constitution" (Pltcs 1310a). Although no code is perfect, it is beneficial for boards to have one as a safeguard against arbitrariness.

Aristotle's biases show in his criteria for the composition of the board. First come the qualifications for citizenship, equivalent to executive shareholdership. He states a preference for elderly males whom he considers superior, fitter for command, in fuller possession of their deliberative faculties and with greater authority (Pltcs 1254b, 1269b, 1260a). He prefers intellectuals to laborers, since governing involves the mind more than the body (Pltcs 1339a). It is more desirable to have many members instead of few, since "the many are more incorruptible than the few; they are like the greater quantity of water which is less easily corrupted than a little" (Pltcs 1286a).

As for the board structure, we must remember that we are legislating with and for ordinary men, since for those of preeminent excellence "there is no law—they are themselves a law" (Pltcs 1283b). Despite being equals, these ordinary men "cannot all rule together, but must change . . . in some order of succession" (Pltcs 1261a). As a result, all citizens rule and are ruled in turn, as justice requires. Another effect is the inhibiting of disproportionate increase in a citizen's prosperity. Aristotle is against a citizen's holding office for life or on account of belonging to a certain family because of arbitrariness and the fact that "the mind grows old as well as the body" (Pltcs 1270b, 1271a). Neither does he approve of the accumulation of offices. He favors short tenures because "it is not easy for a person to do any great harm when his tenure of office is short, whereas long possessions beget tyranny" (Pltcs 1308a). Since "most people are bad judges in their own case" (Pltcs 1280a), board structure has to allow for checks to power.

Most boards delegate functions to committees, specializing in nominations, compensation, compliance, and audit. What advice does Aristotle offer?

The nominations committee is entrusted with the recruitment of board candidates. Aristotle requires three traits: "first of all, loyalty to the constitution; then the highest administrative capacity; and excellence and justice of the kind proper to each form of government" (Pltcs 1309a). Other criteria are birthright, wealth, and chance, but these are overriden by merit. Merit includes foresight and the knowledge of a master, but above all, the excellence of character. Aristotle affirms that "a ruler ought to have excellence of character in perfection, for his function, taken absolutely, demands a master artificer" (Pltcs 1260a). Among the virtues required of a ruler are courage, endurance, temperance, and justice. Ultimately, rulers should be chosen with regard to their personal life and conduct.

The compensation committee determines the remuneration of directors and top management. The objective is not only for a ruler to have enough property to live temperately, but for him to live liberally: both are matters of education rather than resources. Unlike Plato, Aristotle does not forbid citizens from accumulating more than five times the minimum property qualification; yet he still values moderation. Moderation does not mean an equal amount for all, "for it is not the possessions but the desires of mankind which require to be equalized, and this is impossible, unless a sufficient education is provided by the laws" (Pltcs 1266b). Pay should be adequate so that people do not become badly off and prone to bribes. But offices should be run such that rulers do not enrich themselves from them: "people do not take any great offence at being kept out of government—indeed they are rather pleased than otherwise at having leisure for their private business—but what irritates them is to think that their rulers are stealing public money; then they are doubly annoyed; for they lose both honor and profit" (Pltcs 1308b). That an office does not bring profit makes combining democracy with aristocracy possible, because "all would be able to hold office, which is the aim of democracy, and the notables would be magistrates, which is the aim of aristocracy" (Pltcs 1308b, 1309a).

The compliance committee guarantees that board members behave in accordance with rules. Aristotle emphasizes the observance of rules in trifles: "In all well-balanced governments there is nothing which should be more jealously maintained than the spirit of obedience to law, more especially in small matters; for transgression creeps in unperceived and at last ruins the state, just as the constant recurrence of small expenses in time eats up a fortune" (Pltcs 1370b). This also holds true for corporations.

Finally, the audit committee oversees the gathering of information on a company, regulating its flow. Aristotle suggests for transparency, through some sort of general shareholders' meeting, and good record-keeping: "In order to avoid speculation of the public money, the transfer of revenue should be made at a general assembly of the citizens, and duplicates of the accounts deposited with the different brotherhoods, companies, and tribes" (Pltcs 1309a). He recommends that honors be given to magistrates who have earned a reputation of ruling without gain (Pltcs 1309a).

Governing as "Praxis"

To close the gap between the government of states and the governance of firms, we have advocated a wider, more political and ethical view of governing as opposed to a narrow, technical, purely economic, or business perspective. An analogous interpretation of the guidelines found in the *Politics* suggests that governance and government refer to essentially the same kind of action. Good governance demands something more than avoiding that principals be fooled by agents, but neither should it be limited to mere rule-following in the production and distribution of quasi-rents. Governance is the government of the firm as an intermediate institution, one that makes a predominantly economic contribution to the welfare of society as a whole.

The neoclassical economic doctrine and the agency theory underlying most codes of corporate governance assume that individual actors seek above all their own selfish interests, without regard for the common good. Aristotelian anthropology teaches, by contrast, that ordinary people, with their motley set of virtues and vices, have a fundamental inclination towards the common good. Hence, the rules on governance that derive from neoclassical economics and agency theory try to build-up trust among inherently selfish individuals deeply suspicious of each other. Aristotle, on the other hand, focuses on the education of rulers, instilling in them the virtues of mind and helping them cultivate the excellences of character.

Aristotle provides a basis for understanding the task of government through the distinction between "production" (*poieisis*) and "action" (*praxis*) (Pltcs 1254a). "Action" and "production" refer to changes wrought by human intervention on individual, concrete, and contingent realities; they are activities carried out under the guidance of reason in its practical use.

Governing is more akin to "action" or *praxis*, which is superior to "production" or *poieisis*. In "action", the emphasis lies on the qualitative change in the subject, while in "production", the external object is more important (Pltcs 1254a). In "action"—unlike in "production"—it is not possible to perfectly codify a set of objective rules and separate them from the personal dispositions of the agent, in a manner that guarantees the quality of the activity's performance. There are no valid recipe books or instruction manuals for good "action", unlike for good "production". To perform a good "action", aside from following elementary rules, an agent also has to ensure the right intention and moral dispositions. The excellence of "action" is called "prudence"; the excellence of "production", "technique", or "art". Prudence in governing not only requires knowledge of the proper end, but also the right choice of means. As a form of "action", governing comes close to Aristotle's metaphysical model for a "perfect, immanent act", in which the end is internal to the activity itself (Aristotle's Metaphysics 1048b).

The error of most approaches to governance consists in understanding this task as "production" rather than "action". The end then becomes the formulation of codes, the setting up of structures and the design of processes instead of governing the firm well within the wider context of society. Together with this overdependence on codes comes the neglect for the virtues of mind and character in the education of the ruler or executive. Not that Aristotle holds written laws in disdain; they are a safeguard against arbitrariness and exert a powerful influence in moulding habit and custom. But he upholds the superiority of habit and custom over the law, for, absent coercion, it is from habit and custom that the law draws strength.

References

Aristotle. 1971. *Aristotle's Metaphysics* (C. Kirwan, trans. and notes). Oxford: Clarendon Press.
———. 1990. *The Politics* (P. Everson, ed.). Cambridge: Cambridge University Press.
Boatright, John. 1999. *Ethics in Finance*. Malden, MA/Oxford: Blackwell Publishers.
Clarkson, Max, and Michael Deck. 1998. Stockholder. In *The Blackwell EncyclopedicDictionary of Business Ethics*. Patricia Werhane and R. Edward Freeman, eds. Malden, MA/Oxford: Blackwell Publishers, p. 608.

Donaldson, Thomas, and Lee Preston. 1995. The Stakeholder Theory of the Corporation: Concepts, Evidence, and Implications. *Academy of Mangement Review* 20: 65–91.

Freeman, R. Edward. 1998. Stakeholder Theory. In *The Blackwell Encyclopedic Dictionary of Business Ethics*. Patricia Werhane and R. Edward Freeman, eds. Malden, MA/Oxford: Blackwell Publishers, pp. 602–606 .

Friedman, Milton. 1970. The Social Responsibility of Business Is to Increase Its Profits. *The New York Times Magazine* (September 13), 17–20.

Gregory, Holly. 2001. Overview of Corporate Governance Guidelines and Codes of Best Practice in Developing and Emerging Markets. In *Corporate Governance*. Robert Monks and Nell Minow, eds. Oxford/Malden, MA: Blackwell Publishing, pp. 438–446.

Koehn, Daryl. 1999. *An Overview of Issues in Corporate Governance.* <http://www.stthom.edu/cbes/conferences/daryl_koehn.html> (accessed October 16, 2002).

Krasner, Stephen. 1999. *Sovereignty: Organized Hypocrisy*. Princeton, NJ: Princeton University Press.

Monks, Robert, and Nell Minow. 2001. *Corporate Governance*. Oxford/Malden, MA: Blackwell Publishing.

Shleifer, Andrei, and Robert Vishny. 1997. A survey of corporate governance. *Journal of Finance* 52: 737–783.

Zingales, Luigi. 1998. Corporate Governance. In *The New Palgrave Dictionary of Economics and Law*, vol. 1. Peter Newman, ed. London: MacMillan, 497–503.

CHAPTER 7

THE ETHICAL ISSUE OF CORPORATE GOVERNANCE AND MANAGEMENT SCIENCE THEORIES

Wojciech W. Gasparski

States, Corporations, and How They are Governed

States are run by governments and corporations by relevant bodies. The relations between these bodies and company stakeholders creates a system of corporate governance. The use of the word "governance" is partly based on a fad but it emphasizes the focus on the "act, manner, function of government" (Kitson and Campbell 1996, 112).

According to some authors (e.g., Jay 1993) there is "a parallel between the large, modern public corporation and the independent or semi-independent states of the past" (21). Therefore "theories of government offer a way of fully understanding the behavior of these large corporations . . ., management can only be properly studied as a branch of government" (Kitson and Campbell 1996, 111). This does not mean, however, that a corporation board should be considered as a government: "Unfortunately, corporate governance is often misconstrued, and interpreted as if its task were not governing corporations but making them more like governments." (Sternberg 1994, 199).

Although boards of directors are not governments and CEOs are not prime ministers, the ethical issues related to corporate governance are

similar in many aspects to those of state administration. Let us consider the
following issues:

- Who is the principal?: For states it is a party or society; for corporations shareholders or stakeholders;
- What is related to decisions considered as a commodity?: For states it
  is corruption in the worst or *manus puris* in the best; for corporations
  it is excessive remuneration or distributive justice;
- Self-centrism or leadership: For states it is the famous *l'Ėtat c'est
  moi* or the common good; for corporations it is the lord and master or
  Our Credo response;
- Who administers?: For states it is civil servants or the civil service; for
  corporations it is tale-bearers or managers.

No doubt readers will be able to add a few more characteristic issues,
depending on the social context of the state or the corporation with which
they are familiar.

It is not the structure but the functions or social institutions that are
essential for governing, organizational design, theorists say. Some of them
even refer to Locke:

> Each individual, fearing that as he "does his thing," other people are "doing
> their things," and that all the while there may not be enough "things" to
> go around, demands three types of governmental institutions (Locke):
> (1) Objective judges . . ., (2) Objective laws . . ., (3) Institutionalized power . . . .
> In modern organizations, the analogy to scarce resources is clear and work-
> flows of physical technology generate conflict over organizational resources.
> Further, conflict may result from scarce opportunities for self-actualization
> and growth as well as from scarce physical resources. Managers and executives
> become hierarchical judges. Policies, procedures, programs, and other coordi-
> nating mechanisms become objective law. Monetary rewards and various
> opportunities for self-actualization and growth become institutionalized power.
> (Summer 1976, 120–121)

In both states and corporations, governance or institutionalized power
needs legitimacy.

The Issue of Legitimacy

Carroll (1989, 414) differentiates two levels of legitimacy in his inquiry:
(1) The micro or business firm level of "maintaining legitimacy by
conforming with societal expectations" and (2) the macro level of "the

corporate system or the totality of business enterprises." His thesis is that "the issue of corporate governance is a direct outgrowth of the question of legitimacy," that is, there is a gap between what corporations do and what they are expected to do by society.

In essence, the issue depends on the "ontological" question of whether an organization should be considered "as a social organism meeting human needs of the many" or as "an impersonal mechanism for financial processing, creating wealth for the few" (Murray 1997, 142).

Traditional management science literature discusses the issue of running a corporation in terms of organizational structures (Nickels 1987). Some theorists adopt a narrower view. Sternberg, for instance, suggests that corporate governance is nothing more than the need for and the ways of pursuing proper ends of a corporation as defined by its shareholders to whom directors and managers are accountable (Sternberg 1994, 199–200).

Other theorists consider corporations systemically. Authors from organizational design (Baligh 2006; Griffin 1999; Kilmann et al. 1976; Schlesinger et al. 1992) develop the theoretical systems approach. Schlesinger et al. (1992, 5) points to two arguments supporting the systemic nature of an organization. Organizations are complex social systems because of at least two reasons: their internal interdependence and feedback reaction. This means that the parts of an organization affect each other. Therefore the ideal state would be one wherein the "choices managers make about the characteristics of one element depend on choices they make about other elements" (Schlesinger 1992, 5). It also means that once organizations receive information they can use it to improve their operations. They can, but may not. What they really do depends on managers' decisions on how to behave after receiving feedback. The manager decides whether or not "to reach a balance or steady state."

A similar systems perspective is suggested by business ethicists who discuss issues of corporate governance. Collier and Roberts (2001, 70) state that "the view we want to present here is that of a systemic and relational view of the nature of corporate governance and ethics." Business ethicists do not argue for the supremacy of this or that group of stakeholders. Rather, their argument rests on considering a stake or interest as a moral property of relatedness:

> In this sense corporate governance is about the way in which we seek to manage the interdependencies in which we are all immersed. Though we assign the role of governance to particular groups, notably boards of directors within and the state and judiciary beyond the firm, governance in practice is composed of an almost infinite series of responsibilities distributed among the

various stakeholders, and possibly falling between them. The conduct of directors, ministers, lawyers has to be understood in the context of the choices and actions of employees, consumers, citizens, shareholders . . . .From this perspective the problems of governance cannot be resolved at a single site, by board of directors, but only in a change of conduct across these multiple chains of interdependent relationships. At every point there is both a space and a necessity for ethical concern and ethical conduct. Nor are good intentions enough. (Collier and Roberts 2001, 70).

Organizational design specialists and business ethicists join systems theorists in affirming that stakeholder analysis is very important, if not indispensable, in any kind of organized human activity. It is a truly systemic question for it calls for taking into account mutual context dependence—both internal and external—of an organization and its parts (Midgley 2000). Following this argument some authors propose special tools for analysis. One is the stakeholders' matrix, which identifies the interests or stakes to be responded to (Grayson and Hodges 2001, 232–233). Investors need return on investment; employees, jobs, reward, and recognition. Customers are looking for safe and reliable products while suppliers for regular orders and prompt payments. For government, the important stakes are a thriving private sector, providing employment opportunities, serving citizens and paying taxes whereas for local communities, they are employment opportunities and contribution to the local economy.

Corporate Governance and Management Science

It is significant that management theory perceives corporate governance as an issue only for investors and not for other corporate constituencies. According to some management scientists, contemporary investors, hungry for return on investment, put corporate governance and ethics on their agenda "to ensure compliance with best practice in corporate governance" (Grayson and Hodges 2001, 211).

These authors link governance with *Committing to Action*, the fourth of the *Seven Steps*—(1) Recognizing the trigger; (2) Making a business case; (3) Scooping the issues; (4) Committing to action (giving shareholder-added value, putting out signals, governance, demonstrating leadership); (5) Integrating strategies; (6) Engaging stakeholders; and (7) Measuring and reporting—recommended to minimize risk and maximize opportunities in response to 'Emerging Management Issues' (EMI) such as ecology and environment, health and well-being, diversity and human rights, and communities. "With the key issues mapped out, it is necessary to commit to action and articulate that commitment, whether as an individual manager, a department head, or a senior executive. The commitment is to make decisions that minimize risks and maximize opportunities for both business and society, while recognizing their interdependence" (Grayson and Hodges 2001, 211).

In terms of real life practice, authors refer to some of the instruments introduced recently by business organizations. Some of them extensively use approaches sensitive to culture (e.g., Ford's corporate governance group), others introduce corporate governance codes of good practice (for instance, the Polish stock exchange), and a third group uses checklists to control the level of stakeholder participation, such as EMI. Finally, Grayson and Hodges refer to closer cooperation between corporations and public authorities in order to promote and support standards in governance closely related to corporate social responsibility and ethics.

From these details we may conclude with Sternberg that "essential for good corporate governance, business ethics is of value to all businesses everywhere, be they large or small, domestic or international; it is equally necessary for manufacturers and retailers and providers of services" (Sternberg 1994, 18–19). This position is confirmed by contemporary management science according to which "the issue of corporate governance, how well companies' boards of directors represent stockholder and other stakeholder interests, especially around financial performance, is . . . a major concern of activist shareholder" (Waddock 2002, 217).

Toward Good Practice

Waddock (2002, 217) points to the following obstacles to good corporate governance:

- Directors' interests
- Cultural issues
- Board of directors structure, and
- Shareholder rights and activism

To overcome the obstacles, some organizations introduce principles of good corporate governance. The California Public Employees' Retirement System (CalPERS), for example, enumerates accountability, transparency, equity, voting methods, codes of best practices, long-term vision (Waddock 2002, 218–219). Not only established economies make relevant arrangements but also their patterns are followed by emerging economies, for which Central European initiatives serve as a good example. Poland's approach is a good case in point.

In Poland, two relevant codes have been developed: the *Best Practices in Public Companies* of the Corporate Governance Forum and the Warsaw Institute of Business Development (2005) and the *Corporate Governance Code for Public Corporations* of the Gdansk Institute for Market Economics (2002). The World Bank (2005) recently assessed Polish achievements in the area. In its *Report on the Observance of Standards and Codes* (*ROSC*) in OECD countries a special chapter is devoted to the "Corporate governance country assessment: Poland." Other related documents include "Corporate Governance of State-Owned Enterprises in Poland" and the "Note on the enforcement of the 'Comply or Explain' provision in the best practices in public companies 2005 of the Warsaw Stock Exchange."

The "comply or explain" rule was recommended in the Financial Aspect of the Corporate Governance Committee Report (*Cadbury Report*) elaborated for the London Stock Exchange and presented in December 1992. The Polish Code adopted the rule, trying to encourage companies to accept the Code voluntarily. Although this voluntary decision is closely related to the issue of a corporation's reputation ("reputational risk from non-compliance") it is still not clear, according to the World Bank Report (*ROSC*), if the rule is a real trigger or incentive for compliance. Nevertheless, only 3 percent of Polish listed companies comply with none of the principles of the *Best Practices in Public Companies*, also known as the Polish Corporate Governance Code. The percentage of companies complying with all the principles is 14 percent, but as much as 81 percent comply with all but one principle (68 percent do not comply with the principle concerning independent members of the supervisory board, 13 percent with the principle concerning convening shareholders' meetings and adopting resolutions).

The *ROSC* underlines that the Polish Code is an effective instrument to increase awareness of the importance of corporate governance and related reforms. A number of options are mentioned, including flexibility and practicality of imposing sanctions against listed companies that file false compliance statements, requiring audit committees (or auditors) to monitor compliance, providing additional investigation and enforcement power to the Warsaw Stock Exchange, and so forth. The *Report* also lists recommendations that should be revised in the nearest future. First of all, the Code should focus on board issues defining board responsibilities, next, supervisory board members should also be responsible for preparing financial statements, and finally, more training of supervisory board members is necessary.

The following statement should be considered as a conclusion of the Report: "International experience suggests that one of the major benefits of codes of best practice is their utility in 'test marketing' corporate governance legal reforms; many provisions introduced in codes are later migrated to the law" (World Bank 2005, 6).

It is significant that after assessing which OECD corporate governance principles are observed in Poland, the *Report* states that only two are materially not observed. These are the details of the assessment:

- Nine principles were met without significant difficulties, that is, *observed*;
- Twelve principles were *largely observed*, that is, only minor shortcomings plus the intention to achieve full observance were noticed;
- Eight principles were *partially observed*, that is, there were differences in relation to the positive legal and regulatory framework; practice and enforcement diverged;
- Two principles were *materially not observed*, that is, shortcomings were sufficient to raise doubts about the ability to achieve observance. These included (1) "The exercise of ownership right by all shareholders, including institutional investors, should be facilitated" and (2) "Stakeholders, including individual employees and their representative bodies, should be able to freely communicate their concerns about illegal or unethical practices to the board and their rights should not be compromised for doing this" (whistleblowing rules).

Conclusions

Reading the papers, watching TV, or listening to radio programs devoted to corporate misbehavior, one feels that the words written in textbooks published a decade or so ago have been forgotten, or that the students then who are now CEOs and high-ranking managers did not pay attention to what they were taught in their classes on "Business and Society." On the one hand, we learn from the media about Enron, Arthur Andersen in the United States, or about Colloseum, PZU-Zycie and Porta Holding in Poland, and on the other, we recall Carroll's *Business and Society*:

> The giant corporation in the United States is in trouble. Indeed, it could be said that the American system of doing business is in trouble . . . .Shareholder groups have become increasingly critical of how management groups and boards of directors run the firms. They complain about management's lack of accountability, ineffective and complacent boards, excessive managerial compensation, and a general lack of focus on the importance of shareholders relative to management. This later criticism means that management is

looking out for number one, but the number one it is protecting is themselves, not their owners (Carroll 1989, 413).

This gives rise to the following questions:

- Who runs the corporation?
- To whom do board members and top managers report?
- To whom are these people really responsible and accountable?
- Is it perhaps only to themselves?

This applied, and today applies again, mostly to big corporations, that are growing in power and whose managers become richer and richer. Early on, everything was simple and clear: there was the owner who ran his firm by himself. Even when he decided to employ a president or appoint members of the board, he was *the* decision maker; he had *the* power. Company growth and stockholder dispersion induced the separation of two fundamental functions: ownership and control. The positions of individual owners were taken by shareholders. Yesterday's aides to the owners—high-ranking managers—seized control.

The open scissors between shareholder interests (ownership) and management (control) interests gave birth to the question of corporate governance. This is how the truly Montesquian problem of power division emerged. This time in relation not to a state but to corporations, some of which are bigger than many states and function on a global scale, like empires. There are many problems linked to the issue of corporate governance, including:

- The functioning of corporate bodies
- Their effectiveness, efficiency, and ethicality (the "three E's")
- Combining the roles of CEO and Chairman of the Board
- Conflicts of interest
- Hostile mergers and acquisitions
- Practices like greenmail or golden parachutes, and
- Insider trading.

This forces states, business organizations, and international organizations (e.g., the OECD) as well as business ethics specialists to try to solve the Montesquian problem. But the problem has resurfaced. This teaches us that business ethics is a never-ending story, in relation to corporate governance in particular (Zsolnai and Gasparski 2002). With regard to management science theories and their influence on corporate governance and other managerial practices, one should take seriously the warnings from Sumantra Ghoshal of the London Business School: "A management theory, if it gains enough currency, changes the behavior of managers. . . . By incorporating negative, and highly pessimistic assumptions about people and institutions, pseudoscientific theories of management have done much to reinforce, if not create, pathological behavior on the part of managers and companies. It is time the academics who propose these theories, and the business schools and universities that employ them, acknowledged the consequences" (Ghoshal 2003, 4).

It is time to recall the concept of the *humanistic coefficient* introduced a couple of decades ago by Florian Znaniecki, a Polish sociologist, according to whom all cultural phenomena are what they are "only as conscious human endeavors: we study them only in relation to a known or hypothetically construed complex of experiences. . . . All the objective reality of the phenomena . . . are to be missing when . . . the phenomena are to be considered not as subjects of somebody's experience or complexes of one's conscious activities but as 'nobody's' reality of the type postulated by (nature) science" (Gasparski 2003, 6; Znaniecki 1988). This exact warning is echoed in the Ghoshal paper: "The problem is that, unlike theories in the physical sciences, theories in the social sciences tend to be self-fulfilling. . . . This is why it is nonsense to pretend that management theories can be completely objective and value-free" (Ghoshal 2003, 4).

Knowledge vital to conducting business activity comes in two varieties: knowledge about facts and knowledge about values. Knowledge about values—that is, about the axiological context of action—is a sine qua non condition for understanding why people creating the *sensu largo* organization—stakeholders—make particular choices and undertake particular actions. Without such knowledge, familiarity with the facts is only skin deep and is often far from the essence of the issue. What is more, ignoring knowledge about values creates the illusion of the nonexistence of the axiological context, implicitly present at the foundation of decision making and action. Knowledge about the axiological context of business activity is needed. Without it, today's understanding of a knowledge-based economy is deprived of an important component and becomes faulty; practice becomes ineffective and wrong. This is confirmed by recently conducted research relating to the "dominant logic of the company," the outcome of which shows that it is not pure "logic" but a combination of axiology and praxiology manifested in the conduct of the company's people, of which corporate governance is a vital component.

References

Baligh, Helmy H. 2006, *Organization Structures: Theory and Design, Analysis and Prescription*. Springer, New York.

Carroll, Archie B. 1989. *Business and Society: Ethics and Stakeholder Management*. Cincinnati: South-Western.

Collier, Jane, and John Roberts. 2001. Introduction: An Ethic for Corporate Governance? *Business Ethics Quarterly* 11, 1: 67–71.

Corporate Governance Forum and the Warsaw Institute of Business Development. 2005. *Best Practices in Public Companies*, <http://www.wse.com.pl/gpw_e.asp?cel=e_spolki&k=6&i=/corporate/listy_prezesa> (accessed January 23, 2006).

Gasparski, Wojciech W. 2003. Editorial. In *Systemic Change through Praxis and Inquiry*. New Brunswick and London: Transaction Publishers, pp. 5–11.

Gdansk Institute for Market Economics. 2002. *Corporate Governance Code for Public Corporations*, <http://www.pfcg.org.pl/files/download/code_final_complete.pdf> (accessed January 23, 2006).

Ghoshal, Sumantra. 2003. B Schools Share the Blame for Enron: Teaching brutal theories leads naturally to management brutality. *Business Ethics* 17, No. 3 (Fall): 4 (originally appeared in the *Financial Times*, London, July 17, 2003).

Grayson, David, and Adrian Hodges. 2001. *Everybody's Business: Making Risks and Opportunities in Today's Global Society*. London: Dorling Kindersley Ltd.

Griffin, Ricky W. 1999. *Management*. Boston, NY: Houghton Mifflin Co.

Jay, Antony. 1993. *Management and Machiavelli: Power and Authority in Business Life*. London: Century Business.

Kilmann, Ralph H., Louis R. Pondy, and Dennis P. Slevin, eds. 1976. *The Management of Organization Design: Strategies and Implementation*, vols. 1, 2. North Holland, NY: Elsevier.

Kitson, Alan, and Robert Campbell. 1996. *The Ethical Organization: Ethical Theory and Corporate Behaviour*. London: Houndmills.

Midgley, Gerald. 2000. *Systemic Intervention: Philosophy, Methodology and Practice*. New York: Kluwer Academic/ Plenum Publishers.

Murray, David. 1997. *Ethics in Organizations*. London: Kogan Page.

Nickels, William G. 1987. *Understanding Business*. St. Louis, MO: Times Mirror/Mosby.

Schlesinger, Phyllis F., John Kotter, Vijay Sathe, and Leonard Schlesinger. 1992. *Organization: Text, Cases and Readings on the Management of Organizational Design and Change*. Homewood, IL: Irwin.

Sternberg, Elaine. 1994. *Just Business: Business Ethics in Action*. London: Little, Brown & Co.

Summer, Charles E. 1976. Strategies for Organization Design. In *Management of Organization Design: Strategies and Implementation*. Ralph H. Kilman, Louis R. Pondy, and Dennis P. Slevin, eds. North Holland, NY: Elsevier Science & Technology Books, pp. 103–139.

Waddock, Sandra. 2002. *Leading Corporate Citizens: Vision, Values, Value Added.* Boston: McGraw-Hill.

World Bank. 2005. Corporate Governance Country Assessment: Poland. *Report on the Observance of Standards and Codes (ROSC),* <http://www.worldbank.org/ifa/rosc_poland.html> (accessed January 23, 2006).

Znaniecki, Florian. 1988. *Introduction to Sociology* (in Polish—*Wstep do soajologii*). Warsaw: PWN.

Zsolnai, Laslo, and Wojciech W. Gasparski, eds. 2002. *Ethics and the Future of Capitalism.* New Brunswick and London: Transaction Publishers.

PART II

A GLOBAL SURVEY OF BUSINESS ETHICS AND CORPORATE GOVERNANCE

CHAPTER 8

BUSINESS ETHICS AND CORPORATE GOVERNANCE IN AFRICA

G.J. (Deon) Rossouw

Introduction

The rising tide of corporate governance around the globe left its traces on the African continent. Despite the diversity amongst the 53 countries with their varied colonial legacies comprising Africa, some patterns can be discerned with regard to corporate governance. The purpose of this chapter is to identify general trends in how corporate governance is being institutionalized in Africa, and more specifically, to indicate the implications thereof for the prominence and practice of business ethics in African corporations. The most prominent models of corporate governance in Africa are first identified and the implications thereof for business ethics discussed. This discussion touches on stakeholder identification and engagement, the role of business ethics within these corporate governance models, as well as the way in which the ethical performance of corporations are governed in terms of these models. Finally some new corporate governance developments on the African continent are reviewed in order to gauge their possible impact on the prominence and practice of business ethics. Before attending to this agenda, a brief overview of the African landscape is provided to contextualize the ensuing discussion.

The African Context

The 53 countries on the African continent can be roughly divided into three main zones based on their official languages. These three groups are the Arab speaking countries in North Africa (the Maghreb zone), the French speaking countries of central and western Africa (the Franc or Francophone zone), and the English speaking countries of southern, eastern, and western Africa (the commonwealth states or Anglophone zone). Economic activity on the continent is dominated by three countries with Algeria, Egypt, and South Africa contributing 60 percent of Africa's GDP and the other 50 countries sharing the remaining 40 percent (Armstrong 2003, 6). Most private sector companies in Africa are nonlisted small to medium enterprises (SMEs). State-owned enterprises (SOEs) still dominate African markets, with the exception of South Africa. Stock exchanges are relatively small, once more with the exception of South Africa.

The need for corporate governance amongst both listed and nonlisted companies and state-run enterprises are great. The drive toward corporate governance has been fuelled by a number of factors. There is wide recognition that corporate governance can contribute to the economic success of corporations and to their long-term sustainability (Armstrong 2003, 12). It is also recognized that good corporate governance can enhance corporate responsibility and improve the reputation of companies, which in turn can attract local and foreign investors. It is also seen as a deterrent to corruption and unethical business practices that scar Africa's business image. The market discipline and transparency that can result from good corporate governance further drive the quest for good governance in Africa (Armstrong 2003, 25).

There are many obstacles in Africa that frustrate the quest for good corporate governance. Prominent on the list of obstacles are the lack of effective regulatory and institutional frameworks that can ensure the enforcement of the standards of good corporate governance. The exceptions here are the Francophone countries and Mauritius and South Africa that have progressed remarkably in this regard. The lack of transparency and market discipline in those countries without a sound regulatory environment also deter privately owned companies from listing on the stock exchanges that do exist. They fear that the greater scrutiny of their corporate activities and the disclosure demands that inevitably go along with being listed can be exploited by the state and competitors (Armstrong 2003, 18). Consequently there are insufficient incentives for SMEs to join the ranks of listed companies and thus enter the domain in which standards of good corporate governance are required and enforced.

State-owned enterprises often set a poor example of good governance as their boards do not display either the competence or independence that is required for good governance. Not only are boards of state-owned companies not appropriately structured, but also board and senior management appointments are made by the state and often on purely political grounds. It has been realized that the privatization of SOEs is also not the magic solution that it was once purported to be (in the so-called structural adjustment programs of the International Monetary Fund). Simply privatizing a company within the context described here will just perpetuate poor governance practices in the private enterprise domain (Armstrong 2003, 19).

The solution might rather lie in corporate governance reform within SOEs so that a precedent can be created of state-run enterprises in which good corporate governance is being practiced. Exactly this has started to happen in Africa. SOEs are increasingly being included in the scope of corporate governance reform and they can indeed become one of the more promising facilitators of good governance. Other role players who can and are already playing a meaningful role in corporate governance reform are the banking sector, development finance institutions, and institutional investors. Various initiatives by, amongst others, the World Bank, International Monetary Fund, United Nations Development Program (UNDP), Commonwealth Association for Corporate Governance (CSCG), and the Organization for Economic Cooperation and Development (OECD) have all contributed to raise the levels of awareness and expertise with regard to corporate governance in Africa. The Pan African Consultative Forum on Corporate Governance (PACFCG) is also playing an important role in coordinating and stimulating corporate governance reform on the continent.

Amongst the most promising developments in corporate governance reform in Africa count the various initiatives around the continent to develop national codes of corporate governance. These initiatives are often driven by the private sector and professional bodies. Organizations such as institutes of directors or professional bodies such as associations of accountants often take the lead along with other stakeholder groups to produce standards of good governance that is recommended to the local business community. In developing such codes, recognition is taken of corporate governance developments elsewhere on the continent and in the world. Especially three codes of corporate governance are often cited and explicitly referred to as major influences on the development of such national codes of corporate governance. They are the OECD Principles of Corporate Governance, the CACG Principles for Corporate Governance, and either the First or Second King Report on Corporate Governance for South Africa.

These national codes of corporate governance over time tend to find their way in an evolutionary manner into listing requirements of stock exchanges, rules of professional bodies, and also into legislation—thus effecting corporate governance reform from the bottom up. A substantial number of such national codes of corporate governance have already been produced, mostly in the Anglophone countries in Africa. It is in these codes that business ethics is explicitly addressed. Consequently the focus of this chapter is the relation between corporate governance and business ethics found in such national codes. Amongst the countries that already produced and published national codes of corporate governance count Ghana, Kenya, Malawi, Mauritius, Nigeria, South Africa, Tanzania, Uganda, Zimbabwe, and Zambia (see bibliography for reference to these codes). In a number of other countries, such as Botswana, Egypt, Morocco, and Sierra Leone, similar codes are in the process of being developed.

Models of Corporate Governance

The dominant model of corporate governance that emerges in these national codes is an *inclusive* model of corporate governance in which boards of directors are not merely accountable to shareholders, but also responsible to all other stakeholders of the company. The notable exception here is Nigeria that does not commit explicitly to an inclusive model of governance. Without exception, all these codes recommend a *unitary* board structure. All the codes advocate a *self-regulatory* approach in which companies are encouraged to adopt not only the letter, but also the spirit of good corporate governance as best business practice. Although voluntary in nature, all these codes do emphasize the need for an adequate legal and regulatory framework. The codes thus deliberately focus on corporate governance at the enterprise level rather than on the regulatory level.

The inclusive model of corporate governance was first introduced on the African continent in 1994 in the First King Report on Corporate Governance in South Africa and has been further entrenched in the Second King Report on Corporate Governance in 2002 (IoD 2002, 6, 17). The tone and example set in the First and Second King reports found strong and often explicit support in the other national codes produced in Africa. In these national codes a variety of motivations are offered for adopting an inclusive approach. These include the long-term sustainability of companies, respect for the local community, and the society at large in which a company operates, and the need to earn a license to operate from all stakeholders of a corporation. The Second King Report also offers an additional motivation for an inclusive approach by emphasizing the need for a corporate governance model that is attuned to the value system of the context within which it operates. In this regard, explicit mention is made of the value system that Africans across the continent embrace. This African value system is sometimes captured under the term "Ubuntu" that signifies amongst others a commitment to coexistence, consensus, and consultation (IoD 2002, 19, Shonhiwa 2001a, and 2001b, 19). The African value system would render an exclusive focus on shareholders' interest impossible, as it would fly in the face of values such as coexistence, consensus, and consultation that are central to the philosophy of Ubuntu.

The voluntary and self-regulatory nature of the corporate governance model that prevails in Africa also could be explained on a number of grounds. The first factor is the inadequate legal and regulatory framework for controlling corporate activity that is found in the majority of African countries. Given this deficiency many national business communities almost have no other choice than starting the process of corporate governance reform in a voluntary and self-regulatory manner. The expectation often is that this approach will trigger corporate governance reforms on the regulatory and legal level as well. The positive gains that have been made in this regard in countries such as Kenya, Mauritius, and South Africa lend credibility to this strategy.

Another motivation for the voluntary nature of these models can be found in the need to broaden the scope of corporate governance reform. Given the small number of listed companies on the African continent and the prevalence of small and medium nonlisted enterprises as well as state-owned enterprises, a mandatory corporate governance regime that applies only to listed companies would be inadequate and inappropriate as it would leave the vast majority of companies outside the ambit of corporate governance reform. What is required is a wide embracement of corporate governance standards by all types of enterprises. A stringent mandatory corporate governance regime might scare companies away from listing on national stock exchanges in Africa. An evolutionary process is thus foreseen in which all types of companies will voluntarily embrace standards of good governance so that the transition from being nonlisted to being a listed company becomes less extreme.

Stakeholder Identification

The way in which a company treats its stakeholders reflects its ethical standards. It is therefore to be expected that companies for whom ethics is a priority will be sensitive to its stakeholders. This moral sensitivity will be reflected in the identification of stakeholders as well as in the manner in which they are being engaged by the company.

The inclusive model of corporate governance opted for in all national codes of corporate governance in Africa (except Nigeria) imposes an obligation on the board of directors to not only be accountable to their shareholders but also be responsible to all their other stakeholders. This reality is very clearly reflected in the range of stakeholders identified in the various reports. Besides the obvious and conventional relation with shareholders a range of other stakeholders are also identified. These include contractual stakeholders such as employees, customers, suppliers, bankers, and creditors, noncontractual stakeholders such as the media, special interest groups, local communities, society at large, professional bodies, the state, and government of the day. It is, however, evident that certain stakeholders besides shareholders enjoy distinct prominence. It is especially local communities and the society that is being singled out as prominent stakeholders and the social responsibility of companies toward society is consequently emphasized. In some countries it is also clear that other specific stakeholders enjoy an enhanced status. In the Malawian code for example, employees enjoy a privileged status as stakeholder group and the responsibilities toward employees and the need for allowing them the opportunity to participate in decision making is strongly emphasized (7). In the case of the Tanzanian code, this privileged status is awarded to the community (7 and 22), and responsibilities toward the community and communal values receive even more emphasis than in the other national codes.

Stakeholder Engagement

In line with the inclusive model of corporate governance that prevails in Africa, all country codes, with the exception of the Nigerian one, emphasizes that there should be regular engagements with stakeholders. Engagement with shareholders is being effected through the regular channels of communication that exist in the annual general meeting and through regular disclosure of financial reports. In the case of nonshareholding stakeholders more or less all reports propose an outline of what stakeholder engagement should entail. The process should commence with the identification of stakeholders and then policy should be formulated for how a company will engage with its stakeholders. The Zimbabwean code goes even further and recommends that a code of conduct be developed for stakeholder engagement that will ensure that the rights of stakeholders are protected (11). In the codes of countries like Uganda (46) and Tanzania (35) it is emphasized that the policy for stakeholder engagement should not only be developed by the company, but also be agreed with the respective stakeholders of the company.

The content of stakeholder engagement is generally described as an obligation to inform stakeholders on company performance. Although not much clarity is provided on the content of what should be communicated, it is clear that information on both the financial and nonfinancial performance of companies should be disclosed. It is, however, widely emphasized that such communication and disclosure should be prompt, open, relevant, and transparent.

Although the emphasis on stakeholder engagement is pervasive in all these reports, it lacks rigour and discipline. There are, however, a number of notable exceptions. In the Kenyan code reference is made to establishing mechanisms for ensuring performance enhancing stakeholder participation (PSCGT 1999, 20). The *Second King Report for South Africa* brings discipline into this process by recommending that companies follow a triple bottom-line reporting and disclosure approach based on the AA1000 process standard and the GRI reporting principles (100). Adherence to these standards will ensure that stakeholders are not only informed, but that their perceptions of the company are also gauged. It will also ensure that disclosure to stakeholders are done in a disciplined way in which not only reporting on financial performance, but also on the social-ethical and environmental bottom-lines is done according to accepted standards of accounting and auditing. The example set by the King Report has been followed in the Mauritian report, although it is made clear that the commitment to triple bottom-line reporting is still only an aspiration and not yet a requirement (10).

Ethics in Corporate Governance

All the national codes emphasize the ethical nature of good corporate governance. Special emphasis is placed on the fact that good governance is based on a number of cardinal ethical values. Topping the list of the values that should be adhered to in good governance are transparency, accountability, responsibility, and probity. These values should permeate all aspects of governance and be displayed in all actions and decisions of the board. The various aspects of governance such as board compilation and functioning, reporting, disclosure, and risk management are seen as instrumental in realizing these cardinal values of good governance.

Besides these underlying values of corporate governance, mention is also made of specific moral obligations that the board of directors and the company should abide by. Prominent amongst these ethical obligations are ensuring that the company always acts on high ethical standards so that the reputation of the company will be protected as well as respecting the rights of all shareholders, and particularly those of minority shareholders. In line with the inclusive model of governance that prevails in Africa, the duty to protect the human and other rights of all stakeholders enjoys prominence. Stakeholders that are singled out for special protection are cultural or ethnic minorities, women, and children.

The duty of the board and the company to look after the safety and health of its employees is also stressed. The emphasis on health does not surprise if one takes into account that on average 6,500 Africans die of AIDS related illnesses per day (PACFCG 2001, 12). The detrimental impact of HIV/AIDS on business enterprises is well documented and poses a challenge that boards can hardly afford to ignore any longer. Another obligation that commonly occurs in the national codes is the social responsibility of corporations. Given the prominence of local communities and society in general alluded to in the earlier section on stakeholder identification, this emphasis does not surprise and forms an integral part of an inclusive stakeholder model of corporate governance.

Governing Business Ethics

In all the national codes of corporate governance in Africa the need for actively managing the ethical performance of companies is emphasized. The level of detail with which these codes deal with the active management of ethics do, however, differ drastically. All the codes recommend that the board of directors ensure that a code of ethics is developed and that it is endorsed by the board. Most of these corporate governance codes also provide some guidance on the process of developing a code of ethics by either making reference to issues or topics that typically should be addressed in a code, or by outlining a process that could be followed in the process of code design or review.

Few codes go further than that. The Kenyan, Mauritian, and South African codes take the lead in venturing deeper into what the governing of ethical performance entails beyond developing a code of ethics. The most comprehensive recommendations on the governance of ethics are to be found in the Second King Report on Corporate Governance for South Africa. The latter report recommends a six-stage process of governing ethical performance that consists of:

1. identifying through stakeholder engagement the perceptions and expectations that stakeholders have of the ethical performance of a company.
2. Determining the ethical values and standards of the company and codifying it in a code of ethics.
3. Institutionalizing the values and code of ethics of a company on both the strategic and systems levels.

4. Monitoring and evaluating compliance to the code of ethics.
5. Accounting and auditing ethical performance according to emerging global standards on ethical accounting and auditing.
6. Disclosing ethical performance to relevant stakeholders (108–113).

Especially the third stage is emphasized in order to get companies moving beyond merely having a code onto implementing the code of ethics to make a meaningful difference to company performance. Specific interventions that are suggested are regular ethical risk assessment, confidential reporting systems through which unethical or suspicious behavior could be reported, the integration of ethical performance into existing performance appraisal systems, and integrity assessment as part of selection and promotion procedures. This comprehensive treatment of what the governance of ethical performance entails represent a substantial move beyond the guidelines that were provided in the First King Report that was published in 1994, when attention to ethics was still confined to developing and endorsing a code of ethics. The Mauritian report that explicitly follows the lead of the Second King Report reflects this comprehensive approach to the governing of ethics (107–109). It is not unreasonable to expect that other countries in Africa might do the same when they take their national codes of corporate governance in revision in the not too distant future.

The Kenyan code that is also fairly comprehensive in the way it deals with the governing of ethics recommends that companies issue a certificate at the end of every year in which they confirm that to the best knowledge of the board and management no employee of the company has been involved in, amongst others, corruption, money laundering, or the contravention of any national law or international convention (PSCGT 1999, 21).

New Developments

There are a range of initiatives being taken in the field of corporate governance that bears the potential of impacting positively on the improvement of corporate governance standards in general. Some of these corporate governance reform initiatives are on a national level; some are regional, while others are Pan-African in scope. A glimpse of some of the more significant developments on these three levels are provided here.

On a national level various corporate governance initiatives have been taken that have a direct bearing on business ethics. In Ghana, for example, the African Capital Markets Forum (ACMF) launched an anticorruption project within the private sector that targeted the supplyside of corruption. It brought attention to the role that the private sector plays in sustaining corruption by offering bribes to officials (Armstrong 2003, 84). The outcome of this initiative is a greater awareness of the need for adherence to strong ethical standards in both the private and public sectors. In South Africa a concerted effort is being made by professional bodies and tertiary educational institutions alike to introduce programs on corporate governance. Some of these programs have distinct business ethics components in which students in undergraduate and postgraduate levels, as well as extracurricular programs receive formal training on business ethics (Armstrong 2003, 104). Also, in South Africa the JSE Securities Exchange has introduced a Social Responsibility Investment Index for companies listed on its exchange in terms of which they are rated on their triple bottom-line performance, which also includes an ethical dimension. In Kenya the Private Sector Corporate Governance Trust is assisting various organizations in developing codes of ethics (Armstrong 2003, 100). These are just some of the various initiatives that are being taken to increase the standard of not only corporate governance in general, but also of business ethics specifically.

A development on the regional level is the adoption of the Equator Principles by ten leading banks from seven countries. These principles will be used for managing social and environmental issues related to the financing of development projects. Project sponsors in future will have to satisfy these banks that they comply with socially responsible and sound environmental business practices as a precondition for receiving funding from these banks (PACFCG 2001, 11).

On the continental (Pan-African) level the launch of the New Partnership for Africa's Development (NEPAD) also might have a positive bearing on enhancing corporate governance in general and business ethics as an integral part thereof. The aim of the NEPAD initiative is to eradicate poverty and foster socioeconomic growth through democracy and good governance (Armstrong 2003, 66). The heads of state of African countries did not only commit themselves to enhance good political, economic, and corporate governance, but also to engage voluntarily in the African Peer Review Mechanism, in which individual countries will be assessed on their governance performance by their peers in Africa (*Anon.* 2004, 32). The Business Workgroup within NEPAD has also adopted various agreements with a direct bearing on the ethical performance of organizations such as the Business Covenant on Corporate Governance that emphasizes the importance of organizational integrity and the institutionalization thereof, as well as a covenant on the elimination of corruption and bribery. In addition, the Business Declaration on Corporate Social Responsibility was adopted that emphasizes the need for positive stakeholder relationships based on integrity as well as the protection of human rights.

It can be expected that through these various initiatives the tide of corporate governance will raise. Business ethics as an integral part of corporate governance can expect to benefit from this rising tide and gain in prominence as a result.

Conclusion

This survey of the state of business ethics within the context of corporate governance in Africa made it clear that business ethics is considered an integral and essential part of good governance. From the various national codes of corporate governance that were analyzed it is clear that standards of good governance is intimately intertwined with high standards of business ethics. The challenge that faces African enterprises is to translate this commitment to high standards of ethics into organizational practice. It is on this score that most codes of corporate governance in Africa fall short as they provide very little guidance on how business ethics should be institutionalized in enterprises. The second generation codes of corporate governance that are now emerging in Africa tend to recognize this shortfall and address it explicitly. This advance in combination with the new corporate governance developments outlined earlier might facilitate the process of institutionalizing ethics in organizations. It is, however, imperative that these developments on the enterprise level should be reinforced with governance reform on the regulatory and political level.

Note

An earlier version of this chapter was published in *Business & Society* 44(1): 94–106. Permission to reprint this chapter was kindly granted by Sage Publishers.

References

Anon. 2004. African Peer Review Mechanism for Good Governance in Africa. *Good Governance*, 1(March): 32.

Armstrong, P. 2003. *Status Report on Corporate Governance Reform in Africa.* Johannesburg: PACFCG.

CACG. 1999. *CACG guidelines: Principles for corporate governance in the Commonwealth.* Havelock, NZ: CACG.

Code of Corporate Governance in Nigeria. 2003. [n.p.]:[n.pub.].

Corporate Governance Task Force. 2001. *Code of Best Practice for Corporate Governance in Malawi.* Blantyre: Society of Accountants in Malawi.

IoD of South Africa. 1994. *King Report on Corporate Governance.* Johannesburg: Institute of Directors.

IoD of South Africa. 2002. *King Report on Corporate Governance for South Africa 2002.* Johannesburg: Institute of Directors.

IoD of Zambia. 2000. *Manual on Corporate Governance.* Lusaka: IoD of Zambia.

Manual on Corporate Governance and Codes of Conduct—Incorporating Recommended Guidelines for Uganda. [n.d.]: Kampala: ICGU.

Manual on Corporate Governance in Ghana. 2000. [n.p.]: [n.pub.].

Mensah, S. 2000. Opening Address. In *Report on Consultative Meeting on Corporate Governance in Africa.* Nairobi: PSCGT, pp. 19–23.

PACFCG. 2001. *Addendum to Summary of Progress Report for the Second Meeting of the Pan-African Consultative Forum on Corporate Governance.* Johannesburg: PACFCG.

Principles for Corporate Governance in Zimbabwe: Manual of Best Practice. [n.d.]: [n.p.]: African Management Services Company.

PSCGT. 1999. *Principles for Corporate Governance in Kenya and a Sample Code of Best Practice for Corporate Governance.* Nairobi: PSCGT.

Report on Corporate Governance for Mauritius. 2003. Port Louis: Ministry of Economic Development, Financial Services and Corporate Affairs.

Shonhiwa, S. 2001a. African imperatives and transformation leadership, in *Directorship* (March).

——. 2001b. African values for business, in *Financial Mail*, May, 4, p. 19.

Steering Committee on Corporate Governance in Tanzania. 2000. *Manual on Corporate Governance and Codes of Conduct—Incorporating Recommended Guidelines for Tanzania.* Dar es Salaam: Steering Committee on Corporate Governance in Tanzania.

CHAPTER 9

BUSINESS ETHICS AND CORPORATE GOVERNANCE IN THE ASIA-PACIFIC REGION

David Kimber and Phillip Lipton

Introduction

As one considers the characteristics of corporate governance and the impact thereof on stakeholder engagement and business ethics in the Asia-Pacific region, one is struck by the wide diversity of corporate governance models and social and cultural differences that exist in this very large geographic area. This means that in a book of this type, it is only possible to provide an overview of any individual country and it becomes virtually impossible to draw meaningful generalizations regarding the region as a whole. The approach we have taken in this chapter is to draw upon four examples of countries in the region, not because they are representative of certain regional characteristics, but because in themselves they are representative of the diversity that may be found in the Asia-Pacific region. It may then be possible to group other countries with each of the four examples so as to develop a more textured picture of corporate governance and business ethics in the region.

The four countries we have chosen to consider are:

1. Australia
2. China
3. Singapore, and
4. India.

These countries display pronounced differences in terms of inter alia, historical development, cultural and social factors, legal system, corporate governance model, political system, and economic development. It is the complex interaction of all these considerations that provide the context for corporate governance and business ethics in each of the countries chosen.

Overview of the Governance Systems

From the point of view of legal system, Australia, Singapore, and India are all common law jurisdictions in the sense that their legal foundations and principles are based on the English system, having been transplanted during the colonial era. The legal system in China, especially in relation to company law and corporate governance, has developed only since the economic reforms of state. To some extent it draws on German law and practice but to a large degree reflects the social and economic experience of China under the Communist Party and the changes in policy that have occurred over the past 20 years.

At the same time, the three common law countries differ widely in their stage of economic development. Australia and Singapore are relatively wealthy, developed economies with GDP per capita in 2001 of $US 23,300 and $US 27,100 respectively. China and India are developing countries with GDP per capita in 2001 of $US 900 and $US 500 respectively (Energy Information Administration 2003).

China and India are the most populous countries in the world with populations of 1.29 and 1.04 billion respectively. In these terms, Australia and Singapore are small countries with populations of 19.54 and 4.18 million respectively (Energy Information Administration 2003).

China's legal and commercial institutions and practice have developed in the context of, and have been shaped by, the Communist Party and the prevalence of state owned enterprises (SOE). To some extent, a similar history occurred in India that was also dominated by state owned enterprises, albeit to a lesser extent. Until recently both these countries were largely closed to foreign investment but have opened up in recent times to globalization, an inflow of direct foreign investment and greater development of market economies. Australia and Singapore have longer histories of developing international market economies and have been recipients of large foreign investment for a number of decades.

Australia has a mixed regulatory regime that includes mandatory legislation contained in the *Corporations Act* 2001 as well as self-regulation whereby listed companies are required to make disclosure to the market though it is up to the market to draw its conclusions. This can be seen in the Australian Stock Exchange Listing Rule 4.10.3 that requires disclosure of corporate governance practices adopted by a company in its annual report and an explanation of any departures from best practice.

Singapore's corporate governance is also based on the Anglo-American model but departs from this in several important respects. Government involvement in the corporate sector is far greater than that usually associated with this corporate governance model. The government is a major shareholder in many large Singapore companies and government controlled companies play a major role in many key industries.

The CLSA Emerging Markets and the Asian Corporate Governance Association survey, *CG Watch: Corporate Governance in Asia 2003* (ACGA 2003) ranks several Asian markets by their corporate governance practices. China, India, and Singapore are ranked as shown in table 9.1.

This survey did not include Australia. For comparative purposes, similar ratings for slightly different variables were determined by La Porta, Lopez-de-Silanes, Shleifer and Vishny (1998) of 49 countries classified according to legal origin. The ratings in table 9.2 were given in relation to various aspects of enforcement of law for Australia, India, and Singapore.

These tables point out that in relation to several indicators of the corporate governance environment, rule of law, and enforcement, Australia and

Table 9.1   Rating Corporate Governance Criteria

	China	India	Singapore
Rules and regulations	5.0	8.0	8.5
Enforcement	4.0	6.0	7.5
Political/regulatory environment	5.0	6.0	6.0
Adoption of IGAAP	5.0	7.5	9.0
Institutional mechanisms and corporate governance culture	3.0	6.5	8.0
Country score	4.3	6.6	7.7

Table 9.2   Aspects of Law Enforcement

	Australia	India	Singapore
Efficiency of judicial system	10.00	8.00	10.00
Rule of law	10.00	4.17	8.57
Corruption	8.52	4.58	8.22
Risk of expropriation	9.27	7.75	9.30
Risk of contract repudiation	8.71	6.11	8.86
Rating on accounting standards	75	57	78

Singapore rank relatively highly. This accords with the central conclusions put forward by La Porta et al (1998) that investor protection is generally greater in common law countries than in countries whose legal systems originated in France and to a lesser extent, those stemming from the German model. Law enforcement is of higher quality in German and common law origin systems than in French origin models. The quality of law enforcement also bears a relationship to income per capita. Hence law enforcement and transparency is relatively poor in China compared to Australia and Singapore. In *The Economist* in the article "In Praise of Rules" April 7, 2001, PricewaterhouseCoopers has estimated that these factors are equivalent to an extra tax on business of 46 percent.

An illustration of the operation of commercial law in China was described in an article in *The Economist* on April 7, 2001—"Of Laws and Men." In October 1998, the investment arm of the Guangdong province defaulted in repayment of loans from foreign banks. The banks had assumed that the debts were backed by the central government. In fact the central government made it clear that it had no intention of underwriting the debts of provincial government corporations. After two years of inconclusive litigation it became clear that the Bankruptcy Code was of no assistance and the banks settled out of court sustaining substantial losses.

India also has a poor system of corporate insolvency (Goswami 2000). According to Goswami, 32 percent of company liquidations took more than 20 years and 59 percent took more than 10 years to complete. This has important implications for corporate governance because in China and India, management may act in an inefficient way and undertake excessively risky investments without the fear of insolvency and ultimate liquidation when creditors pursue their rights. This is also highly detrimental to the countries' financial sector with a high cost of capital and a significant proportion of nonperforming loans. Financial institutions often allocate capital to nonoptimal uses.

A widespread response to poor investor protection is high concentration of share ownership (Goswami 2000, 23). On the other hand, those countries such as Australia with good investor protection and adherence to high quality accounting standards tend toward having low ownership concentrations. Australia, however, appears to have greater concentration of share ownership than the United States and United Kingdom (Stapledon 1999). Singapore appears to depart from this generalization as it exhibits high ownership concentration despite high ranking in rule of law and accounting standards. This may be explained by the predominance of family controlled companies as well as heavy involvement of government in many listed companies. Companies in India also show high concentration of ownership.

This may be partly explained by poor investor protection and law enforcement. It is also significantly influenced by the social system that has identified the merchant community as a specific caste group. Community and family networks have had a long tradition in India and, as such, have impacted on the structuring of businesses. Thus the Anglo-American model has been superimposed over a cultural framework built up over millennia. Family and government controlled companies are very common. In addition, India has low ratings on rule of law variables and low income per capita.

The Nature of the Corporation

The basis of the Anglo-American model is the primacy of the shareholders as the dominant stakeholders with the ability to exert substantial influence on managerial decision making. In its pure form this has been described as the contractarian model that views the corporation as a nexus of contracts negotiated by self-interested stakeholders. In the pure model, legal constraints and regulation imposed on managers are given less emphasis than voluntary contracting and the operation of market forces as a means of aligning the interests of managers and shareholders (Jensen and Meckling 1976, Fama and Jensen 1983). The alternative view is to see the corporation as a separate entity capable of doing both harm and good in much the same ways as an individual. Rules and legal obligations are required to ensure that corporations discharge their implicit obligations to act in the interests of the society. This has been described as the communitarian view, which sees the corporation as an entity connected to society. In return for the privileges of corporate status, the corporation owes a sense of social responsibility to a wide range of stakeholders (Etzioni 1988, Bradley et al. 1999).

Between these extremes, the notion of the firm as a community of interests for its key operational stakeholders, managers, and employees has had a long history in India. Kipling's (1994) words in a short story, "The Apprentice," written at the end of the nineteenth century gives a strong sense of this which, whilst referring primarily to the English expatriate in India, resonates today.

> They were nearly all sons of old employees, living with their parents in white bungalows off Steam Road or Church Road or Albert Road—on the broad avenues of pounded brick bordered by palms and crotons and bougainvilleas and bamboos which made up the railway town of Ajabpore. They had never seen the sea or a steamer; half their speech was helped out with native slang; they were all volunteers in the D.I.R.'s Railway Corps—grey with red facing— and their talk was exclusively about the Company and its affairs.

They all hoped to become engine-drivers earning six or seven hundred a year, and therefore they despised all mere sit-down clerks in the Store, Audit and Traffic departments, and ducked when they met at the Company's swimming baths.

There were no strikes or tie-ups on the D.I.R. on those days, for the reason that the ten or twelve thousand natives and the two or three thousand whites were doing their best to turn the Company's employment into a caste in which their sons and daughters would be sure of positions and pensions. Everything in India crystallises into a caste sooner or later—the big jute and cotton mills, the leather harness and opium factories, the coal-mines and the dock-yards, and, in years to come, when India begins to be heard from, as one of the manufacturing countries of the world, the labour unions of other lands will learn something about the beauty of caste which will greatly influence them.

While the models noted earlier exist nowhere in their pure form, we may say that, in terms of the prevailing concept of the firm, Australia bears close similarity to the corporate governance models of the United States and United Kingdom. The corporation is largely seen as primarily concerned with the creation of shareholder wealth. The law protects minority shareholders with extensive legislative duties imposed on directors and varied shareholder remedies. It seeks to facilitate a level playing field in financial markets with requirements for continuous disclosure of price sensitive information, heavy penalties for contraventions, and the monitoring of insider trading and detailed requirements for disclosure of corporate governance practices. Takeovers (mergers and acquisitions) are encouraged as a means of imposing market discipline on managers and enhancing shareholder value. Takeovers are regulated in a way that seeks to balance the interests of encouraging takeover bids while ensuring that all target company shareholders are fully informed and given equal opportunity to participate in the benefits of the takeover.

The main objective of corporate governance regulation in Australia is to promote the efficient operation of financial markets and a significant part of this is to protect minority shareholders from exploitation by dominant shareholders (La Porta et al. 1999). Perhaps more important than the regulation itself is the quality of enforcement and the strength of the supporting institutions and gatekeepers. In Australia the corporate regulator is the Australian Securities and Investments Commission (ASIC). It is very active in enforcement of the *Corporations Act* including bringing recent legal proceedings against several prominent company directors. The audit profession is generally highly skilled reflecting a developed education system, and there is an adequate pool of suitably skilled independent directors.

Singapore has a corporate law system that appears very similar to Australia's. In fact the basis of the Singapore Companies Act is the

Australian legislation of the 1960s. The major difference between the two countries lies in the dominance of tightly held family controlled and government controlled listed companies. This means that there is a much higher concentration of share ownership in large Singapore companies than is the case in Australia.

Importance of Stock Markets

While market capitalization gives a broad snapshot of stock market importance, it should also be borne in mind that markets in China and India are more thinly traded than in Australia and Singapore (see table 9.3). This makes the China and India markets less efficient in pricing and more vulnerable to improper market practices especially bearing in mind the poor quality of market regulation and law enforcement.

Taking the population into account it is clear that stock markets play a relatively more important role in Australia and Singapore than in China and India. This is in accordance with the assertion that stock markets play a more important role in Anglo-American countries and Japan (Weimer and Pape 1999, 155). Most Asian companies have relatively low equity and are therefore relatively highly geared, relying on borrowing to raise capital. In many cases conglomerates own banks or other financial institutions to facilitate raising of capital. This has implications for corporate governance in each country because companies in countries in which the stock exchange is relatively important tend to raise capital by raising equity, and this can only be achieved if there is adequate investor protection, transparency, and enforcement of law.

The Importance of the Shareholder

In Australia, the dominant stakeholder is the outside shareholder. In India and China, the state owned enterprises and family controlled companies emerged as the prime type of corporation in the last half of the twentieth

Table 9.3   Market capitalization of stock exchanges

Market capitalization of stock exchanges 2004 (A$ billions)[1]

ASX (Australia)	$948
China	$410
Bombay (India)	$217
Singapore	$204

century. This means that boards and management are often mindful of the interests of these dominant "owner/managers," sometimes at the expense of minority investors. Singapore is somewhere in between. To some extent it exhibits the Anglo-American characteristic of shareholder primacy. The importance of government shareholdings results in the government being a major financial stakeholder as well as a controller/regulator. The effect of shareholder, government, and other stakeholder influence, and how they all impact on the corporation are discussed shortly.

Market for Corporate Control

A major characteristic of Anglo-American systems of corporate governance is the existence of an active market for takeovers. This is perceived as playing a vital corporate governance role because of the discipline it imposes on boards and management. Theoretically, poor performing companies suffer a fall in share price that encourages a bidder to make an above market price bid in the expectation that the assets of the acquired company can be more efficiently utilized. The result of a hostile takeover is that inefficient incumbent management will usually be replaced by more efficient management appointed by the successful bidder. Shareholders are offered a better price than they could hope to achieve under the existing board. This results in greater alignment of interests between management and shareholders. An active market for corporate control benefits shareholders who are able to sell shares in poorly performing companies at above market prices (Jensen 1984).

Supporting the view that financial markets strengthen efficient usage of corporate assets is the belief that even if a takeover does not occur when assets are poorly managed, shareholders will sell off their holdings—the strategy known in the finance industry as "taking the Wall Street walk." Whilst it is possible with relatively low percentage holdings in corporations and liquid stock markets, it is less feasible when fund managers manage large holdings in major corporations. The size of their holdings cannot simply be "dumped" without considerable value loss. This give rise to an alternative view that fund managers are being forced into active governance oversight roles as their capacity to trade securities of poorly performing corporations is diminished. This is the basis for the growth of the finance industry's interest in corporate governance.

In Australia, takeovers play an important role. Hostile takeovers are less common in Singapore and rare if not nonexistent in China. Since 1997 in India, takeover regulation has been reformed but while hostile takeovers are not common, they have occurred on several occasions. The financial markets in these countries are "freeing up" and becoming more liquid, but their evolution is influenced by central governments' concerns relating to economic stability and employment. In India the deregulation of financial markets and "disinvestment" (privatization) of state owned enterprises is occurring but is being resisted largely by employee groups concerned with the potential loss of jobs when state owned enterprises are forced to be more competitive. Arguably, the 2004 elections in India were strongly influenced by concerns that less advantaged sectors of society are losing out to "entrepreneurs and capitalists" as markets free up.

The Regulatory Mix

Australia, Singapore, and India all possess corporate governance regulatory regimes that are based on corporations legislation that provides for mandatory minimum standards dealing with matters such as directors' duties, members' remedies, shareholder rights at meetings and default rules for company constitutions. These mandatory rules may be enforced by civil actions brought by harmed parties and criminal proceedings brought by the respective regulators. These minimum mandatory requirements cannot effectively deal with issues relating to board role, structure and composition, etc. These functional matters are dealt with by codes of internationally recognized corporate governance best practice endorsed by the various stock exchanges and directed at listed companies. This comprises a form of self-regulation because it is not mandatory for companies to follow the best practice principles. The general approach is to require listed companies to disclose in their annual reports the corporate governance practices they have adopted during the relevant year. The listing rules set out detailed endorsed practices, and companies are required to state the extent to which they have adopted these practices. Those companies that depart from the recommended practices are required to explain why they have done so.

The rationale behind this approach is to ensure that the market is informed about a company's corporate governance practices. At the same time there is also recognition that appropriate practice may differ from company to company. In particular smaller listed companies often find it difficult to comply with requirements such as establishment of several board committees where they have relatively small boards.

In Australia, the *Corporations Act* has undergone substantial reform since the early 1990s. Much of this reform has come under the umbrella of the Corporate Law Economic Reform Program that seeks to put corporate regulation in the context of enhancing economic efficiency. The most recent tranche of reforms (known as CLERP 9) addresses matters such as corporate disclosure and auditor independence and in some respects bears similarities to Sarbanes-Oxley in the United States. The ASX established a Corporate Governance Council that issued *Principles of Good Corporate Governance and Best Practice Recommendations* in March 2003. Listed companies must adopt the large number of recommendations set out in this document or explain why they have not, in their annual reports.

Similar developments took place in Singapore where the *Singapore Code of Corporate Governance* was incorporated into the Stock Exchange listing rules in 2001 for compliance starting in 2003 (Singapore Council on Corporate Disclosure and Governance 2001). As in Australia, listed companies must disclose their corporate governance practices and explain any deviation from the Code.

In India, interest in corporate governance sprang from very low levels before the mid-1990s. The Confederation of Indian Industry (CII), India's largest industry association, recognized that good corporate governance was essential in order to enable Indian companies to competitively raise capital. In particular it was necessary to provide greater disclosure, more transparency, and better shareholder value. It released a voluntary code *Desirable Corporate Governance: A Code*. This code (CII 1998) sets out detailed disclosure requirements and has been largely adopted by many of the largest listed companies. A further development occurred with the release of a similar code by the main regulator, the Securities and Exchange Board of India (SEBI). Unlike the position in Australia and Singapore, its corporate governance requirements are mandatory and enforceable by the stock exchanges. The question whether corporate governance codes should be voluntary or mandatory has been the subject of debate. It has been suggested that a mandatory regime encourages a "tick the box" approach with the emphasis on form over substance. Whether this arises in India remains to be seen.

China has developed its corporate law to a significant extent since the late 1980s. A code of corporate governance for listed companies was introduced by the China Securities Regulatory Commission (CSRC), the national securities regulator. It has developed the following guidelines:

- A directive on quarterly reporting in April 2001.
- A set of guidelines on the qualification and appointment of independent directors in August 2001.
- Numerous regulations promulgated over 2001, including rules aimed at enhancing disclosure, improving the functioning of the stock market, outlining rules for inspections of listed companies and management incentive schemes, and so on.

- A national code on corporate governance in January 2002.
- An amended directive on the form and content of quarterly reports in March 2003.

However, there are still serious shortcomings in adopting best practice in corporate governance. The state is still the dominant shareholder of most listed companies. There are few incentives for managers to maximize shareholder value and managers have relatively little market discipline. There is a tendency for controlling shareholders to engage in related party transactions that are not in the interests of minority investors. Managers are protected from the consequences of inefficiency by implicit government support and weak creditors' rights. Investors are more interested in levels of government and parent company support than in demanding good corporate governance.

Private equity markets are undeveloped and the surrounding industries such as institutional investors, auditing and legal professions, and analysts and financial advisers are very much in the early stages of development. Despite corporatization and diversification of share ownership, many of the old structures and political connections have remained intact. Boards of directors often carry out a rubber stamp role with major decisions made behind the scenes. Boards often lack independence and the concept of independent, nonexecutive directors is not well understood.

The Extent of Stakeholder Engagement and Ethics Guidelines

Stakeholder engagement and business ethics concerns in the four countries are growing as corporations grapple with increasingly aware and influential stakeholders. But before one engages too specifically in determining which groups are being the most influential, one needs to clarify the term "stakeholder" and how it is being used in this discussion. The concept of "stakeholder engagement" can be seen as the interaction of members of a number of groupings with the organization—those who have a direct economic relationship with the entity as well as those who have an indirect involvement and interest in the entity's activities. A common list of stakeholders, drawing on the concept of the "triple bottom line"[2] includes:

1. Primary/Direct—financial investors
   - Shareholder/security holders
   - Banks and other finance providers
2. Primary/Direct—other financial stakeholders
   - Employees—Management/Nonmanagement

- Customers and suppliers
- Directly involved government agencies such as the Taxation Office and regulators, ASIC, APRA, etc.

3. Indirect—Social
   - Local communities—Represented by local and state government agencies and lobby groups
   - Regional, national and global communities – represented by NGO's

4. Indirect—Environmental
   - Government agencies such as Environmental Protection Authorities and planning agencies.
   - Nongovernment bodies representing environmental interests—NGOs, research institutes, etc.

SustainAbility's website (SustainAbility 2004) identified stakeholder engagement as shown in figure 9.1.

This initial framework outlined in the figure is used as a basis for the following review of current stakeholder engagement in the Asia–Pacific region.

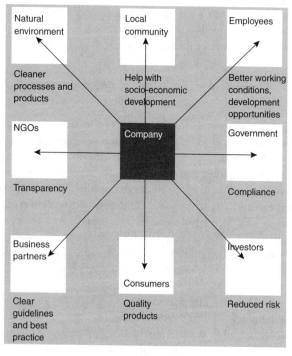

Figure 9.1   Corporate stakeholder Engagement

Primary Direct—Financial Investors

First, we identify in each country the key stakeholder or stakeholder representatives.

In Australia it is evident that a significant community of agencies, associations, and NGOs are involved with stakeholder engagement on behalf of financial investors. They can be identified in three groups as follows and include:[3]

Government Bodies and Authorities

Attorney General, Australian Competition & Consumer Commission (ACCC), National Competition Council, Reserve Bank, Australian Securities & Investments Commission (ASIC), Takeovers Panel, and Australian Prudential Regulation Authority (APRA).

Professional Associations

Chartered Institute of Company Secretaries, CPA Australia and Institute of Chartered Accountants (professional accounting bodies), Institute of Company Directors, Law Council, Law Institute and Australian Corporate Lawyers Association, and other legal professional bodies.

Securities and Exchange Organizations

Australian Stock Exchange (ASX), Financial Markets Association, Independent Shareholder Services, Investment & Financial Services Association, Newcastle Stock Exchange, Securities Institute, Australian Shareholders' Association, and Sydney Futures Exchange.

Most of these groups have secretariats, boards, or committees of management and extensive groups of managers and employees. They significantly influence the way corporate governance is perceived and practiced in Australia and have significant impact in terms of stakeholder engagement. They have protocols, standards, and codes that clarify how they support their clients or members and their relationships with corporations in Australia. They are a more extensive group in Australia than in any of the other countries considered, primarily because Australia has had a free financial market for over 100 years. Although as noted in the following passages, extensive Australian corporate ownership of shares is a relatively recent phenomenon, regulating and managing the share market has a long history in Australia, going back to the gold mining company stock exchanges in the nineteenth century.[4]

The growth of entities involved in financial stakeholder engagement has been fostered by increasing shareholding participation through direct shareholdings and superannuation funds. As the average age of Australians rises and the government limits the amount of and eligibility for age pensions, increasing numbers have become interested in saving for retirement and are doing so through direct investment in shares, through share purchasing in self-managed superannuation funds and contributions to superannuation funds.

Rather than considering each entity, only one is reviewed in this chapter in terms of how they "engage" with corporations.

The superannuation (pension fund) industry has established the Australian Council of Superannuation Investors (ACSI 2005) with the main objective of ensuring superannuation trustees are properly equipped to deal with corporate governance issues in relation to companies in which they invest. Among the services provided by ACSI to its members is a Voting Alert Service to aid with voting and engagement issues. ACSI has also issued its *Corporate Governance Guidelines.*

Another organization representing financial service providers is the Investment and Financial Services Association Limited (IFSA 2005). Its primary role is to represent members to the government and the community on issues affecting institutional investors such as the managed investments, superannuation, and life insurance industries. This body guides corporate governance through its recommendations on corporate governance practice. The IFSA corporate governance guide (the "Blue Book") was one of the first major documents in Australia to extensively recommend corporate governance principles in Australia. As the peak body for superannuation funds and fund managers it represents a powerful voice on behalf of institutional shareholders.

IFSA notes in the Blue Book that corporations should establish a code of ethics that is endorsed by the board. In terms of its own members in 2001, IFSA established a code of conduct for its members, as the first of its "standards." At the same time it laid out a process for standard setting and compliance procedures—in effect a procedural framework.

In the other countries, the issue of stakeholder engagement with the primary investor groups seems to have a shorter history and is less clearly identified. In India, community and state based investor associations and NGOs have emerged recently and are likely to become influential at state and federal control levels, as financial markets grow.[5] Since independence and arguably up until the early 1990s, the central government in India has had a strong influence over the economy and kept tight control over capital markets. There was substantial government control over investment and consequently state owned enterprises were major asset managers in India. This factor, alongside a close-knit framework of family based enterprise management, has meant investor activism is a relatively new phenomenon in India.

One body, representing the fund management industry, the Association of Mutual Funds in India (AMFI 2005) "is dedicated to developing the Indian Mutual Fund Industry on professional, healthy and ethical lines and to enhance and maintain standards in all areas with a view to protecting and promoting the interests of mutual funds and their unit holders."

Ethics and standards are clearly a concern for AMFI. It has a code of ethics drawn up in 1997 with assistance from Price Waterhouse and USAID, the U.S. government aid agency. According to its website, it is closely associated with the Securities and Exchange Board (SEBI) and seeks to ensure its members maintain high standards. It is not clear from its website that it has a direct involvement in the governance arena, unlike ACSI and IFSA in Australia.

As noted earlier, SOEs are a key issue in stakeholder engagement in India. State owned banks and financial institutions have direct investment in many state owned enterprises. Unit Trust of India, the government managed fund, looks after a large proportion of the funds under management in India. An ongoing debate in India is around whether the extensively state owned and managed enterprise system should be dismantled. Social objectives such as poverty alleviation, employment, food production, and distribution create significant tensions relating to the governance of such entities. The influence of government as an owner and stakeholder in India, either directly or through the public sector banking and finance industry, is complicated by this factor (Reddy 2004).

In China there is less evidence of representative bodies supporting financial stakeholders. Prime reliance seems to be focussed on government initiated codes, such as that created by the China Securities Regulatory Commission (CSRC 2005).

Much of the regulation in China is aimed at protecting minority shareholders and ensuring the corporation is not used by "some controlling shareholders . . . as their own little ATM machines" (AGCA 2003). Thus the key concern about ethics is protection of the financial interests of shareholders from unscrupulous controlling shareholders. It is evident from a Hong Kong shareholder activist corporate governance website[6] that there is a distinction between the private investment community in Hong Kong and investors in other cities in China. In Hong Kong there is greater concern about the way corporations are being managed either by the state or other majority shareholder groups. The strength of investor activism appears less in Beijing or Shanghai because of the lack of a democratic heritage and the more recent emergence of the corporation as a business framework in mainland Chinese cities.[7]

However, other stakeholders are not ignored in the national Code of Conduct for Corporations in China. Chapter 6 identifies stakeholders as those with primarily direct financial interests in the corporation including shareholders, banks, creditors, employees, consumers, and suppliers, but also notes "the community and other stakeholders." Whilst the Code directly refers to codes of ethical conduct, it does include statements such as:

- controlling shareholders owe a duty of good faith,
- directors shall faithfully, honestly and diligently perform their duties for the best interests of the company and all the shareholders, and
- the company shall be concerned with the welfare, environmental protection and public interests of the community in which it resides, and shall pay attention to the company's social responsibilities. (CSRC 2005)

The Code also requires "comply-or-explain" disclosure relating to corporate governance practices.

In Singapore, the Investment Management Association of Singapore (IMAS 2005) has been set up to "serve as a forum for members in discussions as well as a collective voice where representation is needed on behalf of the investment management industry, facilitating training for its members, and contributing towards investor education."

Unlike its equivalent associations in Australia, which take a strong stance on influencing corporate governance principles, IMAS seems to concentrate on investment knowledge and training for its members.

Directors

A major interest group primarily representing the share/security-holders' interests is the board directors. Directors are in effect the recipient of control models as well as the major protagonists in the corporate governance debate. In Australia their voice is collectively represented by the Australian Institute of Company Directors (AICD 2005). This body sees its role as being "the peak body for directors, offering board level professional development, director specific information services, and representation of directors' interests to government and the regulators."

The AICD has identified its main corporate governance roles as to:

- meet the information and education needs of directors;
- be the recognized advocate for corporate governance and directors' issues; and
- provide a valued directors' network.

The AICD, originally a chapter of the U.K. Institute of Directors, was formed as a separate body in 1971. It now has over 18,500 members and has emerged as a strong body, seeking to professionalize the role of directors and growing significantly in the last two decades. It runs a number of education and training programs that form the basis for membership and links with other professional bodies to advocate for corporate governance reform and development. It has an excellent journal, runs a mail order bookshop, and produces its own monographs on corporate governance issues.

In the other countries the role of directors is less clearly emphasized as a stakeholder representative. In India the Indian Institute of Directors exists but it is a body that appears to have grown from the quality control movement. Recently it has linked with a university to establish a director training institute. However, other bodies such as the accounting and auditing professional bodies, CII and SEBI seem to have had a stronger influence over corporate governance reform.

In Singapore the Institute of Directors was set up in 1998 and now has over 700 members (SIOD 2005). It is structured in a similar way to the AICD and is developing along similar lines as a professional member association. In China the former U.K. Institute of Directors chapter became the Hong Kong Institute of Directors in 1997, and like the other IoDs, conducts various professional development and education programs. At the time of writing, there appear to be no other Chinese director associations.

The discrepancy of development between the director community as a profession in Australia compared to the other three countries can be seen as a direct result of different cultural backgrounds. The higher emphasis on individualism and self-regulation has encouraged the growth of professional associations. These cultural aspects have become more important elements impacting on business behavior and corporate governance. This is less evident in countries in which government control over corporate behavior has been stronger and family grouping and communitarianism is a core social influence. In India, where arguably individualism and self-control is also emphasized, one can posit that the sense of identity comes from both religious influence and professional standing. These factors are likely to have a direct bearing on the potential impact of corporate governance models on business behavior. The cultural overlay should not be underestimated, as is discussed shortly.

Other Direct Stakeholders

Employees
In Australia, employees have traditionally been represented by trade unions and professional associations. The Sunshine Harvester Case in 1907 helped

establish the principles of a basic wage and a centralized arbitration and conciliation system that lasted for some 90 years (Hancock 2004). It underpinned the power of the union movement that has only diminished in the last decade with the impact of globalization and enterprise bargaining. The union movement is still strong and has in recent years become involved in corporate governance issues, through member based superannuation funds and links with shareholder association activities. Professional associations likewise often are concerned with corporate behavior and act on behalf of members to pressure senior managers, boards, and owners to act legally and ethically.

In India, traditionally, the employees have been more closely aligned to the business and its owners or to a caste community. As such, whilst the trade union movement exists, its influence is arguably ameliorated by loyalty to the business entity. This view would be offset by perceptions of increasing militancy of unions that are concerned with issues of privatization, especially of state owned enterprises.

In the last few decades, NGOs have taken an increasingly active role in supporting social causes in India, often focussing on issues such as child or indentured labor, poor labor conditions, equal opportunity, and discrimination. Such groups are often supported by international agencies such as Oxfam, Care or World Vision and United Nations (UN) agencies such as the International Labor Organization. This has meant the pressure exerted by these stakeholder groups is linked to such influences as the Global Compact (GC 2005) or the Caux Round Table (CAUX 2005).

In China and Singapore the role of employees as stakeholders has been strongly influenced by government driven regulation. Union or NGO activism is less influential than in either Australia or India. Such direct activism is likely to be discouraged by government, in China particularly. However, relationships between individual employees, employee groups and associations, and government agencies are likely to be informally influential (Park and Luo 2001).

Customers and Suppliers

In Australia, industry groups and associations, such as chambers of commerce, the Mining Industry Council, consumer advocacy bodies such as Australian Consumer Association and government agencies such as the State Department of Consumer Affairs can, and do, engage with corporations to protect customers and suppliers interests. Legislation directed at regulatory issues such as maintaining competition, protecting consumers rights, and fair trading is relatively strong and is administered by a large number of regulatory bodies.

In other countries similar groups exist. In India, the Ministry of Consumer Affairs, Food and Public Distribution focuses on managing food distribution and regulating markets to protect consumers from market manipulation. A China Consumers Association website (CCA 2005) indicates that a focus on "consumer rights" is growing. However, a web search on consumer affairs activities did not indicate an extensive network of organizations. In Singapore, an Inspectorate & Consumer Affairs Department exists but has little information about its activities listed on its website (SGD 2005).

It seems from web based research that the free market environment evident in Australia has spawned a much wider network of stakeholder agencies and organizations than in the other countries reviewed. Again this reiterates the wide divergence of national systems that have had, and will continue to have, significant impact on how corporate governance processes are likely to develop.

Indirect Stakeholders—Social

Local Communities

In Australia local community stakeholder engagement could take place in a number of ways. Local government departments are likely to have an interest in businesses located in their regions. Planning and industry policy departments will administer regulations relating to: constructions, harmonization with existing infrastructure, and integration with local services. Such departments are likely to manage stakeholder engagement via community engagement projects, discussion groups, and in other ways, especially if there are major potential conflicts likely to emerge. NGOs or semigovernment authorities, interested in social development issues, have a potentially strong influence in specific regions or industries, for example the Northern Lands Council has protocols for doing business in designated Aboriginal reserve areas (NLC 2005).

In India, whilst local government bodies vary significantly in terms of sophistication and ability to interact with business, NGOs, including religious institutions such as temples and ashrams may have a significant capacity to influence stakeholder engagement with corporations. This has become very evident in campaigns relating to land usage, such as the Narmada Dam project (Naramada 2005) and multinational corporation (MNC) activity in India.[8] The ability of NGOs to have considerable influence in India is partly related to a high level of mistrust of government and public sector officials as well as a history of support for social action from local volunteer community bodies in India.

China and Singapore appear to have less indirect local social engagement with business, again reiterating the tradition of reliance on government intervention on behalf of local community stakeholders.

Regional, National, and Global Communities
In all countries the impact of networks representing the social interests of broader based stakeholder groups is growing. The influence of such initiatives as the Global Compact (GC 2005), the Global Reporting Initiative[9] and Fair Trade,[10] is having an impact on how corporations, especially MNCs, are approaching their social policies in all countries. In Australia, social reporting indexes are being openly acknowledged by major corporations as important.[11] In the other countries local community responses are likely to be specific issue related.[12] However, given the growing concerns about MNC impact on society and as markets in China and India grow, these networks may establish a broader influence.

Indirect Stakeholders—Environment

The environmental movement is represented by a wide range of agencies or individuals. These fall into two broad categories. First formal approved bodies such as national or regional government departments or U.N. accredited agencies exist and are active in the field. Second, individuals concerned by environmental destruction or NGOs whose charters are to protect the environment emerge and seek legitimacy as indirect stakeholders. The latter group has emerged often in response to concerns about "capture" of the formal agencies by the opponents of the environmental movement.

In Australia, government agencies concerned with the environment fall into two groups. First are those who have an interest in promoting the use of natural resources such as departments of agriculture, water storage, and forestry. Second are those who have been established specifically to monitor and respond to growing community concerns about environmental degradation such as the Environment Protection Agency (EPA), LandCare, and Parks Victoria. The way such bodies engage with corporations varies and is influenced by community attitudes and political interests. Some may take opposing views in response to natural resource utilization. For example, some departments work with and support agribusinesses using irrigation, whilst other departments may openly seek to reduce the amount of water usage devoted to agriculture. Government policy in response to environment protection is often influenced by electoral considerations. Up to two decades ago economic usage dominated issues such as forestry logging and dams for irrigation. Since then greater emphasis on sustainable usage has driven government policy and is impacting on how departments engage with corporations. There is now greater concern for issues such as forest degradation, land salinity, and other environmental issues. Consequently corporations are increasingly required to monitor their environmental impact. The EPA regularly checks water and air pollution and fines corporations who are guilty of breaking laws aimed at protecting the environment.

In India and China, with considerably more economic and demographic pressure on the environment, the trends are the same but the impact different. A decade ago, economic growth was seen as paramount and government agencies' work was directed primarily toward this.[13] Today, things seem to have changed—concerns for the environment are growing as pollution, especially in cities, is increasing. Attitudes are changing and government bodies' policies are likewise changing.[14] How extensive these changes are in terms of active engagement with corporations is hard to determine without further fieldwork research (Balasubramanian and Siemensma 2005).

In Singapore, again demographic and economic factors have considerable influence on the way agencies relate to corporations' environmental impact. Environmentalism is an important government concern because of the small land area, the dense population and strong political influence. Traffic in the city area has been tightly controlled, ensuring reasonable air quality. Singapore has sought to reduce the industry effect, by establishing an economic development zone on the nearby Indonesian area of the Bataan Islands.

Ethics and Governance

The main business ethics issue, from a corporate governance perspective, is the establishment of systems that manage ethical concerns and establish control procedures that seek to enhance business integrity and ethical conduct. One can reflect on ethics and governance from two perspectives in the context of cross country comparisons. First, how have various approaches to governance implicitly or explicitly focused on improving ethics in organizations? Second, how do social or organizational culture factors influence how "best practice" models "work" in different cultural settings? Does "ethics drive governance" or "governance drive ethics"? Whilst these two concepts may be interrelated, they do identify a number of significant and different issues. It is not possible to cover the full gamut of ethics and governance concerns in a brief intercountry comparison.

Consequently a number of issues that are important considerations for the four countries involved are highlighted.

Protection of Minority Shareholders and "Powerless" Stakeholders

The protection of the less powerful stakeholders is an issue, with different perspectives, for all countries reviewed. In China and India the "minority shareholder" is openly acknowledged as a potentially "endangered species" in reports on corporation governance and in new codes (Balasubramanian 2004, IFF 2004). In Australia, the prime concern to be addressed is that the dominant shareholders, directors, or senior executives, will maintain control to serve their personal interests.

In China a number of sections in their new code directly note this concern, advising controlling shareholders that they owe a duty of good faith toward the listed company and other shareholders. The Code also requires related party transactions to be properly, ethically, and transparently managed—a clear reference to the controlling shareholders' capability to manage the company inappropriately.[15] The Code implies that a relatively simple set of principles can be outlined that will guide the controlling shareholders' behavior.

In the other countries, the emphasis on protection focuses on independence, transparency, and audits. This approach to governance suggests that minority interests can best be protected by having an independent voice on the board that will offset the potential for unethical behavior by those in control.

In India, one can posit, given the limited capacity for legal enforcement, the strength of individual integrity of independent directors is seen as a key influence. Also, one can suggest that the personal values of individuals acting as, or on behalf of, the "controlling shareholders" are often openly appealed to.

Duty to Act Honestly, with Due Care and Diligence

In Australia the strength of the legal process has reinforced the notions of fiduciary duties of directors especially in the last 20 years. In this period a number of changes in corporate law and decisions in courtrooms have significantly sharpened directors' awareness of these issues. Recent corporate failures such as One-Tel, HIH, and Harris Scarfe[16] have all led to either commissions of inquiry, law reform amendments, or court cases whose judgments are likely to reconfirm or extend directors' responsibilities. In this environment, governance practices that lead to more ethical behavior have been reinforced by law. Today the potential for Australian directors to incur legal liability is high, as shown by the recent litigation arising from the collapse of HIH (Lipton 2006).

Social pressure to "do the right thing" is also growing as business commentators and the media have enjoyed the opportunity to highlight the unethical behavior of senior executives, especially when they appear to be overpaid at the same time (Arbouw 2001).

In India the inability of the legal system to effectively prosecute suggests that this issue is less likely to be driven by regulation and enforcement than by personal values and an inner sense of concern for ethics (Abhishek 2004). This pressure comes via the business media, as well as active business professional groups such as the Confederation of Indian Industry and the accounting and commercial law communities. The NGO movement is also a significant force in India. In summary, stakeholder pressure and a strong, often spiritually based, personal value system support good governance principles aimed at protecting minority interests.

In China, and to a lesser extent Singapore, one might suggest these ethical issues, honesty, due care, and diligence rely more on culture and less on governance regimes supported by a strong legal system enforcing compliance. This is discussed in detail shortly.

Managing Conflicts of Interest

The ability of senior executives and directors to appropriately deal with potential conflicts of interest is an ethical issue governance models seek to address. In Australia, statute and case law, codes of conduct and ASX guidelines address this issue to a greater or lesser extent. Statutory duties in this regard are spelt out in sections of the *Corporations Act*. Disclosure and other statutory obligations are mandatory. In China, the Code addresses this concern, primarily from the perspective of related party transactions and duties of good governance for directors. In India, task force reports in the past five years have emphasized the need for greater disclosure, reflecting on related party transactions in particular. The development of draft codes and the move toward more stringent listing regulations and corporate law are likely to incorporate this concern. However, it is not as specifically regulated in any of the other countries as in Australia. In all countries disclosure is emphasized as a way of managing this concern. It suggests open acknowledgment of a conflict of interest will limit the potential negative impact. This issue is discussed further shortly.

Impact of Social and Cultural Ethical Factors
on Corporate Governance

Whilst governance models are capable of encouraging ethical practice, one is immediately aware of potential tensions and paradoxes. The following issues, whilst by no means exhaustive, suggest that a "universal model" approach to corporate governance may be problematic and not necessarily able to produce optimal ethical outcomes. As ethics theorists are well aware,[17] much of what is perceived to be good ethics is influenced by the norms of cultures and society. Consequently corporate governance principles may well be interpreted via norms coming from social patterns and culture. "Actual Practice" may not follow "Idealized Theory."

However, one cannot be too "absolutist" in relation to this issue. Clearly when local companies are seeking international funding and legitimacy, they are likely to adopt the "best practice" models, as perceived by international financial markets, at least on paper. This is less likely when international legitimacy is not considered important or is not in the interests of existing managers such as in poorly performing former SOEs, or in family based corporations.

The Influence of Transparency and Disclosure to Encourage Ethical Behavior

This issue needs to be considered in the light of both culture and business practice. A valuable article by Velayutham and Perera (2004) reflects on how culture may impact on the ability of disclosure and transparency to foster better practice. They note that societies that identify "guilt" as a strong social factor are likely to be more responsive to "confession" or disclosure as a way of dealing with ethical dilemmas. They argue that such cultures are likely to be, in Hofstede's dimensions, individualistic, low power distance, and low uncertainty avoidance cultures (Hofstede 1984). Such cultures are likely to be Judaeo-Christian and typified by America or Australia. Accountability and transparent reporting are practices that "come naturally."

Alternatively, the authors suggest, cultures that respond more strongly to "shame" as an influence on behavior are less likely to feel comfortable with disclosure. To be identified by others as involved in an unacceptable act is the last thing individuals will be prepared to acknowledge. This may be equated to the "loss of face" concern often discussed as a dominant feature in communal cultures. Shame relates to unacceptability. Velayutham and Perera (2004) suggest such societies, in Hofstede's terms, are likely to be "collectivistic, large power distance and high uncertainty avoidance" cultures—those cultures typically associated with China and Singapore.

This argument provides a clue as to why disclosure of potentially difficult issues such as those related to potential conflicts of interest and individual remuneration as a means of encouraging good behavior may be resisted strongly. This factor underpins much of what is considered "good governance" in the "universal model." It may be difficult to genuinely instil it as a practice in China and Singapore.

Hofstede's initial findings in countries like Singapore were published three decades ago. In view of the economic development since then, and with the increasing influence of business practices from the United States, some of these cultural influences may be changing, albeit slowly, especially in international trading cities in North Asia or Singapore (Lyngaas 2003).

Alongside this hypothesis, in highly competitive, high population regions, is a belief that the competitor should never be given an advantage. Much of the Chinese business literature reflects historic war strategies that prize secrecy (Lao Tzu 2006). To highlight disclosure, as a process of good governance, may conflict with much "common sense" about doing business. Also it is likely that increasing disclosure about wealth will pose personal security risks for senior executives, especially in regions in which corruption and extortion are realistic business threats. This issue is likely to be a significant concern in some regions of India and China.

All these factors suggest that the idea of transparency, as a means of managing conflicts of interest as practiced in Australia, may be resisted in other countries in the region.

Independence and Loyalty

Independence has come to be seen as a cornerstone issue in corporate governance. It is the prime means of giving assurance that conflicts of interest are being managed and that appropriate monitoring of the senior executives is being properly handled by the board. The role of the independent nonexecutive director (NED) has been emphasized as paramount in many reports and in legislation (Higgs Report 2003).

However, this can be seen as a "culture laden" notion. In some societies "belonging" is a major cultural influence. To seek to be independent from the group, to hold an independent perspective, and to stand as an individual against a group position is undertaken only after all other possible alternatives have been exhausted. Being loyal to the group's leader, and to others in the group, may be regarded as more ethical than taking account of other consequences or upholding alternative principles. Harmony is the dominant social concern.

In some countries, independence of mind is regarded as an admired strength, whereas in community oriented societies it may be seen as socially undesirable. Fukuyama's (1995) work on high and low trust societies alludes to these themes, as do many cultural researchers' findings, on group or individual driven behaviors (Trompenaars and Turner 1997). The quote from Kipling (1994) similarly emphasizes the importance of being identified as part of a group.

In terms of governance, loyalty to the group's norms may be a key factor that inhibits the likelihood that "independent minds" can ensure equity and fairness in boardroom decision making. This is not to say independent directors in countries that are strongly "group" focussed will not be deeply troubled by inappropriate behavior. Rather it simply emphasizes that the "loyalty ethic" may override the capacity for directors to be truly independent. It is likely to be a factor in India, where family and community relationships are important, as well as in China, and Singapore.

Importance of Leadership

A corollary of the loyalty issue is the recognition by many researchers that attitudes about leadership vary considerably across cultures. Hofstede (1984) identifies this as a power distance dimension of culture. He suggests that countries like Singapore, China, and India register a high power distance score indicating most people do not expect to have a relationship with, or influence, senior organizational officials. Hofstede noted, in contrast, that Australia has a low power distance score, indicating most employees expect to have closer interaction with senior managers. Trompenaars and Turner (1997) use flat or steep triangles images to represent the relationship between leaders and employees in organizations. Their work confirmed Hofstedes' findings suggesting China, India, and Singapore businesses are likely to have "tall triangles," whereas in Australia, they are more likely to be equidistant.

This can also be related to the power of the individual leader. Political history clearly emphasizes a different approach to leadership. India, China, and Singapore have been more accepting of autocratic leaders (Gandhi and Nehru in India, Mao and Deng in China, and Lee Kuan Yew in Singapore) than is the case in Australia.[18]

Hence a clear difference between acceptance of the authority of the key figures between Australia and the other three countries appears likely. It relates to the theoretical assumption that strong debate in the boardroom, combined with the capacity of the board to represent its "electors"—the shareholders, is likely to occur in all countries. Cultural/social theorists, as noted earlier, would probably suggest otherwise. The capacity for individuals to speak out against the "clan leader," the majority shareholder representative, the senior family director/manager is less likely to be a way that ensures corporate or social ethics are sustained, in countries where this is "against culture."

These are presented as three examples of a wide variety of ethics and culture-related notions that will influence different countries' pragmatic responses to the "best practice" model in the Asia-Pacific region. Ultimately they support the view that "ethics" will influence "governance" as much as the other way around.

Ethics, the Senior Executive and the Director

Whilst ethics relating to board members and their actions are not ignored in Australia, it does seem the corporate governance "profession" is largely focused on the legal liability of its members. There is little evidence in the AICD website of a focus on business ethics processes and procedures.[19] A search of the AICD library website indicates that only a few publications that directly focussing on ethics approaches are available. Whilst such themes are certainly likely to be incorporated in the AICD publications on roles and duties of directors and their training programs, the lack of usage of terms "integrity" or "business ethics" in their website, given the concerns about business behavior over the last decade, suggests a degree of reticence that is surprising.

In other countries the concerns about ethics and behavior of professionals seem more evident. Institute of Director websites in Singapore and India gave direct reference to director training and development programs that address ethics and social responsibility issues.[20] In India, academic research on corporate reputation, corporate social responsibility ethics, and values is extensive and developing (Kimber and Balasubramanian 2000). Management and director education in this area is growing. The role of the "virtuous business leader" is well known and has traditionally been encouraged through social and spiritual movements (Balasubramanian and Siemensma 2005).

It appears that there are two diverging belief systems underpinning attitudes toward directors and senior executives. One is that directors are all driven by self-interest and are potentially corruptible. Therefore stringent regulations and compliance regimes are necessary to constrain their natural behavior. This seems to be the underlying orientation in the recent legislation in the United States. The other, more traditional, attitude emphasizes that directors have an innate capacity to be "good stewards" and "virtuous leaders" and that their personal sense of high moral standards underpins good ethical behavior in business. This orientation is evident in principle-based corporate governance regimes that are more focused on "ethics maintenance" than "legal compliance." Which perspective predominates is likely to be strongly influenced by the way different cultures respond to the relationship between ethics and leadership.

This suggests that ethics in the governance arena will be directed more by social and cultural pressures than legal or compliance regimes—a comment that is becoming increasingly emphasized in debates about the applicability of "black letter law" in countries outside the United States. In Australia, Karen Hamilton, Chief Integrity Officer of the ASX, recently commented on the principles and guidelines approach that she sees as more relevant in Australia than the "Sarbanes Oxley approach" coming from the United States (Hamilton 2004). If this is so for Australia, given its Anglo-American connections, it can only be more of an issue for Asia-Pacific countries that have different legal systems, business approaches, and cultural practices.

Conclusion

Corporate governance is an emerging and developing field in many parts of the world. However, to suggest that a convergence model is about to appear seems unlikely. As John Lyngaas (2003) suggests, this will not develop quickly because of well-entrenched corporate practices in China, Singapore, and India, as well as other Asian countries, which focus on family management/ownership[21] or majority ownership by government.[22] He goes on to note that examples of good corporate governance are easier to describe than to implement, especially in Asia.

This chapter highlights not only this issue, but also the different orientations to stakeholder management and integrity behavior in the boardroom and executives' offices. Different stages of business development, emerging industrialization, different political and legal systems, and traditional cultural and ethical practices all have considerable impact. Whilst globalization and financial market hegemony suggests a convergent model is theoretically desirable, the human capacity to protect diversity and enshrine regional and local interests seems likely to minimize rapid change, especially in the SME and national corporation arena. We hope that those in senior roles are aware that the sustainability of corporations, economies, and societies rests ultimately on their personal capacity to maintain high standards, principles, and foster ethical practices.

Notes

An earlier version of this chapter was published in *Business & Society* 44(2): 178–210. Permission to reprint it was kindly granted by Sage Publishers.

1. Australian market capitalization for ASX/S&P All Ordinaries sourced from Ipress Market Technology. China, India, and Singapore data sourced from Bloomberg.com and converted to Australian dollars. All data is at December 31, 2004.

2. The "Triple Bottom Line" or "3BL" is a term "used to capture the whole set of values, issues and processes that companies must address in order to minimize any harm resulting from their activities and to create economic, social and environmental value" SustainAbility website (an NGO established to encourage sustainable business practice in the UK). <http://www.sustainability.com/philosophy/triple-bottom/tbl-intro. asp> (accessed May 4, 2004 updated January 25, 2005.)

3. List primarily derived from corporate governance website portal Webb-site.com <http://www.webb-site.com/cg/default.htm> (Accessed December 15, 2005).

4. The Bendigo Stock Exchange, one of the three registered exchanges in Australia, was formed in the 1850s and reached its zenith in 1870. Then, it was noted, "mining companies were being floated . . . at the rate of half-a-dozen a day. Gaslights glimmered all night in the brokers' offices as staff struggled to cope with the deluge of business. In the latter half of 1870 some three hundred new companies registered and there was little abatement of the fever in the months that followed." Refer BXS Website <http://www.bsx. com.au/about_history.asp> (accessed December 15, 2005.)

5. A web Portal in India has been established to link all information relating to NGOs at <http://www.indianngos.com/> (accessed January 10, 2006).

6. See Hong Kong shareholder activist website at <http://www. webb-site.com/> (accessed January 10, 2006).

7. Ten years ago when working in Shanghai, I was fascinated to see that the Stock Exchange had set up branches in shops in main streets, not unlike a Totalizer Agency Board betting shop in Melbourne. It appeared that screens were flashing "buy" and "sell" quotes for listed shares and that the "punters" could go over to a wire screen to register their transactions. It brought new meaning to the notion of "day trading" and seemed to indicate that the "gambling" factor of owning shares was the main motive. Notions of good corporate governance were unlikely to be of key concerns.

8. For a news analysis of the debate on the Dabhol power project see website <http://news.bbc.co.uk/1/hi/world/south_asia/1113996.stm> (accessed January 11, 2006).

9. An NGO whose mission is to develop and disseminate globally applicable Sustainability Reporting Guidelines. See <http://www.globalreporting.org/> (accessed January 11, 2006).

10. An NGO aimed and encouraging fair international trade. See <http://www.fairtradefederation.com/> (accessed January 11, 2006).

11. Reputex Ratings and Research Services launched its Socially Responsible Investment Index in 2005. For an example of a company given a high rating by Reputex, see the corporate responsibility statement of Westpac Bank at <http://www.westpac. com.au/internet/publish.nsf/Content/ WI+Corporate+responsibility> (accessed January 11, 2006).

12. See Narmada (2005) and note 8.

13. As teachers in a university in Shanghai in 1995, we were told by senior officials, "after development we can worry about pollution."

14. Since 2004 in New Delhi in India all motorized taxis, once bad polluters using two stroke engines, have been required to change to natural gas. Trucks and buses some years ago were able to spew out black clouds of diesel smoke with gay abandon. Today, according to discussions with colleagues in Bangalore, they are being forced off the roads because environmental laws are being enforced.

15. See Code of Corporate Governance for Listed Companies in China issued by China Securities Regulatory Commission, Chapters 1 and 2 (CSRC 2005).

16. For the circumstances surrounding these and other corporate collapses see Australian Corporate Governance website <http://www.australian-corporate-governance.com.au/case_studies.htm> (accessed January 11, 2006).

17. The debate around universal versus relative ethics is extensive and ongoing. For an analysis of this issue, refer to Bowie (2004). This chapter cannot fully address all the dimensions. It simply posits that some culture/society issues have to be taken into account.

18. It could be argued, in Australia, Prime Ministers Menzies, Hawke, and Howard were/are accepted as strong leaders. However, their impact and influence is realistically far less than the leaders mentioned earlier in the other countries.

19. A 2005 search on the AICD website for ethics related information only gave seven "hits." Three of the seven references were to titles of books that could be purchased through the online bookshop. Two were to speeches and reports presented. One was a reference to the constitution. There were no references to integrity or ethics systems.

20. Refer Indian IoD website at http://www.iodonline.com/ and Singapore IOD http://www.sid.org.sg/index.php (accessed January 11, 2006).

21. "25% of 450 listed corporations in Singapore are controlled by 10 families according to David Gerald, the Chairman of the Securities Investors Association (Singapore)" (Lyngaas 2003, 12).

22. "(In China) . . . the state on average, owns 45% on each listed company" (Lyngaas 2003, 12).

References

ACGA. 2003. Asia Corporate Governance Association Survey 2003. Available at <http://www.acga-asia.org/> (accessed December 13, 2005).

ACSI. 2005. The Corporate Governance Guidelines. <http://www.acsi.org.au/dsp_viewcontent.cfm?news=2&nid=15> (accessed January 2006, 10).

AICD. 2005. The Australian Institute of Company Directors Website. <http://www.companydirectors.com.au/default.htm> (accessed January 10, 2006).

AMFI. 2005. Website for the Association of Mutual Funds in India. Available at <http://www.amfiindia.com/> (January10, 2006).

ACGA. 2003. Asia Corporate Governance Association. Available at <http://www.acga-asia.org/> (December 13, 2005).

Abhishek, Manu. 2004. The Legal Context of Corporate Governance. *Corporate Governance—Issues and Perspectives*. Arora R. and Saxena T, eds. Jaipur: Mangal Deep Publications.

Arbouw, John. 2001. Show Me the Money! *The Company Director*. Vol. 17 No. 7. Available at <http://www.companydirectors. com.au/Media/Company+Director+Journal+Archive/2001/August/Show+me+the+money.htm> (accessed January 11, 2006).

ASX. 2003. Corporate Governance Council *Principles of Good Corporate Governance and Best Practice Recommendations*. Available at: http://www.asx.com.au/about/pdf/ASXRecommendations.pdf> (accessed December 13, 2005).

Balasubramanian, N. 2004. Mainstreaming Corporate Governance in South Asia. Paper presented at ISBEE Conference, Melbourne, July 14–18, 2004.

Balasubrumanian, N., Kimber, D., and Fran Siemensma. 2005. Emerging Opportunities or Traditions Reinforced?—An Analysis of the Attitudes towards CSR, and Trends of Thinking about CSR, in India. *Journal of Corporate Citizenship* 17: 79–92.

Bowie, Norman. 1997. The Moral Obligations of Multinational Corporations. In *Ethical Theory and Business*, 5th Edition, T. L. Beauchamp and N. E. Bowie, eds. New Jersey, Prentice Hall.

Bradley, M., Schipani, C., Sundaram, A., and J. Walsh, 1999. The Purposes and Accountability of the Corporation in Contemporary Society: Corporate Governance at a Crossroads. 1999. *Law and Contemporary Problems* 62: 35–47. This is available at <http://papers.ssrn.com/sol3/papers.cfm?abstract_ id=220570> (accessed December 15, 2005).

CAUX. 2005. Caux Round Table Principles. Available at <http://www. cauxroundtable.org/> (accessed January 10, 2006).

CCA. 2005. China Consumer Association Website. Available at <http://eng.cca.org.cn> (accessed January 10, 2006).

CII. 1998. Confederation of Indian Industry. *Desirable Corporate Governance: A Code* 1998. Available at <http://www.ecgi.org/codes/code.php?code_id=59> (accessed December 15, 2005).

CSRC. 2005. China Securities Regulatory Commission. *The Code of Corporate Governance for Listed Companies in China* 2001. Available at <http://www.ecgi.org/codes/code.php?code_id=23.> (accessed December 15, 2005).

Energy Information Administration. 2003. World Per Capita Gross Domestic Product Using Market Exchange Rates, 1980–2003. US Department of Energy International *Energy Annual 2003*. Available at <http://www.eia.doe.gov/pub/international/iealf/tableb2c.xls> (accessed December 13, 2005).

Etzioni, Amitai. 1988. *The Moral Dimension: Toward a New Economics.* New York: Free Press.

Fama, Eugene, and Michael. Jensen 1983. Separation of Ownership and Control. *Journal of Financial Economics* 26: 301.

Fukuyama, Francis. 1995. *Trust: The Social Virtues and the Creation of Prosperity.* England: Penguin Books.

GC. 2005. The Global Compact Available at <http://www.unglobalcompact.org/Portal/Default.asp> (accessed January 10, 2006).

Goswami, Omkar. 2000. The Tide Rises Gradually, Corporate Governance in India. OECD: 19–23. Workshop April 3–4, Paris. Available at <http://www.oecd.org/dataoecd/6/47/1931364.pdf> (accessed December 15, 2005).

Hamilton, Karen. 2004 Corpulent Governance: The Supersizing of Corporate Governance, Ethics and Regulation and the ASX's Role in Achieving a Healthy Balance. Melbourne: Partners in Business Luncheon Law Insitute. Available at <http://www.asx.com.au/about/pdf/Law_Institute_and_ICA_Melb_Oct04_Final.pdf> (accessed January 10, 2006).

Hancock, Keith. 2004. The Wage of the Unskilled Worker and Family Needs, 1907 and 1920. Adelaide: National Institute of Labour Studies, pp. 2–12. Available at <http://www.ssn.flinders.edu.au/nils/publications/workingpapers/wp152.pdf.> (accessed January 10, 2006).

Higgs Report. 2003. *UK Review of the Role and Effectiveness of Non-Executive Directors* Available at <http://www.dti.gov.uk/cld/non_exec_review/pdfs/higgsreport.pdf> (accessed January 10, 2006).

HKIOD. 2005. The Hong Kong Institute of Directors Website. Available at <http://www.hkiod.com/eng/cpd_core.asp> (accessed January 10, 2006).

Hofstede, Geert. 1984, *Cultures Consequences: International Differences in Work-Related Values.* London: Sage Publications.

IFF. 2004. Corporate Governance in China—an Investor Perspective. Available at <http://www.iif.com/data/public/china_task_force_final.pdf> (accessed January 11, 2006).

IFSA, 2005. Investment and Financial Services Association Limited Website. Available at <http://www.ifsa.com.au> (accessed January 11, 2006).

IMAS 2005. The Investment Management Association of Singapore Website. Available at <http://www.imas.org.sg/imas/about/overview.do> (accessed January 10, 2006).

Jensen, Michael. 1984. Takeovers: Folklore and Science. *Harvard Business Review.* Available at <http://papers.ssrn.com/sol3/papers.cfm?abstract_id=350425> (accessed December 15, 2005).

Jensen, Michael, and William Meckling. 1976. Theory of the Firm: Managerial Behaviour, Agency Costs and Ownership Structure. *Journal of Financial Economics* 3: 305.

Kimber, D., and N. Balasubrumanian 2000. Corporate Governance, Reputation and Competitive Credibility. *Indian Institute of Management Bangalore—Management Review* 12 (2 June): 67–75.

Kipling, Rudyard. 1994. The Apprentice. In *The Penguin Book of Indian Railway Stories*, Bond R. (ed.). New Delhi: Penguin Books. Available at <http://whitewolf.newcastle.edu.au/words/authors/k/KiplingRudyard/prose/landandsea/boldprentice.html> (accessed July 5, 2006).

La Porta, R., Lopez-de-Silanes, F., Shleifer, A., and R. Vishny. 1998. Law and Finance. *Journal of Political Economy* 106: 1113–1155. Available at <http://post.economics.harvard.edu/faculty/shleifer/papers/lawandfinance.pdf> (accessed December 15, 2005).

———. 1999. Investor Protection and Corporate Governance. *World Bank* Available at <http://rru.worldbank.org/Documents/PapersLinks/investor_protection_origins_consequences_reform_latest.pdf> (accessed December 15, 2005).

Lao Tzu, 2006. *The Art of War.* Available at <http://www.westmeet-east.com/edusuntsu2.htm#ch6> (accessed January 10, 2006).

Lipton, Phillip. 2006. The Demise of HIH: Corporate Governance Lessons. Available at <http://www.australian-corporate-governance.com.au/hih_royal_commission.pdf> (accessed January 11, 2006).

Lyngaas J. 2003. Corporate Governance: Will Asia Buy It? Available at <http://www.ey.com/global/download.nsf/Singapore/Spotbiz_Iss_1_(2003)_ar3_Will_Asia_Buy_It/$file/3_CGWillAsiaBuyIt.pdf> (accessed January 11, 2006).

Narmada. 2005. Available at http://www.narmada.org/> (accessed January 11, 2006).

NLC. 2005. Northern Lands Council website. Available at <http://www.nlc.org.au/html/busi_menu.html> (accessed January 11, 2006).

Park, Seung Ho., and Yadong Luo. 2001. Guanxi and Organizational Dynamics: Organizational Networking in Chinese Firms. *Strategic Management Journal* 22: 455–477.

Reddy, Y. R. K. 2004. First Principles of Corporate Governance for Public Enterprise. In *Corporate Governance—Issues and Perspectives*, Arora R. and T. Saxena (eds.). Jaipur: Mangal Deep Publications.

SGD. 2005. Singapore Government Directory. Available at <http://app.sgdi.gov.sg/listing_print.asp?agency_subtype=dept&agency_id=0000006068> (accessed January 10, 2006).

SIOD. 2005. The Singapore Institute of Directors Website. Available at <http://www.sid.org.sg/index.php> (accessed January 10, 2006).

Singapore Council on Corporate Disclosure and Governance. 2001. *Code of Corporate Governance.* Available at http://www.ecgi.org/ codes/documents/cg_code.pdf (accessed December 15, 2005).

Stapledon, Geof. 1999. Share Ownership and Control in Listed Australian Companies. Social Science Research Network. Available at <http://papers. ssrn.com/sol3/papers.cfm?abstract_id=164129> (accessed December 15, 2005).

SustainAbility 2004. Who Are the Stakeholders?" Available at <http:// www. sustainability.com/issues/who-are-stakeholders.asp> (accessed May 1, 2004).

Trompenaars, Fons, and Charles Hampden Turner. 1997. *Riding the Waves of Culture*. London: Nicholas Brierley Publishing.

Velayutham, Sivakumar and Hector Perera. 2004. The Influence of Emotions and Culture on Accountability and Governance. *International Journal of Business in Society*. Vol. 4 No. 1: 52–64. Available at <http://ariel. emeraldinsight. com/ vl=4041581/cl=57/nw=1/rpsv/cgi-bin/linker?ini=&reqidx=/cw/ mcb/14720701/v4n1/s5/p52> (accessed January 11, 2006).

Weimer, Jeroen, and Joost Pape. 1999. A Taxonomy of Systems of Corporate Governance *Corporate Governance: An International Review* 7: 152–165.

CHAPTER 10

BUSINESS ETHICS AND CORPORATE GOVERNANCE IN JAPAN

Nobuyuki Demise

Introduction

Since the 1990s, many company executives, lawyers, and scholars have been debating the issue of corporate governance in Japan.[1] However, differences in opinion on the appropriate approach to corporate governance prevented them from coming to a unified conclusion. Given the lack of consensus, some companies took the initiative and started reforming their corporate governance structures voluntarily. They focused mainly on the compilation and functions of their boards of directors.

The recent exposure of corporate malpractice fuelled interest in the ethical aspect of corporate governance. There is a growing conviction that business ethics should be institutionalized in companies. This further stimulated the corporate governance reform agenda. It also received support by the government, which recognized these problems and enacted legislation to deal with and prevent corporate malpractice.

Different Models of Corporate Governance in Japan

Japanese companies use a one-tier board system. All directors are elected at the shareholders meeting, and the elected directors constitute the board. Many directors in Japanese companies are former employees of the companies on which boards they serve. The majority of members on the board tend to come from the ranks of the executive managers in the company.

Many large companies have a board of auditors.[2] The company auditors are elected at the shareholders' meeting and at least one of them must be from outside the company. According to the company law, the board of company auditors must monitor the management and report on their performance to the shareholders. A large number of outside directors and company auditors are executives of other companies in the same group as the one on whose board they serve (Learmount 2002, 125). This gives rise to the phenomenon of cross-directorships. The Mitsubishi Group is an example of this.

The Japanese Commercial Code that was revised in 2003 enables Japanese companies to abolish the board of auditors system. Instead thereof, it introduces a board committee system. The board committee system is composed of the audit committee, the nominating committee, and the remuneration committee. The majority of members of each committee has to be directors from outside the company. In 2005 about 100 companies including Sony and Hitachi adopted this model. Many large companies, including Toyota Motor, Matsushita Electric, and Canon, however, did not follow suit.

Companies like Toyota Motor and Matsushita Electric chose a different method of corporate governance reform. They reduced the number of directors on their boards by removing executive managers from the board. At the same time they elected more outside company auditors to their boards and also appointed more executive officers in the company. This approach is called the separation of execution from decision-making. The company law that was legislated in 2005 permits both these models.

The extent of Stakeholder Engagement in Japan

Previously banks and employees were considered to be the main stakeholders in Japanese corporations (Hopt and Wymeersch 1997, 185–193). Many of the large companies would hold equal shares of other large companies. This is referred to as cross-shareholdings. It was used as a measure to prevent takeovers. Within this system banks would finance many companies that belong to the same group of cross-shareholdings. This created dependency by such a cross-shareholding group on the bank (Hoshi and Kasyap 2001, 91). Consequently, when the company faces financial difficulties, the bank would send its executives in to restructure and rescue the company. More recently the practice of cross-shareholdings has been decreasing, causing more Japanese companies to become vulnerable to takeover bids. A number of hostile takeovers of large public companies were attempted in 2005, but they ended in failure.

The powerful position that banks were in with regard to companies are, however, changing as banks themselves were forced to restructure. This has resulted in banks becoming less likely to intervene in the affairs of the companies that they finance. New stakeholders, like managers of pension funds and foreign investors are at the same time becoming more influential. They do not shy away from contesting proposals and decisions by the CEOs of the companies in which they invest.

The situation is equally changing with regard to employees. Employees in Japanese large companies are regarded as "core members" of companies, though employees include managers under the lifetime employment system and the seniority system. The time has come to reconsider the lifetime employment system. In this system employees used to make a lifetime commitment to the growth of the company that they were employed in. In return the company provided them with secure employment for their entire working life. This psychological contract is, however, changing as new terms of employment are introduced, which offer less security to employees. Despite this changing employment situation, ethical issues like *karoshi* (death from overwork) and harassment at work remain a concern in Japanese companies. The persistence of these ethical issues can be seen as a direct result of the fact that Japanese employees are unlikely to raise these ethical issues. The reason for this is the fact that many top managers in Japanese companies were once low-level employees, who were willing to sacrifice in order to be promoted. Hard work and personal sacrifices guaranteed them promotion, and they now expect similar behavior from their subordinates. This attitude will be perpetuated as long as the concept of lifetime employment prevails. Thus, employees are not encouraged to stand up for their own needs and rights.

The Relevance and Role of Business Ethics in Corporate Governance

After the recent exposure of corporate malpractices, many companies are more prepared to engage with ethics as part of their corporate governance reform. Companies may bring in directors from outside to sit on their ethics committees or appoint experts in business ethics from outside the company to be members of the ethics committee. They start to manage their ethics more actively, through ethics officers, ethics communication systems, and ethics training programs. Some companies emphasize the improvement of transparency and accountability by establishing a code of conduct.

In Japan there are some companies that have the tendency to be embroiled in scandals repeatedly. The Mitsubishi Motors Corporation

(MMC) for example was embroiled in a scandal in 1997 when it was disclosed that it paid a third party who illegally "fixed" shareholder meetings. In 2000, it was brought to light that MMC managed for years to cover up defects in cars. After that revelation a business ethics program was introduced, but MMC still refrained from electing independent directors to its board. The program that was introduced included a code of conduct, an ethics committee, and an ethics help-line. In 2004, however, Mitsubishi Fuso Truck & Bus Corporation that was separated from MMC in 2003 once more became embroiled in another scandal.

Nowadays, the top management of most companies has a commitment to business ethics. They recognize that it is important for their business to be perceived as trustworthy by consumers. They understand what their stakeholders require from their business and they seem to be well acquainted with procedures to be taken to reinforce the business ethics of their organizations.

The company law that was legislated in 2005 requires top managers to establish an internal control system. Establishing such a system involves the introduction of a compliance program and the institutionalization of business ethics.

Management and Reporting of Business Ethics

The process of managing ethics in companies was stimulated with the publication of *The Charter of Corporate Behavior* in 1991 by Nippon Keidanren (the Federation of Economic Organizations in Japan). In response to the publication of this charter, many large companies have established a code of ethics or a code of conduct. In 2004 Nippon Keidanren revised the Charter of Corporate Behavior. The revised charter puts greater emphasis on corporate social responsibility. Also concepts like "human rights," "communication with the stakeholders" and "supply chain management" are introduced in the revised charter.

In 2003 Keizai Doyukai, the Japan Association of Corporate Executives, published the fifteenth Corporate White Paper on "*Market Evolution and CSR Management: Toward Building Integrity and Creating Stakeholder Value*".[3] Keizai Doyukai regarded corporate social responsibility and corporate governance as the most important elements for companies to build trust and create sustainable stakeholder value. In 2004 Keizai Doyukai published the findings of a survey on corporate social responsibility and corporate governance in Japan. It concluded that Japanese companies need to build compliance systems with more effective control mechanisms to ensure sustained corporate social responsibility and good corporate governance.

Some companies have adopted standards such as ECS2000,[4] GRI, and the United Nations Global Compact. Furthermore, many companies in Japan have also formulated environmental policies. Companies that take their environmental responsibility seriously also publish environmental reports. Recently more companies have started publishing environmental and social reports, as well as sustainability reports, that result in more reporting and disclosure on the social performance of companies.

New Developments with Regard to Business Ethics and Corporate Governance

There are a number of new developments that have the potential to result in improved corporate governance and business ethics. These initiatives have been taken by the Japan government, the Tokyo Stock Exchange, and the Pension Fund Association in Japan respectively.

In Japan the government plays an important role in reforming corporate governance and business ethics. The Japanese government is seriously considering making whistleblowing systems and codes of conduct mandatory for all companies. The whistleblowing system is intended to protect whistleblowers from retaliation. The government also has the authority to compel companies to publish their codes of conduct.

In 2004 the Tokyo Stock Exchange published its *Principles of Corporate Governance for Listed Companies*.[5] The *Principles* covered the following:

- Rights of shareholders
- Equitable treatment of shareholders
- Relationship with stakeholders in corporate governance
- Disclosure and transparency
- Responsibilities of board of directors, auditors, or board of corporate auditors and other relevant groups

These Principles have many points in common with the 1999 OECD Principles on Corporate Governance.

In 2004 the Pension Fund Association in Japan published recommendations on corporate governance. In addition the association published guidelines on the exercise of shareholder's rights. This is a clear indication that nongovernmental organizations are also getting involved in corporate governance.

In 2005 a new company law was legislated and a draft of enforcement regulations was published by the Ministry of Justice. In that draft it is emphasized that one of the duties of directors is to ensure the maximization of interests of shareholders. This directive coincides with the norms of the Japanese society.

In reaction to large illegal collusions (*dangou*) that were detected in 2005, the Japanese Antitrust Act was revised. It will come into force in 2006 and will make it easier to expose illegal collusion to the Fair Trade Commission.

Conclusion

In Japan corporate governance reform is most likely to take place at the level of the board of directors. Top managers usually carry out the reforms that the board has decided upon as they are expected to have a commitment to business ethics. There are, however, companies that resist corporate governance reform and the introduction of any ethics programs. These companies therefore lack transparency, which ultimately prevents them from achieving credibility. A number of critical ethical issues such as death from overwork (*karoshi*), harassment at work, discrimination at work, illegal collusion (*dangou*), and defrauding consumers and governments still remain unresolved and persistent in Japanese business.

Notes

An earlier version of this chapter was published in *Business & Society* 44(2): 211–217. Permission to reprint this was kindly granted by Sage Publishers.

1. The Japanese Corporate Governance Forum was established in 1994. The members of JCGF are company executives, lawyers, and scholars. See http://www.jcgf.org (accessed January 5, 2006).
2. The board of auditors comprises company auditors, whom we call "Kansayaku." See <http://www.kansa.or.jp.> (accessed January 5, 2006).
3. See <http://www.doyukai.or.jp/en/policyproposals/articles/pdf/030326_1.pdf.> (accessed January 6, 2006).
4. See <http://r-bec.reitaku-u.ac.jp/files/ECS 200E.pdf> (accessed June, 2006).
5. See http://www.tse.or.jp/english/listing/cg/principles.pdf. (accessed January 6, 2006).

References

Hopt, Klaus, and Eddy Wymeersch, eds. 1997. *Comparative Corporate Governance.* New York: Walter de Gruuyter.

Hoshi, Takeo, and Anil Kasyap. 2001. *Corporate Financing and Governance in Japan.* London: MIT.

Learmount, Simon. 2002. *Corporate Governance.* London: Oxford University Press.

CHAPTER 11

BUSINESS ETHICS AND CORPORATE GOVERNANCE IN EUROPE

Josef Wieland

Corporate Governance and Business Ethics

For some years now, the question of how to implement and operationalize moral values, convictions, and intentions in firms has received increasing attention in the business and corporate ethics literature. The main issue is to develop management systems capable of integrating the moral dimension of economic transactions and questions of value into firms' strategies, policies, and procedures. The challenge for such management systems is to achieve this in a sustained way, and to carry the moral dimensions and questions of values down to the level of typical decisions taken in everyday business. In Germany, this discussion has unfolded under the label "values management," emphasizing the link between value creation and moral values. It parallels the manifold endeavors on the European level to secure the credibility and verifiability of value management systems, as well as their documentation and reporting structures, by imposing standards or guidelines and assurance processes to evaluate those.[1] In Germany, the main standard is the "ValuesManagementSystem[ZfW]" developed by the Zentrum für Wirtschaftsethik (Center for Business Ethics).[2] It has been developed on the basis of a decade of practical experience and cooperation with leading German firms, ranging from SMEs to multinationals. The German standard aims at sustainable management by integrating its economic, moral, legal, and political dimensions. Governance structures that implement such an approach are comprehensive and integrative in nature and are part of corporate strategy (Wieland, 2003). No consensus has yet been reached on the question of who should verify or enforce such programs—the firms themselves, NGOs, or state regulation. Self-enforcement and third party enforcement thus appear as two opposing alternatives. I want to propose a different perspective on the matter: It is conceivable that third party enforcement could be an expression of self-governance. Third party enforcement could be based on a voluntary decision on the part of the firm (Wieland, 2003).

The endeavor of developing standards for individual and collective action is not at all confined to the relationship between economics and ethics. We also find such endeavors in the many disciplines that lie at the interface between economics, law, and politics (Brunsson and Jacobsson, 2000). Certainly, the globalization of economic activity and the lack of regulation and institutions that address it are amongst the drivers of such endeavors. The global movement for the creation of corporate governance codes can serve as example. On the one hand, there was a drive toward homogenizing rules and transparency for international investors. On the other hand, the uninterrupted series of recent scandals, capricious behavior on the part of top management and the gaps and weaknesses of conventional risk management that correspond to such behavior have certainly also driven that movement. The starting point of the corporate governance discussion has therefore always been the compliance aspect of business ethics. It has always, however, been interpreted from a legal point of view. Rarely have actors adopted a values orientation when implementing it.

In what follows, I argue that efforts of standardization need to be synchronized in both areas, and finally be integrated. From the perspective of the corporate governance movement, the central insight is that effective and efficient leadership, management and control of the firm will be impossible without integrating moral attitudes and requirements with behavior. From the perspective of business ethics it is important, in my view, to acknowledge that such a comprehensive understanding of corporate governance actually means to consider the objective of values management a strategic management task and thus anchor it on the top management level. From such a perspective, increasing the importance that business ethics has in all corporate processes and structures would then be decisive. I also argue that a discussion of high relevance to the social sciences is connected to the topic "corporate governance," that is, the discussion of the question of the objective and purpose of firms as organizations in market economies. From the perspective of business ethics, such a discussion only makes sense if an adequate notion of corporate governance is available. For this reason, in what follows I also review the European research frontier on this issue.

For this purpose, I propose a definition of governance that aims to be integrative: I define corporate governance as leadership, management, and control of a firm by formal and informal, public and private rules. The governance matrix in table 11.1 formalizes such an understanding of comprehensive corporate governance as institutionalization and organization of formal and informal, private and public rules.

The "leadership" element covers codified guidelines in firms as well as informal leadership standards and the function of managers to serve as role models. The "management" aspect covers the formal decision mechanisms of a firm as well as the informal values of its corporate culture. Firm-specific control, finally, covers audits and other assurance processes, as well as the exclusion of risks by moral individual conduct. The public formal rules we consider here are of the type of the Sarbanes-Oxley Act in the United States, the German laws on the control and transparency (KonTraG) and on the transparency and publicity (TransPuG) of transactions or the widely diffused type of "comply-or-explain" regulation contained in many governance codes that directly influence the corporate governance of a firm. Public informal rules include such things as the impact of a national or regional culture on social or ecological responsibility of firms, or on how to deal with corruption.

Adopting such a comprehensive interpretation of corporate governance leads to the conviction that any efficient and effective governance structure needs to serve two functions: to constrain and to enable. Corporate governance cannot be interpreted solely as constraint of behavior (for instance as limitation of exposure to risk). It should also be understood as enabler of behavior (for instance, in "grey zones") for managing transactions with integrity (on this distinction see Wieland 2001b). A crucial objective of the notion of governance I propose here is to realize both functions in everyday business conduct.

It is obvious and beyond dispute that no broad agreement with such a definition of corporate governance exists in many countries and regions.

Table 11.1 Governance Matrix and Management of Rules

	Formal Rules	Informal Rules
Public	• Sarbanes Oxley • Comply-or-Explain	• Economic culture • Tradition, mores, conventions
Private	• Corporate Governance Code • Values Management System	• Corporate culture • Corporate values

The Anglo-Saxon countries and Switzerland, for instance, emphasize management control and the defensive aspects of monitoring. The Danish or Dutch, on the other hand, interpret corporate governance as effective stakeholder management. From such a perspective, monitoring and management control also have an important role to play. They are, however, embedded in a conception of the firm that sees it as part of the society at large, and that takes the interests of different stakeholders into consideration. I discuss these issues in detail shortly. At this point I just want to emphasize once more that only a comprehensive and integrative understanding of corporate governance is capable of providing a link between questions of business and corporate ethics, and the strategic and operative management of firms. At the same time, only the process of understanding corporate governance in a comprehensive and integrative way creates the conditions that enable the governance structure as a whole to be effective, including its public and private rules of compliance. Public and private, formal and informal rules form a network. The network linkages support the individual components and increase their effectiveness. This indeed appears to be the lesson from the recent scandals: firms such as WorldCom, Enron, and Arthur Andersen all had formally implemented brilliant systems of corporate governance and compliance but they, and especially the top management of these firms, did not live according to them. There are two problems with corporate governance that is not backed by a corporate culture suited to it, and with formal rules not backed by the mobilization of informal values that support the enforcement of the formal rules. First, their effectiveness is limited. Second, they can also serve to disguise risks. They can lead to the impression that means for risk prevention would be available within the firm. I have discussed this in detail elsewhere (Wieland and Fuerst 2004).

There are additional important arguments for coupling questions of corporate governance with those of business ethics in the way proposed here, bundling them into the "ethics of governance" (for this research program see Wieland 1999, 2001a).

First, questions of corporate governance relate to all processes taking place in firms. They arise on both the strategic and the operative level of management and span all hierarchical levels. Moreover, the decision to codify a corporate governance code is a top management decision. Coupling questions of corporate governance with those of business ethics will help to strengthen the endeavor to pursue an applicable and practically relevant approach to business ethics within firms. It will add to both import and importance.

Second, corporate governance provides an interface between the legal and moral aspects of transactions, the notion of compliance and corporate culture, and the process of implementation and that of enforcement of systems of ethics management or value management. Such an interface is provided precisely when and if corporate governance is conceived as a self-enforcement process, conditioned by a "comply-or-explain" rule. Such a process is an instance of structural coupling, which is characteristic of the governance of modern societies.

Third, it is important to note an aspect often rather neglected in the corporate governance discussion. The discussion in all countries includes the question on what the goals and tasks of firms in a global economy should be. Should they be purely economic, or also include social goals and tasks? This question leads to a discussion of the definition and raison d'être of firms from an economic perspective, and from the perspective of the society. That discussion carries normative baggage and aims at providing legitimation. The answer we arrive at will therefore be of the utmost importance for further theoretical and practical development of business ethics.

In what follows, I focus on the third aspect. My aim is to identify the European perspective at present, and sketch out what it could be in the future.

Diversity of Corporate Governance

The term "corporate governance" is used on a global scale. Nevertheless, interpretations of what it means are not at all homogenous. Divergences relate to the terms "corporation" and "governance." Both on the definition and raison d'être of corporations and on the interpretation of the term governance, large differences in opinion prevail. The causes of those divergences in interpretation are to be found both in theories and in the cultural background. The next paragraph is dedicated to explain this in depth.

The notion of corporate governance is much less sharply defined than one might expect at first glance. In fact, many different interpretations exist of what is a corporation (firm) and which types of transactions the systems of leadership, management, and control—that is, the governance system—should be focused on. What is the objective of a firm? What are its aims? Who are its relevant actors? What do the relevant governance structures need to look like in order to achieve the purposes chosen? What is the role of the firm as an economic organization situated within the context of society? It is not difficult to see that all those questions and the answers that are given have a crucial impact on the positioning of a firm in terms of ethics. For the moment it seems to make sense to make an attempt to assemble a theoretical framework for dealing with those differences, in order to facilitate their understanding and estimate their consequences.

Based upon the theoretical findings of the Institutionalist Theory of the Firm and the New Economics of Organization (Kroszner 1996) three theories of corporate governance can be distinguished: (1) Agency theory, (2) Transaction cost theory, and (3) Organization theory (as shown in table 11.2).

Agency Theory

Agency theory is focused on the problems relating to the separation of ownership and control. The personal separation of owners and managers, and the legal separation of ownership rights and decision rights lead to the core problem of agency theory: the conflict of different utility functions and interests between owners and managers in a firm.

The assumption shared by all economists is that managers, like all other economic actors, strictly maximize their own utility. Furthermore, economists also share the assumption that managers' interest does not need to converge with the owner's interest. Under such assumptions, adequate governance structures are required for allowing owners to monitor and control managers (Jensen and Meckling 1976; cf. Berle and Means 1932/1991; Shleifer and Vishny 1997). The point of reference of this model of corporate governance is the market. Its competitive mechanisms, however, fail where they encounter the limits posed by incomplete contracts and insurmountable information asymmetries. That, precisely, is the meaning of Jensen and Meckling's (1976: 310) term "residual loss," which refers to the difference between a pure market solution and an agency solution.

These three aspects are of fundamental importance for any corporate governance system: the fact that actors who are in relations with the firm have different objectives; the incompleteness of the contracts of which the

Table 11.2   Theoretical Diversity of Corporate Governance

Theory	Focus	Governance Regimes	Reference
Agency Theory	Ownership / control	Control, monitoring Performance based compensation	Market
Transaction Cost Theory	Allocation of governance to distinct transactions	Informal / formal rules, structures	Hierarchy
Organizational Theory	Rights / responsibilities of stakeholders	Organizational resources, competences	Strategic management

business cooperation is made of, and which comes to the surface in its everyday practice; and finally, the problem of asymmetric and incomplete information, which can concern any team member or stakeholder. Against this backdrop, it is clear why governance structures can be understood as instruments for "structuring, monitoring, and bonding a set of contracts among agents with conflicting interests" (Fama and Jensen, 1983: 304).

At the present moment, principal-agency theory dominates the theoretical discussion of corporate governance. I show shortly that this is not true for the practical discussion of the respective national corporate governance codes—in particular, if one considers them from a European perspective. In terms of the matrix presented in table 11.1, agency theory focuses exclusively on the problems in the left-hand column.

Transaction Cost Theory

Contrary to agency theory, transaction cost economics uses the term "governance" explicitly and at a point that is decisive from a theoretical perspective. From a transaction cost economics vantage point, the firm is a comparatively efficient hierarchical structure that serves for accomplishing contractual relations. The firm is a nexus of contracts that organize and regulate transactions of products and services. The central problem of transaction cost economics is therefore to explain the carrying out of economic transactions by the efficiency of the chosen governance structures that have been tailored to carry out the transactions at hand. Oliver E. Williamson, the founder of transaction cost economics, defines governance structure as follows: "A governance structure is thus usefully thought of as an institutional framework in which the integrity of a transaction or related set of transactions, is decided." (Williamson, 1996: 11). For Williamson, governance regimes consist of formal and informal structures and rules that enable carrying out economic transactions in an economic manner. Transaction cost economics focuses on hierarchical governance structures— such as firms and other organizations—as alternative to the market as governance structure. The corporate governance problem of transaction cost economics is therefore not the protection of ownership rights of shareholders, rather the effective and efficient accomplishment of transactions by firms in their cultural and political environment (Williamson 1996: 322–324). From such a vantage point, law and contracts are considered governance structures, just like corporate culture and the moral atmosphere of an economic transaction (Wieland 1996, Williamson 1996). Transaction cost economics therefore refers to all four quadrants of the comprehensive corporate governance approach presented in table 11.1.

Organization Theory

The most interesting contributions of organization theory for our topic
here are the Resource-based view and the Competence-based view.
Where economic organizations are understood as a pool of human and
organizational resources, capabilities or competences, the objective of the
governance regime is to generate, combine, and activate such resources in
order to attain a competitive advantage. Daily, Dalton, and Cannella (2003:
371), for instance, write: "We define governance as a determination of the
broad uses to which organizational resources will be deployed and the resolutions of conflicts among the myriad participants in organizations." For
Aoki (2001: 11), corporate governance refers to "the structure of rights and
responsibilities among the parties with a stake in the firm." The point of
reference of organization theory is neither market nor hierarchy. Rather, it
is strategic management of resources and competences within and by means
of an organization. Accordingly, for both transaction cost economics and
organization theory, the firm is considered fundamentally different from
market solutions. In this regard, both are in contrast to agency theory. The
consequences for the notion of stakeholder are important. In the pure market model, stakeholders are reduced to being the counterpart to shareholders.
They are not part of the economic problem. In the other two approaches,
exactly the opposite is the case: there, shareholders are just one type of
stakeholder, even though the most important one.

The Empirics of Corporate Governance

In the following, I refer to the results of an empirical analysis on corporate
governance codes of 21 states that I have carried out. Some of these only
have one code, such as Hungary. Others have several documents, such as
Great Britain. Some are purely technical, others more political in character.
They are edited by economic and political organizations. All those are covered in the empirical analysis (see appendix for details).

Several distinctions have been proposed for building taxonomies of the
European corporate governance regimes. White (2003) distinguishes
between shareholder value and stakeholder value approaches. Others propose a distinction between "market or blockholder system" (Bratton and
McCahery 2002), or between shareholder, stakeholder and enterprise
interest approaches (Wymeersch 2002; cf. Becht et al. 2002). As opposed
to these proposals, from the perspective of the ethics of governance that I
have proposed and in the light of the empirical results, it is important to
start by acknowledging that different ideas on the meaning and the objectives

of the firm are attributed to each code. From a pure shareholder perspective, usually built on the theoretical foundation of agency theory, a firm is a vehicle for increasing the capital invested by the owners. I call this the *maximization model*. From a transaction cost economics perspective, the firm is a formal or informal organization structure that can accomplish economic transactions in an economizing way. I call this the *economizing model* of the firm. The organization theory perspective sees the firm in the context of cooperation between owners of internal and external resources in order to realize pecuniary and nonpecuniary income from their resources. I call this the *cooperation model* of the firm.

These three different perspectives, based on different theoretical foundations, are mirrored in the European corporate governance codes. The Swiss Code of Best Practice for Corporate Governance for instance, refers exclusively to agency theory and the maximization model. It says, for example: "Corporate Governance is the sum total of the principles focussed on the interest of shareholders" (6). To the contrary, the French code, Viénot, basis for the French system of corporate governance, says: "In Anglo-American countries, the emphasis in this area is on enhancing share value, whereas in continental Europe and particularly in France it tends to be on the company's interest. . . . The interest of the company may be understood as the overriding claim of the company considered as a separate economic agent pursuing its own objectives which are distinct from those of shareholders, employees, creditors including the internal revenue authorities, suppliers and customers. It nonetheless represents the common interest, which is for the company to remain in business and prosper. The committee thus believes that directors should at all time be concerned solely to promote the interests of the company" (I.1). Here, the firm as a distinct organizational form is the point of reference. It is conceived as consisting of independent objectives and interests, which corporate governance structures are supposed to realize. These independent objectives and interests need to be distinguished from those of their members and stakeholders. Here, we meet a classic example of a firm-oriented corporate governance perspective. It corresponds to what I call the economizing model. Finally, as an example for the cooperation model I would like to cite the Dutch Corporate Governance Code of 2003. Point three of its preamble states: "The code is based on the principle accepted in the Netherlands that a company is a long-term form of cooperation between the various parts involved."

If we align the European corporate governance codes according to the models distinguished a little while ago, the huge diversity of codes in Europe becomes apparent very clearly.

Table 11.3   Concepts of Shareholder vs. Stakeholder

Perspective	Shareholder Value	Stakeholder Value	
Focus	Shareholder Management	Shareholder Stakeholder	Corporation Stakeholder
Countries	Switzerland, Czech Republic, Portugal, Sweden, Finland, Great Britain, Ireland	Denmark, Netherlands, Spain, Lithuania, Poland, Romania, Slovakia	Austria, Belgium, Germany, France, Italy, Hungary, Russia, Turkey
Entries	7	7	8

As the table 11.3 shows, most European corporate governance codes do not refer to agency theory and its focus on shareholder interest. Rather, they focus either on the conflict of interests between shareholder and stakeholder, or the conflict of interests between the firm as a legal and moral actor in itself and the stakeholders (including shareholders, which might be identified as the crucial stakeholders). In a certain sense, the latter category is a theoretical challenge for conventional stakeholder theory. The reason is that conventional stakeholder theory does not have an explicit, theoretically based notion of the organization. Therefore, it is just the inverse of agency theory. The crucial point, though, is that the distinction of organization and stakeholder (including shareholder) is indispensable for those who want to understand firms not just as organizations of the economy, but also as organizations of society—as forms of social cooperation. That, precisely, is the declared intention of stakeholder theory. My diagnosis is that the lack of a notion of organization could well be at the root of the unsatisfactory analysis of the stakeholder problem. Further research is needed on the issue. It should perhaps not go unnoticed that stakeholder approaches and approaches focused on the firm do of course mention the paramount importance of shareholder interest—while approaches focused exclusively on shareholders do not mention stakeholders and their interest at all.

Stakeholders and Values in Codes

If we investigate the diversity of European corporate governance codes a little more in depth, we find further differences that are of importance for the corporate ethics discussion. Of particular interest in this context is the question of which stakeholders are acknowledged and identified as having

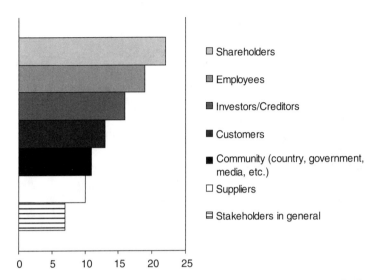

Figure 11.1   **Stakeholders in European Corporate Governance Codes**

an interest in the firm (see figure 11.1). This particularly depends on the
committees responsible for issuing the corporate governance codes, that is,
on the fact whether they are appointed by government departments, stock
exchange bodies, or professional bodies. Also, the stakeholder engagement in
reality depends on law and the common national practice. Moreover, most
codes follow the recommendations of the according OECD principles.[3]

As mentioned, the Swiss corporate governance code is the only one that
exclusively identifies shareholders as stakeholders. The Dutch code, to the
contrary, identifies shareholders, employees, whistleblowers, investors,
suppliers, customers, government, and the civil society. In most of the
European corporate governance codes, shareholders, customers, employees, suppliers, and creditors constitute the core of stakeholders. Depending
on the function of the particular code, some of these stakeholders are then
dropped or others added.

An especially telling example is the Russian corporate governance
code.[4] It says: "Corporate Governance is a broad term that encompasses a
variety of activities connected with the management of joint stock companies. A company's Corporate Governance practices affects its performance
and its ability to attract the capital required for economic growth (2.)" The
Russian standard therefore belongs to the firm-oriented standards. It men-
tions the interests of "all" shareholders (private and public shareholders
included), the benefit of the Russian economy as a whole and high ethical

standards. But no other stakeholders are identified. This is probably an expression, in cryptic form, of the orientation toward the state that Russian firms have. Coded as respect of the law and the social morale, it refers back to the socialist tradition.

A further differentiation of corporate governance codes shows up via an analysis of the values mentioned in the corporate governance codes.

Shareholder-oriented codes emphasize the interests of owners, problems of incomplete information, transparency, accountability, performance based remuneration, and sustained financial solidity. Stakeholder-oriented codes, on the other hand, have a wider frame of reference, as table 11.4 shows. In addition to the points emphasized by shareholder-oriented codes, they highlight the relevance of ethical standards for management, the importance of cooperation and partnership in the firm, the importance of reporting, communication, and dialogue; they also put the interest in social welfare and prosperity and the creation of jobs, as well as taking social and ecological responsibility, at par with shareholders' profit interests. A similar differentiation can also be identified in the respective control regimes.

Table 11.4   Issues in European Corporate Governance Codes

Stakeholder Related Issues

Issue	Entries
Code of Ethics, and ethical standards	11
Cooperation codetermination, and partnership	10
Reports, dialogue, and communication	7
Wealth, prosperity, and jobs	6
Environmental protection	6
Social responsibility	5
Sum	45

Table 11.5   Regimes of Control

Shareholder Perspective	Stakeholder Perspective
voting	internal / external assurance
market (manager, capital)	internal / external whistleblowing
liability	reporting systems
reporting	standards
boards	(VMS^{ZfW}, SA 8,000, AA, Q-RES, etc.)[5]
incentives	

Shareholder-oriented codes work by control through the market (market for managers, capital market, and incentive systems) and the organization of the firm (relations of voting rights, legal responsibilities, reporting system, and board structure). For stakeholder-approaches, on the other hand, imposing morally sensible standards, reporting-systems, and internal and external assurance systems are the important working mechanisms as illustrated in table 11.5.

A synoptic summary of the fundamental principles of European corporate governance codes confirms this impression. Such a synoptic summary of a comprehensive and complete corporate governance code of European enterprises is available from the study "Corporate Governance Principles for listed companies," carried out by the European Corporate Governance Service in 2003/2004 as shown in figure 11.2.[6]

From the analysis we can see that a "typical" European benchmark code deals with questions relating to the board of directors (e.g., board structure, board size, role of chairman, and director training) and to shareholder rights (e.g., equitable treatment, controlling shareholders, and antitakeover devices). Furthermore, aspects of transparency and reporting and audit-systems of transparency (e.g., transparency, auditing process, reporting structures, and internal control), and instruments for the adjusting interests (e.g., company constitution, shareholder resolutions, and extraordinary general meetings) are also important. The imposition of a remuneration policy for managers (e.g., framework, incentives, pensions, and contractual

Figure 11.2 European Principles for Corporate Governance

terms) and of guidelines for the area of corporate social responsibility (e.g., environment, social standards, and human rights) complete the picture.

Conclusion

In conclusion we can now recognize the following: Corporate governance codes that focus exclusively on the agency problem and pursue the maximization model offer no entry points whatsoever for a dimension of business ethics that goes beyond the honoring of contracts on the part of the managers. Corporate governance codes, on the other hand, that pursue the economizing or cooperation model, directly and immediately lead to the integration of questions of moral and social responsibility of firms and their engagement in terms of corporate citizenship. Most of the European states follow one of the latter two models. This assessment appears to be a good foundation for a practically applicable and theoretically interesting discussion of the notion of corporate governance. After all, the discussion of a European approach to corporate governance has not at all come to a conclusion, but has just begun. Despite all historical differences, a tendency for codes to converge can now be discerned. Take for instance the idea of corporate governance as a process of self-governance of firms. Adopting such an idea implies that the role of the state should be contained within the framework set by a "comply-or-explain" rule. It cannot, moreover, escape the observer that in codes such as the German one, Anglo-Saxon influences are attaining an increasing weight, such as when shareholder interests are emphasized more. At the same time, the Sarbanes-Oxley Act in the United States that is of international importance because of its transterritorial impact, explicitly demands moral standards and value management systems for risk prevention (Wieland and Fuerst 2004). In this context also notable seems the Corporate Governance action plan of the EU commission of May 21, 2003 that is based on the preparatory work of the Winter reports of 2002. Though this action plan negates the establishment of a standardized European Corporate Governance Code, it stipulates requirements that are to be implemented according to the national perspective of each member state. And in the context of the Global Compact, the Financial Sector Initiative of European Banks' "Who cares wins. Connecting financial markets to a changing world" is of eminent importance as well.[7] It contains detailed "Recommendations by the financial industry to better integrate environmental, social and governance issues in analysis, asset management and securities brokerage" and is endorsed by major banks such as AXA Group, Banco do Brasil, CNP Assurances, Credit Suisse Group, Deutsche Bank, Goldman Sachs, HSBC, ISIS Asset Management, KLP Insurance, Morgan Stanley, UBS, and Westpac.

We can take these examples as instances of reciprocal learning processes
that have clarified that a modern economic and moral focus on corporate
governance does not necessarily need to end up in the inadequate and not
very fruitful reductionism of agency theory. Nowadays, the economic and
business ethics literature contains theoretical approaches that integrate economic calculation and the pursuit of social responsibility by framing it as an
allocation problem of economic resources, to be solved with the help of
organizations.

Appendix: European Corporate Governance Codes
Western and Middle Europe

Austria	*Austrian Code of Corporate Governance* (Austrian Group on Corporate Governance in Austria)
Belgium	1. Merged Code (Brussels Stock Exchange BXS and Finance Commission) 2. *Recommendation from the Federation of Belgian Companies* 3. *Directors Charta* (Belgian Directors Foundation)
France	1. *Viènot 1* (French employers' association CNPF and private business ass. AFEP) 2. *Viènot 2* (Committee on Corporate Governance MEDEF and AFEP) 3. *Recommendations on Corporate Governance* (Commission on Corporate Governance AFG–ASFFI) 4. *Promoting Better Corporate Governance in Listed Companies* (MEDEF & AFEP) 5. *The Corporate Governance of Listed Corporations* (MEDEF & AFEP)
Germany	1. *German Code of Corporate Governance* (Berlin Initiative Group) 2. *Corporate Governance Rules for Quoted German Companies* (German Panel on Corporate Governance) 3. *Baums Commission Report* (German Government Panel on Corporate Governance) 4. *German Corporate Governance Code* (Government Commission German Corporate Governance Code)
Netherlands	*The Dutch Corporate Governance Code* (Corporate Governance Committee)
Switzerland	*Swiss Code of Best Practice for Corporate Governance* (Economie Suisse) *Richtlinien Corporate Governance der Schweizer Boerse* (RLCGSWX)

South Europe

Italy	1. *Preda Report* (Committee for the Corporate Governance of Listed Companies)
	2. *Corporate Governance Code* (Committee for the Corporate Governance of Listed Companies)
Portugal	*Recommendations on Corporate Governance*
Spain	1. *The Corporate Governance of Listed Companies* (The Olivencia Commission)
	2. *The Aldama Report* (Aldama Special Commission)
Turkey	*TÜSIAD Corporate Governance Code of Best Practice: Composition and Functioning of the Board of Directors* (Corporate Governance Association of Turkey)

North Europe

Denmark	1. *Guidelines on Good Management of a Listed Company* (Danish Shareholders' Association)
	2. *Recommendations for Good Corporate Governance in Denmark* (Norby Committee)
Finland	1. *Corporate Governance Code for Public Limited Companies* (Central Chamber of Commerce and Confederation of Finnish Industry and Employers)
	2. *Ministry of Trade and Industry Guidelines* (Finnish Ministry of Industry and Trade)
Ireland	*Corporate Governance, Share Option, and Other Incentive Schemes* (Irish Association of Investment Managers)
Sweden	1. *Corporate Governance Policy* (Swedish Shareholders' Association)
	2. *The NBK Rules* (Naringslivets Borskommitte)
UK	1. *Cadbury Report* (Financial Reporting Council and London Stock Exchange)
	2. *Greenbury Report* (Confederation of British Industry Committee)
	3. *Hampel Report*
	4. *Hermes Statement on International Voting Principles* (Hermes Investmt. Mgt. Ltd.)
	5. *Code of Good Practice* (Association of Unit Trusts and Investment Funds)
	6. *The Hermes Principles* (Hermes Investment Management Ltd.)
	7. *The Combined Code on Corporate Governance* (The Financial Reporting Council)

East Europe

Czech Rep.	*Revised Corporate Governance Code* (Czech Securities Commission)
Hungary	*Corporate Governance Recommendations* (Budapest Stock Exchange Company Limited by Shares)
Lithuania	*The Corporate Governance Code for Companies Listed on the National Stock Exchange of Lithuania* (National Stock Exchange of Lithuania)
Poland	1. *Best Practices in Public Companies in 2002* (Best Practices Committee at the Corporate Governance Forum) 2. *The Corporate Governance Code for Polish Listed Companies* (Polish Corporate Governance Forum)
Romania	*Corporate Governance Code in Romania* (Corporate Governance Initiative for economic democracy in Romania)
Russia	*Russian Corporate Governance Code*
Slovakia	*Corporate Governance Code* (Financial Market Authority and others)

Notes

An earlier version of this chapter was published in *Business & Society* 44(1): 74–93. Permission to reprint this was kindly granted by Sage Publishers.

1. <http://europa.eu.int/comm/employment_social/soc-dial/csr/greenpaper.htm> (accessed March 6, 2006).
2. <http://www.dnwe.de/2/content/bb_01.htm> (accessed April 3, 2006).
3. Cf. <www.oecd.org/document/49/0,2340, en_2649_34813_ 31530865_ 1_1_1_1,00.html> (accessed March 10, 2006).
4. <http://www.cipe.org/pdf/programs/corp_gov/RusCGCodedraft.pdf> (accessed June 25, 2006).
5. The VMS[ZfW] can be downloaded at <http://www.dnwe.de/2/content/bb_01.htm> (accessed June 25, 2006). The other codes can be found on the following websites: http://www.sa-intl.org (Social Aoountability International; accessed June 25, 2006); http://www. accountability.org.uk (accessed March 16, 2006) and http://www.qres.it (accessed June 25, 2006).
6. Available at <www.ecgs.org.> European Corporate Governance Service Ltd. (accessed June 25, 2006).
7. Download the report at <http://www.wbcsd.org/web/projects/sl/whocareswins.pdf.>

References

Aoki, M. 2001. *Information, Corporate Governance and Institutional Diversity: Competitiveness in Japan, the USA and the Transnational Economies.* Oxford: Oxford University Press.

Becht, Marco, Patride Bolton, and Ailsa Röell. 2002. *Corporate Governance and Control*. National Bureau of Economic Research (NBER) Working Paper No. 9371 of Dec. 2002.

Berle, A., and G. Means. 1932/1991. *The Modern Corporation and Private Property*. New York and New Brunswick, NJ: Transaction Publishers.

Bratton, W.W., and J.A. McCahery, 2002. Comparative Corporate Governance and Barriers to Global Cross Reference. In *Corporate Governance Regimes*, McCahery, J.A., Piet Moerland, Theo Raaijmakers, Luc Renneboog (eds). *Convergence and Diversity*. New York: Oxford University Press.

Brunsson, N., and B. Jacobsson. 2000. *A World of Standards*. Oxford: Oxford University Press.

Daily, C.M., D.R. Dalton, and A.A. Cannella. 2003. Corporate Governance: Decades of Dialogue and Data. *Academy of Management Review*, 28(3): 371.

EU Commission. 2003. *Modernisierung des Gesellschaftsrechts und Verbesserung der Corporate Governance in der Europäischen Union*. Brussels, May 21, 2003.

Fama, E.F., and M.C. Jensen. 1983. Separation of Ownership and Control. *Journal of Law and Economics*, 26 (June): 304.

Jensen, M.C., and W. Meckling. 1976. Theory of the Firm: Managerial Behavior, Agency Costs and Ownership Structure. *The Journal of Financial Economics*, 3(305): 305–306.

Kroszner, R.S. 1996. *The Economic Nature of the Firm*. Reader, NY: Cambridge University Press.

Shleifer, A., and R.W. Vishny. 1997. A Survey of Corporate Governance. *The Journal of Finance*, LII(2): 737–783.

Wieland, J. 1996. *Oekonomische Organisation, Allokation und Status*. Tuebingen: Mohr (Siebeck).

———. 1999, 2004. *Die Ethik der Governance*. Marburg: Metropolis.

———. 2000. Corporate Governance und Unternehmensethik. In Mittelstrass, J. (ed.) *Die Zukunft des Wissens*. Berlin: Akademie Verlag.

———. 2001a. The Ethics of Governance. *Business Ethics Quarterly*, Vol. 11(1): 73–87.

———. 2001b. *Die moralische Verantwortung kollektiver Akteure*. Heidelberg: Physica.

———. 2003. *Standards and Audits for Ethics Management Systems—The European Perspective*. Heidelberg: Springer.

Wieland, J., and M. Fuerst. 2004. Moral als Element der Good Corporate Governance in Banken. In *Ethik in der Bankenpraxis*, Wagner, A., and C. Seidel, eds. Frankfurt AM: Bankakademie Verlag.

Williamson, O.E. 1996. *The Mechanisms of Governance*. New York: Oxford University Press.

Winter, J. (Winter-Report). 2002. *Report of the High Level Group of Company Law Experts on a Modern Regulatory Framework for Company Law*. Brussels, November 4, 2002.

Wymeersch, E. 2002. Convergence or Divergence in Corporate Governance Patterns in Western Europe? In *Corporate Governance Regimes. Convergence and Diversity*, McCahery, J., Piet Moerland, Theo Raaijmakers, and Luc Renneboog (eds.). New York: Oxford University Press, 242 ff.

CHAPTER 12

BUSINESS ETHICS AND CORPORATE GOVERNANCE IN LATIN AMERICA

Heloisa Bedicks and Maria Cecilia Coutinho de Arruda

Introduction

The most important characteristics of Latin American economies that influence the development of corporate governance are: rapid technological change, economic globalization, concentration of ownership, defined control, and the need for capital. Most companies are controlled by dominant groups (often families that fulfill the role of owners as well as managers). Controlling shareholders have on average 60 percent–70 percent of the voting rights. Family control remains the norm for most of the region's nonlisted small and medium-sized enterprises. About 25 percent of public companies have shareholder agreements. Majority shareholders—clearly identified and actively engaged—can be a great strength for a company by ensuring active oversight of management and providing a ready source of financial support to the company at critical moments (OECD 2003, 9). Nevertheless, if earnings are limited and financial resources considered insufficient to attain the desired growth rate, the challenge is to find domestic and international sources of capital. This often implies that governance practices have to be adapted to meet the demands of outside sources of finance, without sacrificing the benefits of the alignment of ownership and defined control.

Latin American has experienced a decline in the number of companies listed in domestic markets as companies have delisted and gone private due to the increasing internationalization of industry and finance. Larger regional companies have shifted the trading of their shares to the deeper depository receipt markets in the United States. Consequently, domestic trading markets are under pressure. Companies that have shifted their trading to the North American stock exchanges are subjected to the regulation of the Sarbannes-Oxley Act and have to align their corporate governance practices to the requirements of that law.

The shift in trading of blue chip firms to the international market has called into question the viability of domestic stock exchanges and their contribution to national economies. There is consensus in the region that it is a matter of priority to establish a legal framework that allows shares with different voting rights. The motivation for this is to ensure that stronger and more effective protection is given to minority shareholders. This will encourage boards of directors of companies to engage with stakeholders, and more specifically with minority shareholders. Institutional investors, who have been passive in the past, are starting to exercise their ownership rights in a more informed manner (OECD 2003, 13). Particularly the larger pension funds and a few asset managers have become increasingly vocal and are demanding more participation in boards.

The Role of Business Ethics in Corporate Governance in Latin America

The purpose of this chapter is to determine what the role of business ethics is within the Latin American corporate governance context. This is done by analyzing five sources of information that provide vital information on the state of corporate governance in Latin America. These sources are:

1. The meetings of the Latin American Corporate Governance Network, which culminated in the establishment of the ILAGC (Latin American Institute of Corporate Governance);
2. The debates in the Latin America Corporate Governance Roundtables (OECD 2000, 2001, 2002, 2003, 2004, 2005);
3. The study *Panorama Atual da Governança Corporativa no Brasil* (Overview of Corporate Governance in Brazil), developed by the IBGC (Brazilian Institute of Corporate Governance) in partnership with Booz Allen Hamilton in 2003 (IBGC—Booz Allen 2003); and
4. The third version of the *Código das Melhores Práticas de Governança Corporativa* (Code of Best Practices of Corporate Governance) produced by the IBGC in March 2004 (IBGC 2004).
5. The IBGC Corporate Governance Survey in Brazil.

Based on the analysis of these sources, conclusions are drawn on the role of business ethics within Latin American corporate governance.

The Latin American Corporate Governance Network

The Latin American Corporate Governance Network was created in Mexico City, in April 2002, when organizations related to corporate governance in Latin America met for the first time. The objectives of the Network were to discuss the best ways to build the capacity of members of boards of directors and to disseminate best practice in corporate governance. The promotion of best practice among members of boards of directors is an essential element in the drive to improve the corporate governance of companies. A further objective of the Latin American Corporate Governance Network is to strengthen local institutes of corporate governance through the exchange of research data and knowledge. It also offers advice on the creation of new similar institutes in other countries. Due to its experience since 1998, when the first Course for Members of Boards of Directors was offered, the IBGC—Instituto Brasileiro de Governança Corporativa (Brazilian Institute of Corporate Governance) played a leading role in the discussions about the best ways to train and build the capacity of directors (IBGC 2006).

The member institutions of the Latin American Corporate Governance Network are indicated in table 12.1.

The Latin American Corporate Governance Network has the support of the IFC (International Financial Corporation), the GCGF (Global

Table 12.1   Countries in the Latin American Corporate Governance Network

Countries	Institutions
Argentina	IAGO—Instituto Argentino para El Gobierno de las Organizaciones (Argentinean Institute for the Government of the Organizations)
Brazil	IBGC—Instituto Brasileiro de Governança Corporativa (Brazilian Institute of Corporate Governance)
Chile	SVS—Superintendencia de Valores y Seguros de Chile y Universidad de Chile (Superintendence of Values and Insurance of Chile and University of Chile)

Continued

Table 12.1 **Continued**

Countries	Institutions
Colombia	Confecamaras—Confederación Colombiana de Camaras de Comercio (Colombian Confederation of Chambers of Commerce)
Mexico	IMGC—Instituto Mexicano de Gobernabilidad Corporativa (Mexican Institute of Corporate Governance) CCE—Consejo Coordinador Empresarial del Mexico (Business Coordinating Council of Mexico)
Peru	ASDIC—Asociación de Directores Corporativos (Association of Corporate Directors)
Venezuela	AVE—Asociación Venezoelana de Ejecutivos (Venezuelan Association of Executives)

Source: Latin American Corporate Governance Network, 2003.

Corporate Governance Forum), CIPE (Center for International Private Enterprise), and the International Institute of Corporate Governance of the University of Yale, in the United States.

In July 2003, the ILAGC—Instituto Latino-Americano de Gobierno Corporativo (Latin American Institute of Corporate Governance) succeeded the Latin American Corporate Governance Network.

The Latin American Corporate Governance Roundtables

The Latin American Corporate Governance Roundtables is a regional forum that promotes dialogue about policies on corporate governance. It came into being through cooperation between the OECD (Organisation for Economic Co-operation and Development), the World Bank, the International Finance Corporation (IFC), the Global Corporate Governance Forum, and regional public and private strategic institutions in Latin America.

Among the participants of the Latin American Roundtables count policymakers, regulatory entities, business leaders, investors, labor unions, other nongovernmental organizations, and multilateral institutions with an interest in corporate governance. The following countries participate in the Roundtables: Argentina, Brazil, Chile, Colombia, Peru, Mexico, and Venezuela.

The first Roundtable was held in Sao Paulo, Brazil, in 2000. Subsequent meetings were held in Buenos Aires, Argentina (2001), in Mexico City

(2002), in Santiago, Chile (2003), in Rio de Janeiro, Brazil (2004) and Lima, Peru (2005). The Roundtables held from 2000 to 2005 in Latin America provided an exchange of knowledge and experiences. It served as a forum for debates on changes that are needed to ensure that good corporate governance practices are effectively implemented in the private and the public sectors. It is expected that the ILAGC—Instituto Latino-Americano de Governança Corporativa (Latin American Institute of Corporate Governance) will remain a forum to continue this discourse.

The OECD's White Paper on Corporate Governance in Latin America

In April 2000, at the first Roundtable, it was decided to develop an Official Report on Regional Corporate Governance, which became known as the *White Paper*. It was prepared through several meetings that were held since and was published in 2003, with the following intentions:

- To provide policymakers and private sector leaders, including international institutional investors, experts, and multilateral institutions, with an overview of the main issues and developments in the Latin American region. It also aims at providing them with benchmarks for measuring progress.
- To provide a set of recommendations for reforming and improving corporate governance in the region that can be implemented by governmental authorities, multilaterals and private sector institutions.
- To generate input for the reassessment of the OECD Principles of Corporate Governance that was to be completed in 2004 (OECD 2003, 5).

Some regional characteristics were defined that had a major impact on the four largest capital markets in the region: Argentina, Brazil, Chile, and Mexico. These were the following:

- Privatization.
- Concentration of ownership, defined control, and the need for capital.
- Importance of industrial groups.
- Restructuring of banking systems.
- Regionalization and the importance of multinational enterprises.
- Limited domestic capital markets and growing importance of foreign listings.
- Mandatory privately managed pension schemes.
- Legal traditions and enforcement patterns (OECD 2003, 9–11).

Ethical perspectives in the "White Paper"

In two chapters of the *White Paper* ethical issues are specifically addressed. Chapter 2 stresses the importance of good corporate governance for Latin America and chapter 5 presents a set of recommendations. In these chapters the *White Paper* encourages corporations to act morally responsible by creating jobs, generating tax revenue, rendering goods and services to consumers, providing secure retirement for employees, ensuring a maximum degree of transparency and internal and external accountability, and building strong domestic capital markets to assure tomorrow's new enterprises and industries (OECD 2003, 7). Besides all the technical benefits of good corporate governance, the *White Paper* suggests that disclosure, transparency, and accountability strengthen private sector firms substantially, increase the likelihood of success of the wide and varied efforts being taken in the region to contain official corruption, and restore public faith in government (OECD 2003, 8).

A long row of recommendations deals with business ethics either implicitly or explicitly. Some aspects that deserve mentioning are:

- Respect for the rights of shareholders (specifically minority shareholders) and taking voting rights seriously.
- Emergence of active and informed owners (transparency practices).
- Equitable treatment of shareholders especially in changes of control and in delistings.
- Emphasis on the role of stakeholders in corporate governance.
- Quality and integrity of financial reporting.
- Disclosure of ownership and control (transparency).
- Conflicts of interest and related party transactions.
- Reporting on internal corporate governance structures and practices.
- Board integrity and director independence (i.e., acting in the best interest of the company).
- Improved compliance and effective enforcement.
- Encouragement in reporting illegal or unethical behavior (OECD 2003, 15–34).

The IBGC's Code of Best Practice of Corporate Governance

In 2004 The IBGC—Instituto Brasileiro de Governança Corporativa (Brazilian Institute of Corporate Governance) launched the third version of its *Code of Best Practice of Corporate Governance*. It is a work that summarizes recommendations about best practices in corporate governance. In these

Table 12.2 Ethical Issues in the Code of *Best Practice of Corporate Governance*

Ethical Issues—IBGC's Code of Best Practice of Corporate Governance	
• compliance with laws and payment of taxes;	• political activities;
• inappropriate payments or receipts;	• community relations;
• conflicts of interests;	• use of alcohol and drugs;
• privileged information;	• right to privacy;
• receiving gifts;	• nepotism;
• unequal opportunities;	• exploitation of adult and child labor;
• donations;	• share-trading policies;
• environment;	• judicial processes and arbitrage;
• sexual and moral harassment;	• intercompany transactions;
• occupational safety;	• prevention and handling of fraud.

Source: IBGC—*Code of Best Practice of Corporate Governance* (2004).

recommendations reference is made to the importance of having a code of conduct in a company, as well as to its importance for the auditing committee, members of the board of directors, managers, employees, and executives (IBGC 2004).

The *Code of Best Practice of Corporate Governance* has a series of topics related to ethics, grouped under the title of Code of Conduct (table 12.2).

Although it is recommended that each company has a code of conduct with specific items to be considered, nearly 50 percent of companies in Brazil still do not have a code of ethics. There is also no report that business ethics management is required. Companies are, however, encouraged to report their activities with regard to corporate social and environmental responsibility, using tools already available such as the Global Reporting Initiative's (GRI) guidelines and the Brazilian IBASE's Social Balance Sheet (IBASE 2006) and Instituto Ethos' Social Responsibility Index (Instituto Ethos de Responsabilidade Social das Empresas 2006).

Brazil was the first country in Latin America to have *a Code of Best Practice of Corporate Governance*. This code stresses the importance of ethical principles and recommends that all companies have a code of conduct. Other countries in Latin America have followed suit whilst some are yet to develop such codes of best practice for corporate governance. This process of developing such codes will further strengthen business ethics as an important part of good governance. Table 12.3 provides an overview of where countries in Latin America stand with regard to having a code of best practice.

Table 12.3 Codes of Best Practice by Countries in Latin America

Country	CG Discussion Leaders	Code of Best Practice	CG and Directors' Training
Argentina	IAGO—Argentinean Institute for the Government of the Organizations	No	No
Brazil	IBGC—Brazilian Institute of Corporate Governance and São Paulo Stock Exchange—Bovespa	Code of Best Practice of Corporate Governance—Brazilian Institute of Corporate Governance—Corporativa— 1999 CVM—Cartilha de Governança Corporativa— 2002	Yes
Chile	SVS—Superintendence of Values and Insurance of Chile and University of Chile	No	No
Colombia	Confecamaras—Colombian Confederation of Chambers of Commerce	Corporate Governance Code—2002	No
Mexico	IMGC—Mexican Institute of Corporate Governance and Business Coordinator Council of Mexico.	Código de Mejores Prácticas Corporativas, Mexican Stock Exchange, the Mexican Bankers' Association, the Mexican Institute of Finance Executives, and the Mexican Institute of Public Accountants—2001	No
Peru	ASDIC—Association of Corporate Directors	Principios de Buen Gobierno para las Sociedades Peruanas, Comisió Nacional Supervisora de Empresas y Valores (CONASEV)—2002	No
Venezuela	AVE—Venezuelan Association of Executives	No	No

Source: Instituto Latino-Americano de Governança Corporativa (2006).

The IBGC Corporate Governance Survey in Brazil

In 2003 the IBGC—Instituto Brasileiro de Governança Corporativa (Brazilian Institute of Corporate Governance) in partnership with Booz Allen Hamilton conducted a survey on corporate governance in Brazil (IBGC—Booz Allen 2003). The objective of the study was to identify the current level of compliance with best practices in corporate governance. The sample was 285 nationally controlled companies (Editora Abril 2001). The questionnaires could be answered by chairpersons or members of boards of directors, CEOs, and investor relation officers. Seventy companies participated, generating 110 responses to the questionnaire.

Some of the findings of this survey are presented here. Concerning the perception of current practices of governance, see table 12.4). –

The most important benefits for a company to comply with the practices of governance are listed in table 12.5.

When asked what aspects of governance are effective in obtaining these benefits, the respondents indicate a *code of ethics* as shown in table 12.6.

Table 12.7 shows the most important qualifications that a member of a board of directors should have.

The following were considered the most important responsibilities of the Board of Directors in the company: Monitoring the performance of the

Table 12.4   Current Practices of Governance

Perception of Practices	% of Respondents
Know the *Code of Best Practive*	66
Consider Good	55
Consider Satisfactory	38

Source: IBGC—Booz Allen (2003).

Table 12.5   Benefits of Good Governance

Benefits	% of Respondents
To improve the management	46
To have easier access to capital	44
To allow better alignment between shareholders and directors	44
To assure shareholders' representation	32
To reduce capital cost	31

Source: IBGC—Booz Allen (2003).

Table 12.6   Effectiveness of Governance

Effectiveness of a Code of Ethics	% of Respondents
Consider effective	52
Consider very effective	23
Consider less effective	17
Consider irrelevant	5

Source: IBGC—Booz Allen (2003).

Table 12.7   Qualifications for Board of Directors' Members

Qualifications	% of Respondents
Personal integrity	88
Independence	52
Awareness of the shareholders' interest	40
Awareness of the Best Practice of Governance	40
Ability to read and understand accounting Reports	28

Source: IBGC—Booz Allen (2003).

Table 12.8   Companies with Codes of Ethics

Existence of a Code of Ethics	% of Respondents
Yes, and I believe that everyone follows it	56
Yes, and I believe that most people follow it	11
No	31

Source: IBGC—Booz Allen (2003).

company business; assuring compliance with ethical and legal standards; verifying that the financial statements are a reliable reflection of the company's situation (IBGC—Booz Allen 2003).

Respondents were asked whether the company had councils or committees for ethics and only 1 percent agreed, saying that there is a committee for ethics. Finally they were asked whether the company had a code of ethical principles. The results are indicated in table 12.8.

This survey shows that there is awareness about business ethics, and a lot remains to be done in this regard. Should the same survey be repeated in other Latin American countries, the expectation is that the level of awareness could be even a bit lower than in Brazil. In most meetings with Latin American representatives of the corporate governance institutions, ethical principles have rarely come up as a significant topic. Discussions usually revolve around capital and ownership structure, the role and responsibilities of the board of directors, and market situations.

Conclusion

The analysis in this chapter has shown that corporate governance is gaining in prominence in Latin America. The networks and institutions that have been formed to facilitate discussion on best practice with regard to corporate governance underline this. Institutions such as the Latin American Institute of Corporate Governance as well as the Latin American Corporate Governance Roundtable will ensure that the discourse on best practice in corporate governance is continued. It is furthermore clear that the incline in corporate governance awareness is also leading to a similar incline in awareness of the role and importance of business ethics as an integral part of good corporate governance. There is, however, much to be done to ensure that this awareness of the importance and role of business ethics in corporate governance is translated into organizational practice. This has been clearly demonstrated by the findings of the IBGC corporate governance survey in Brazil.

Note

An earlier version of this chapter was published in *Business & Society* 44(2): 218–228. Permission to reprint this chapter was kindly granted by Sage Publishers.

References

Bologna, Marco Antonio. 2005. Governança Corporativa. *TAM Magazine*, 11: 3.

BOVESPA. 2002. *Novo Mercado*. São Paulo, Brazil.

Editora Abril. 2001. *Exame. Edição Especial: 500 Maiores e Melhores*. São Paulo, Brazil.

Fischer, Rosa Maria, and Luciano Sathler. 2005. *Corporate Governance, Corporate Social Responsibility and Civil Society Organizations*. Handout of the authors' paper presentation in the 2005 BALAS Annual Conference (BALAS—Business Association of Latin American Studies—Conference hosted by the Instituto de Empresa—Madrid, Spain—May 25–28, 2005.)

IBASE—Instituto Brasileiro de Análises Sociais e Econômicas. 2006. *Balanço Social das Empresas* (Social Balance Sheet). Available at <http://www.ibase.org.br> (accessed January 24, 2006).

IBGC—Booz Allen. 2003. *Panorama Atual da Governança Corporativa no Brasil.* São Paulo, Brazil.

IBGC—Instituto Brasileiro de Governança Corporativa. 2004. *Código das Melhores Práticas de Governança Corporativa.* São Paulo, Brazil.

———. 2006. Available at <http://www.ibgc.org.br> (accessed January 24, 2006).

Instituto Ethos de Responsabilidade Social das Empresas. 2006. *Indicadores Ethos de Responsabilidade Social.* Available at <http://www.ethos.org.br> (accessed January 24, 2006).

ISAR—Intergovernmental Working Group of Experts on International Standards and Reporting. 2003. Geneve: Minute of the 20th ISAR Session, September 29, 2003.

Mendonça, Luciana Rocha de, and Cláudio Antonio Pinheiro Machado Filho. 2004. Governança nas Organizações do Terceiro Setor: Considerações Teóricas. *Revista de Administração / Faculdade de Economia, Administração e Contabilidade da Universidade de São Paulo*, 1: 302–308.

OECD—Organisation for Economic Co-operation and Development—Centre for Co-operation with Non-Members—Emerging Economies Transition. 2003. *White Paper on Corporate Governance in Latin America.*

OECD—Organisation for Economic Co-operation and Development. 2004. *Latin American Corporate Governance Roundtables.* Throughout the Roundtables, numerous papers and reports have been prepared by participants (Brazil, 2000; Argentina, 2001; Mexico, 2002; Chile, 2003; Brazil, 2004; Peru, 2005). Available at <http://www.oecd.org/daf/corporate-affairs> (accessed December 25, 2005).

Perazzo, Alberto Augusto. 2004. Ética e Responsabilidade Social: Uma Questão de Estratégia Empresarial. *Bem Comum*, 81: 13–35.

Rabelo, Flavio M., and Flavio C. Vasconcelos. 2002. Corporate Governance in Brazil. *Journal of Business Ethics*, 37: 321–335.

Schiehll, Eduardo, and Igor Oliveira dos Santos. Ownership Structure and Composition of Boards of Directors: Evidence on Brazilian Publicly Traded companies. *Revista de Administração / Faculdade de Economia, Administração e Contabilidade da Universidade de São Paulo*, 1: 373–384.

Steinberg, Herbert. 2003. *A Dimensão Humana da Governança Corporativa: Pessoas Criam as Melhores e Piores Práticas.* São Paulo: Editora Gente.

CHAPTER 13

BUSINESS ETHICS AND CORPORATE GOVERNANCE IN NORTH AMERICA

Lori Verstegen Ryan

Introduction

At first glance, the three North American countries' geographic proximity suggests a similarity that proves to be illusory. Even those observers who assume that Latino Mexico differs from its northern, Anglo neighbors may be tempted to presume that the United States and Canada must surely shadow one another. However, dissimilarities prevail even in the realm of corporate ownership and corporate governance. Along some dimensions, the United States and Canada do share characteristics apart from Mexico, but in other cases, Canada and Mexico align, with the United States as the contrast country, and in still others Mexico and the United States differ from Canada.

We attempt here to present a snapshot of the current state of corporate governance and business ethics in these three countries. For the purposes of comparison, the upcoming analysis has been outlined in table 13.1. After noting some key distinctions, we discuss the state of corporate governance and business ethics in each of the three countries in turn. We begin with the corporate governance system's economic and legal backdrop, then more specifically the economic regulations affecting corporate governance and the corporate governance structures that have emerged in that context. Finally, in terms of business ethics, we examine corruption and recent scandals for each country, along with companies' treatment of stakeholders.

Table 13.1 Comparison of North American Corporate Governance and Business Ethics Contexts and Characteristics

	Mexico	United States	Canada
Economy	Moderate; stabilizing; low per capita GDP	Large and robust; high real per capita GDP and producitivity	Moderate; persistent unemployment
Legal System	Civil; codified rules; sluggish judiciary	Common; case law; strong civil system	Common; case law; efficient judiciary
Economic Regulation	Comply or explain; reforms underway	Rules; Sarbanes-Oxley backlash	Comply or disclose; decentralized
Corporate Governance	Concentrated, family control; poor shareholder protections	Dispersed ownership; shareholder-focused board	Concentrated, family control; poor shareholder protections
Corruption	Pervasive; in fundamental reform	Low to moderate	Low; minimal discretion
Corporate Scandals	Pemex; TVAzteca	Enron, WorldCom, Tyco, Adelphia.	Livent, YBM Magnex
Stakeholder Management	Minimal; diminishing paternalism	Mutually instrumental	Moderate; reliant on social programs

The final section draws points of comparison from this analysis, as discussed in the other continental analyses in this volume, and consider whether corporate governance in North American countries is tending toward convergence or divergence.

Key Distinctions

Several key distinctions help to inform the upcoming analysis. We consider here common versus civil law systems, French versus Anglo-American cultural roots, insider versus outsider systems of corporate governance, and principle- versus rule-based forms of corporate-governance regulation.

Countries differ in systematic ways on their approaches to the development and application of the rule of law. In common law countries, the law is based on precedents and general principles (Creel 2001; La Porta et al. 2000). In corporate governance cases, judges can extrapolate from such principles as "fiduciary duty" or "fairness" to determine if a behavior is against the spirit of the law, leaving corporate directors and executives unsure of their culpability in gray areas (La Porta et al. 2000). Civil law, on the other hand, is codified and not rooted in legal precedent. Legislation and judges' decisions are intended to be applied only in specific cases, and principles such as fiduciary duty are not applied in the courts. Therefore, slight variations on previously illegal behaviors are considered legal unless specifically prohibited. In terms of corporate governance, this distinction has evolved with common law countries having among the strongest shareholder protections around the world and civil law countries the weakest (La Porta, Lopez-de-Silanes, and Shleifer 1999).

Systems of government have been further distinguished based on their historical sources. French-origin countries on average have poorer shareholder protections, far lower gross national products, and more corruption than English-, German-, or Scandinavian-origin countries (La Porta et al. 1998). Across countries, the level of ownership dispersion rises with the level of shareholder protection (La Porta et al. 1999), so the weaker protection of minority investors has led to much higher ownership concentration of large firms in French-origin countries (La Porta et al. 1998).

Ownership dispersion is also a core component of the distinction between insider and outsider systems of corporate governance (Nestor and Thompson 2000). Outsider systems are characterized by dispersed ownership with increasing levels of institutional holdings, the primacy of shareholders in decision making, protection of minority shareholders, strict disclosure requirements, strong capital markets, and a greater reliance on equity financing than on debt. Insider systems are much the opposite, with concentrated ownership or voting control, weak minority shareholder protections, relaxed disclosure requirements, less institutionalization, a greater reliance on debt over equity, and the state and families acting as countervailing powers in the economy.

Legal and regulatory approaches to corporate governance can also be distinguished based on where they fall along a "rule-based versus principle-based" continuum (Garrett 2004). The more rule-based approach focuses on enforceable laws, in which actions that are not prohibited are permitted. The principle-based approach relies on voluntary compliance with stated guidelines, using either a "comply or disclose" or a "comply or explain" form of enforcement. In the first system, companies must act in accordance with stated guidelines or disclose to investors and the public that they do not; in the second, they must disclose not only where they depart from the guidelines, but also explain why.

Mexico

Expectations of Mexico's business community are changing rapidly, as it enters the global credit and equity markets. Long-held beliefs and practices are being challenged, leaving open the question of whether Mexico's corporate governance practices and business ethics must be fundamentally transformed to succeed in global markets. This section discusses the state of the country's corporate governance practices, along with several aspects of the state of business ethics in Mexico.

Corporate Governance

Corporate governance in Mexico is characterized by consolidated family ownership and very weak protections for minority shareholders. After a brief examination of the current state of Mexico's economy and legal system, which provide a context for its corporate governance practices, we outline the country's rapidly evolving economic regulations and the country's corporate governance practices themselves.

Economy

Mexico's $925 billion GDP economy embodies one of the lowest per capita GDPs among OECD countries, at $6,200 (OECD 2004a). Recent governmental reforms have led to low inflation rates and a stable peso, but GDP growth rates of 4 percent will not bring much of the country out of abject poverty (Conger 2004; OECD 2004d).

Mexico's economy currently finds itself suffering from a "triple whammy": the conclusion of protective tariff agreements under NAFTA, China's emergence as a leader in low-cost manufacturing, and the globalization of the labor pool (Conger 2004, 5). Unfortunately, Mexican businesses did not take advantage of their years of protection under NAFTA to build their research and development capabilities, but instead remained focused on low-level manufacturing jobs that have now moved on to China. Nor did they increase the skills in the Mexican work force over that period, a major contributor to its low GDP: The countries' populace ranks twenty-sixth out of 27 OECD countries in its amount of formal schooling, averaging just nine years. A key reason for the weakness of public education is Mexico's small federal budget. Analysts agree that the country should increase its tax rates; it has one of the lowest proportions of any country in the world (Conger 2004; OECD 2004d). Improved enforcement is also critical. Even at the current low level of taxation, tax evasion is widespread (Conger 2004).

Mexico's stock market, the BMV, is small, and the country has no over-the-counter equity trading (Kappaz 2004). The economy is also enormously concentrated: Just five companies make up 60 percent of the BMV's stock index (Husted & Serrano 2002). Movements in this main index follow the variations of the U.S. market more closely than do those in other Latin American countries (*Economist* 2003).

Having weathered the 1994 massive peso devaluation with loans from the United States and the International Monetary Fund (Conger 2004), the country now possesses a solid banking system with regulations close to best practices for OECD countries (OECD 2004d). Recent, successful reforms are credited to the newly appointed, Stanford-trained central banker, Guillermo Ortiz (Conger 2004).

Legal

The rule of law is weak in Mexico, as demonstrated by a 5.35/10 score on an international comparison (La Porta et al. 1998). According to observers, in Mexico "the rule of law has often seemed more like a tool for the powerful to get away with robbery than an effective institution to punish such offenses" (O'Boyle 2003, 38), "finance ministry officials acknowledge that many violations go undetected or unpunished" (Luhnow 2004, A1), and the "Mexican legal system is considered slow and unreliable" (Kappaz 2004, 2).

One factor contributing to this weakness is the 71-year reign of the PRI political party in Mexico, which has reportedly allowed systemic abuses to evolve in all branches of government, including the judiciary (Conger 2004). The election of PAN party reformer Vicente Fox to the presidency in 2000 may begin to reverse this trend, but he continues to face an entrenched PRI majority in Congress.

Mexico's French legal tradition often coincides with the poor levels of economic performance noted earlier, as well as with weak shareholder protections and significant legal corruption (La Porta et al. 1998). In addition, its reliance on civil law encourages creative rule breaking by allowing white-collar criminals to engage with impunity in minor variations of illegal activities (La Porta et al. 2000).

Both of Mexico's two judiciary branches adjudicate business law: the judicial, under the judicial branch of the government, covers criminal, civil, and commercial cases; and the jurisdictional, under the executive branch, covers a broad area that includes labor, trade, and foreign investment issues (Creel 2001). Because it has no jury system, judges are pivotal, and historically judicial corruption has been rampant. However, after significant constitutional and legal reform in 1994, the judiciary has strengthened and become more independent. While judicial decision making has improved over the last decade, a huge case backlog remains and rulings are generally made after lengthy delays. Thus, on an international comparison of the efficiency of judiciaries, Mexico earned a score of "6" on a 10-point scale (La Porta et al. 1998).

Economic regulation

Corporations in Mexico are covered by the General Law of Mercantile Companies, which codifies the basic rights of minority shareholders (IFLR 2003), and gives 25 percent owners the right to name a director, a right held by 10 percent owners if the company is publicly traded (Husted and Serrano 2002). Under the Securities Act, Mexican corporations must have both a board of directors and a *comisario* or statutory auditor (Garrett 2004).

Mexico's current corporate governance guidelines have evolved from the 1999 Code of Better Business Practices created by a private/public committee (IFLR 2003). The code coincides with many OECD standards, such as those concerning the establishment of committees and outside directors on boards, but also suggests more Mexican-specific requirements such as "patrimonial directors" chosen because of major shareholdings. While the code itself is not enforceable, many of its recommendations have since been built into the 2001 Securities Market Law, which includes requirements for 25 percent independent directors, audit committees, insider trading restrictions, and protection of minority shareholders (IFLR 2003; Ritch Grande Ampudia 2002). In addition, in March 2003 the National Banking and Securities Commission (CNBV) passed provisions that require its listed companies to engage in "comply or explain" observance of the code (Garrett 2004; IFLR 2003). The Mexican Stock Exchange (BMV) places additional requirements on listed companies and engages in member surveillance (IFLR 2003).

Historically, Mexico's strong federal government has engaged in extensive economic intervention (Hood and Logsdon 2002). Developing countries have tended to favor either "import-substitution" or "export-led" industrialization (Reed 2002). The former system, historically emphasized in Mexico, leads to governmental protection and support of the industrial base, with a focus on producing for a domestic market. As these systems expand, they generally lead to inefficiency and corruption, and to economies dominated by large groups of family owned businesses in which families control far more than they own, through interlocking directorates and intercorporate arrangements. In contrast, export-led industrialization, while also interventionist and protective of domestic markets, focuses on exporting to world markets. While competitive pressure has tended to make these economies more successful than import-substitution systems in the global economy, they are generally associated with repressive regimes that do not recognize workers' or minority shareholders' rights, and also feature consolidated, family owned business networks. Mexico has been observed to be shifting from an import-substitution to an export-led economy through its involvement in free-trade agreements such as NAFTA and GATT (Husted & Serrano 2002). Many developing countries have engaged in these more interventionist approaches to business in the early stages of their development, after which successful economies move toward freer markets (Reed 2002).

Other economic reforms are also underway, including a program of privatization and deregulation (Husted and Serrano 2002; OECD 2004d). However, many of President Fox's wideranging economic reform proposals are being thwarted by the PRI-controlled Congress (Barham 2004; O'Boyle 2003). Since his election, Fox has indicted a number of PRI members on corruption charges, and the party has retaliated by withdrawing support for his reforms.

One key corporate governance constituency has benefited from recent reforms, however. To date, institutional investors have not been a force in Mexican corporate governance. Pension funds (afores) were established just seven years ago in Mexico, and now hold $35 billion in assets (Barham 2004). Experts expect their involvement to ultimately help to boost the domestic financial market (Husted and Serrano 2002; Ritch Grande Ampudia 2002). However, since their inception, regulations have precluded afores from investing in corporate equity, so it is in their role as corporate creditor that they have begun to demand improved transparency from debtor firms (Ritch Grande Ampudia 2002). Only in May 2004 did the government modify the regulations to allow pension funds to invest up to 20 percent of their holdings in equity securities, both foreign and domestic, starting in December 2004 (Lyons 2004a; Lyons 2004b). The increased competition for these funds' capital could compel further improvements in Mexico's corporate governance practices, including improved minority shareholder protection.

Some argue that countries with weak shareholder protections like Mexico may ultimately gain access to foreign capital even without explicit legal reforms (La Porta, Lopez-de-Silanes, and Shleifer 1999). Many Mexican companies have recently issued American Depository Receipts, in which U.S. purchasers buy shares in a holding company that actually holds the shares in the Mexican firms. While this technique increases Mexican companies' disclosure requirements somewhat, it involves fewer reporting responsibilities and fiduciary duties than those faced by companies resident in the United States (La Porta, Lopez-de-Silanes, and Shleifer 1999; Pliego 2001). Also, foreign capital and reforms may be infused into the economy when Mexican companies are acquired by and assimilated into foreign firms based in countries with strong shareholder protections.

Corporate Governance Structures

As noted earlier, large firms in French-origin countries tend toward much higher ownership concentration than those from other traditions, and, even further, Mexico's is the second most concentrated economy of the 21 French-origin countries (La Porta et al. 1998). Mexico's handful of large business groups have been characterized as "family run empires" (Luhnow 2004) led by "impresarios" (Hummings 2004) focused on the betterment of the family's welfare regardless of their actions' impact on poorly protected minority shareholders.

A major study of ownership structures around the world offers useful statistics (La Porta et al. 1999). In Mexico, 100 percent of the major firms have a single family in control of at least 20 percent of the voting rights. Countries with controlling shareholders tend to rely on either pyramid structures, in which controlling shares of companies are owned by other companies, or on differentiating voting classes of stock. In Mexico, shareholders must, on average, own 16.44 percent of a company's stock to control 20 percent of the votes, suggesting that shareholder power is derived more from pyramid structures than from varying the voting rights of stock classes. In fact, 25 percent of Mexican companies are held through pyramids. The average controlling shareholder family in Mexico controls 1.05 firms, and 95 percent of major firms have a family member in management or on the board of directors. In 20 percent of firms, controlling families share control with at least one other shareholder who controls a 10 percent bloc.

These large Mexican companies started out family owned, then went public, selling only a minority of the equity and maintaining family members in key management roles (Pliego 2001). Boards are characterized as "friendly," and in practice are "closed" to new members. Board interlocks are pervasive: Among the largest firms that constitute the bulk of the Mexican stock market, five directors sit on at least ten different boards (Husted and Serrano 2002). Mexican business groups are actually holding companies that invest in other integrated companies, with cross-holdings within groups.

On the one hand, in these "insider" systems (Nestor and Thompson 2000), the leading families tend toward risk aversion both because of cultural antirisk norms and because their interests are more concentrated than those of their diversified minority shareholders (Kappaz 2004; La Porta et al. 1999). On the other hand, controlling shareholders may take advantage of their relative autonomy and their access to minority shareholders' funds to engage in high-risk expropriation or other corrupt practices (La Porta et al. 1999). Family-based power systems reduce the risk of exposure by fellow corporate leaders. Some have observed, though, that as family ownership and interests diffuse through now second- and third-generation family members, some intrafamily conflict concerning corporate goals is arising and is likely to increase (Husted and Serrano 2002).

Mexican firms also face fewer corporate governance controls than in most countries. The country has virtually no market for corporate control (Creel 2001; Husted and Serrano 2002), and banks are not involved in corporate governance (Husted and Serrano 2002). However, as noted earlier, *afores* have begun to demand increased transparency as creditors, and are likely to intensify their pressure as they begin to amass equity stakes (Husted and Serrano 2002; Ritch Grande Ampudia 2002). Cross-listing of shares on U.S. stock markets is also beginning to increase external pressure for transparency and corporate governance reform. The number of Mexican companies traded on U.S. markets has increased from 13 to 23 over the last decade (Luhnow 2004), a number that represents a significant proportion of their consolidated market.

Recent discussions of instituting "corporate governance reforms" to protect minority shareholders have met with defensiveness from Mexican business leaders, who view the idea as an Anglo-American intrusion into Mexican methods and culture (Ritch Grande Ampudia 2002). By association, many have concluded that all forms of corporate governance reform are suspect. Nevertheless, most major Mexican companies have recently begun establishing audit committees and drafting committee charters, generally following U.S. models (Garrett 2004). Notably, Mexican companies are not likely to face pressure to eliminate CEO duality in their firms, as fewer than 25 percent of major firms have the same person as both chairman and CEO (Husted and Serrano 2002). The chairman is generally the founder of the company, and the president a member of the family's second generation.

Enforcement will be key to the success of planned corporate governance reforms (Husted and Serrano 2002; Ritch Grande Ampudia 2002). To date, they are backed by little force, and many may constitute empty investor relations gestures.

Business Ethics

Stories of corruption and fraud abound in the Mexican press, suggesting that the Mexican populace may have a different perspective on business ethics than do American or Canadian publics. Researchers have suggested that Mexicans' view of human nature as fundamentally both good and evil, coupled with their high respect for authority, may make them more acquiescent in the face of high-level abuses (Hood and Logsdon 2002). Nevertheless, after a history of few companies developing codes of ethics, their numbers are now increasing sharply (Dorroh 2003). This section examines corruption in Mexican corporate governance, along with reports of recent corporate governance scandals and companies' treatment of their stakeholders.

Corruption

Corruption runs rampant in Mexico: The World Bank estimates that it costs the country nearly 10 percent of its gross domestic product (Dorroh 2003). On Transparency International's latest Corruption Perceptions Index, Mexico ranked sixty-fourth out of 133 countries with a score of 3.6/10, behind Belarus and Latvia (Transparency International 2004), and La Porta and his colleagues (1998) reported Mexico's scores as 4.77/10 for corruption, 7.29/10 for risk of expropriation, and 6.55/10 for contract risk.

Cleaning up corruption was a key campaign promise of Vicente Fox, who has made some progress since taking office despite his efforts being thwarted by the PRI Congress (Luhnow and Fritsch 2002). For example, Secodam, the government's auditing agency, initiated 13,000 audits in 2002, causing the firing or suspension of thousands of low- and medium-level government officials. The agency employs 120 internal auditors and contracts 12,000 more from other government agencies. However, compliance with Secodam's bureaucratic demands is costing businesses millions of dollars and has slowed many sectors to a crawl. The agency may even suffer from corruption among its own numbers: As a precaution, the Secodam offices themselves are equipped with cameras to watch the auditors at work.

In addition to internal reforms, Mexico is now visible in international anticorruption circles. Mexican officials entered into the OECD antibribery convention of 35 countries and the Inter-American Convention against Corruption with 30 other countries (Dorroh 2003). Mexico also signed a U.N. anticorruption treaty in December 2003 (*Wall Street Journal* 2003).

Despite the Fox administration's efforts at reform, the country still houses a huge black market with a high level of police and government involvement (Grillo 2003). Police are also implicated in corporate scams. Kraft Foods recently had to lock out their corrupt, subcontracted security team, led by an off-duty police officer, and replace it overnight with young, educated, highly paid replacements under Kraft's direct control

(Gips 2003). Some question how successful Fox will be at rooting out such corruption in "a government built around an almost medieval concept of patronage" (Luhnow and Fritsch 2002, A1).

Scandals

Like many countries, Mexico has had its share of corporate governance scandals in recent years, but they take on a different cast than those of its northern neighbors, one involving corruption in a state-owned enterprise and the other an "impresario" that employs masked bandits.

"Pemexgate," the scandal involving the country's state-owned oil company Pemex, demonstrates the depth of governmental and union corruption inherent in Mexican businesses (Estudillo 2003; O'Boyle 2003). Members of the nation's leading political party, PRI, have been accused of embezzling 1.5 billion pesos from the oil giant to help fund the unsuccessful campaign of PRI presidential candidate Francisco Labastida in 2000. In a key effort to begin cleaning up government corruption, President Fox has had PRI leaders arrested for their roles in the scandal, some of whom have turned state's evidence in exchange for protective custody (O'Boyle 2003). The oil workers' union chief, Carlos Deschamps, and other union officials have also been accused of playing a central role in the scandal, but for three years Deschamps has been protected by Mexico's shield of immunity given to all members of Congress. As his term expired, he simply filed a series of *"amparos"* or injunctions that will enable him to block his arrest until he chooses to volunteer himself to the courts. Other indicted union officials have fled the country. Throughout, Deschamps has remained president of the union, even weathering an election as members claim to be afraid to vote against him. Pemex is currently filled with auditors poring over a complex mass of bureaucratic paperwork, in search of further evidence (Luhnow and Fritsch 2002).

Another set of highly visible recent scandals involve Ricardo Salinas Pliego, the irrepressible head of a network of seven companies, including the country's second largest broadcaster, TV Azteca SA (Hummings 2004; Luhnow 2004). Unknown to TV Azteca's minority shareholders, controlling shareholder Pliego purchased a 46 percent stake in the troubled cellular telephone company Unefon, then engaged in a variety of financial maneuvers that culminated in spinning off the communications company. In the process, $218 million in profits were absorbed by two "unidentified creditors." An expert at maneuvering through the maze of Mexico's civil law courts for decades, Pliego is now facing a fraud investigation by the SEC under the U.S. Sarbanes-Oxley Act, after being turned in by Unefon's U.S. attorneys. If found guilty, Pliego and several confederates could be barred from serving on the board of any company trading in the United States, and the firm could be delisted from the New York Stock Exchange. Unefon fallout also includes a minority shareholder class action suit in the United States, and an investigation by a U.S. law firm at the request of TV Azteca's board of directors. In a separate TV Azteca event, Pliego sent masked gunmen to take over and hold another broadcasting studio for a week when his contract claim was under review in court (Luhnow 2004). These and other high-risk maneuvers cause the companies Pliego controls to trade at a discount that brokers call the "Salinas factor."

Stakeholder Management
Mexican firms are at a more rudimentary stage of corporate governance development than those that engage in formal programs of stakeholder management. They do not yet protect the interests of minority sharehold-ers or safeguard their communities: In urban areas, air and water pollution are among the worst in OECD countries (OECD 2004d). The employee stakeholder group has the most developed relationship with Mexican firms.

Corporate leaders demonstrate loyalty to their family members, so nepotism is high and management tends to be paternalistic toward their employees overall (Hood and Logsdon 2002). As competitive pressures have increased in Mexico, however, some generous employee programs have been suspended (Husted and Serrano 2002). Lower level workers in Mexico tend to work in the informal economy, given the lack of disincen-tives to do so and the high cost of social security for workers in the formal sector (OECD 2004d). Companies now face another cost to formal hiring, with 10 percent of gross profits required to be distributed to employees as profit sharing (Conger 2004; Husted and Serrano 2002). Unions have also been weakening over the last two decades, and particularly since PRI left power with the election of President Fox (Husted and Serrano 2002). Mexican business leaders show no propensity for following the OECD's recommendation that workers be included in the boards of directors.

The United States

Corporate governance and business ethics abuses in the United States have caused enormous upheaval in global markets since 2001. In the United States, numerous scandals caused a public outcry that led the government to intervene in existing practices and replace principles with legislated rules intended to curb business ethics infractions. The adjustment to this new restrictive regime is ongoing.

Corporate governance
These new legislative rules are fundamentally changing the roles of and relationships among executives, directors, and shareholders in the United States. We first note the current economic and legal situation in the United States, followed by a detailed examination of current U.S. economic regulations and corporate governance practices.

Economy
The U.S. economy is approximately 15 times the size of Mexico's and Canada's, with a 2002 GDP of $10,383 billion (OECD 2004a). The country's real GDP growth exceeds all other G7 countries' (OECD 2004b), and, on a per capita basis, U.S. GDP is $36,100, six times that of Mexico and more than 50 percent higher than Canada's (OECD 2004a). Americans' per capita real income is second only to Norwegians' among OECD countries (OECD 2004c).

The economic recovery following the post–9/11 and Enron recession has gained a broad base, with spending now increasing in households, government, and business capital formation (OECD 2004b). The economy's long-term performance has been strong, in part due to robust, ongoing open competition and an increasingly adaptable labor force (OECD 2004e). Productivity has increased significantly over the last decade (OECD 2004b), with the United States leading most OECD countries in both labor utilization and labor productivity (OECD 2004c). Millions of Americans are actively involved in equity markets. As of the end of 2003, Americans held $12 trillion in equities, both United States and foreign, constituting 38 percent of the market capitalization traded in the world's major exchanges (Thain 2004).

Legal
Unlike Mexico, the United States has a common law system (Creel 2001) based on its roots in the English legal tradition (La Porta et al. 1998). Therefore, the law is grounded in legal precedent and the application of legal principles. According to cross–country comparisons, the United States rates a 10/10 on the Rule of Law, and another 10/10 for the efficiency of its judiciary (La Porta et al. 1998).

The civil courts are of unusual significance to U.S. corporate governance. American judges take an activist stance in interpreting legislation and general principles such as "fairness" (Burke 2002). The combination of an active judiciary and shareholder-friendly procedural devices, such as derivative and class action lawsuits, enable investors to enforce directors' fiduciary duties to investors. The U.S. contingency-fee system also reduces shareholders' financial risk in bringing suit, allowing them to avoid all attorney's fees except in the case of a successful verdict. Although, historically, few directors have actually been held liable for corporate abuses, the ongoing threat of a shareholder suit may help to rein in potentially abusive behavior.

Economic Regulation

Much of the U.S. regulation of corporations has its roots in the American stock market crash of 1929, which led to regulations preventing the development of powerful voting blocs in American corporations (Roe 1994). The resulting Securities Acts of 1933 and 1934, which governed U.S. corporate law for much of the twentieth century, prohibited banks from owning corporate equity, shareholders from owning 5 percent of a firm's stock without disclosure, and more than ten investors from communicating with one another, all laying the groundwork for the United States's current highly dispersed corporate ownership (Davis and Thompson 1994). These acts also established the Securities and Exchange Commission (SEC) to oversee the activities of the New York Stock Exchange (NYSE). Since that time, the SEC has had authority over American exchanges' proposed rule changes, but it does not have the power to make changes unilaterally (Burke 2002). Because American firms incorporate under state law, the federal SEC does not have authority to regulate their corporate governance practices, except through its supervisory power over the exchanges in which the firms list their stock.

Investor pressure led to many of the United States's long-standing strict regulations being loosened in the 1980s and 1990s (Ward 1997), allowing for greater consolidation of shareholdings and increased investor activism with portfolio firms (Davis and Thompson 1994). This increasing institutional investor vigilance, combined with strong shareholder protections, judicial activism, and the courts' broad interpretations of such principles as fiduciary duty and fairness allowed the NYSE corporate governance guidelines to remain quite relaxed during the 1990s (Burke 2002).

However, the various U.S. corporate governance scandals of the early 2000s, to be discussed shortly, led to an avalanche of new, restrictive legislation and regulation of the "rule" variety. The Sarbanes-Oxley Act constituted the most all-encompassing change in American corporate law since 1934. The Act requires that all publicly traded U.S. firms adopt outside auditor independence, independent internal audit committees, CEO and CFO certification of financial reports, a prohibition of personal loans to corporate officers, and whistleblower protection, in addition to a "comply or explain" recommendation to adopt a code of ethics for senior financial officers (Schlesinger 2002; Snell and Wilmer 2002). In addition, the Act significantly increases the personal penalties—in terms of both monetary fines and imprisonment—for perpetrators of corporate financial fraud, and clarifies its determination to bar any "unfit" securities violator from serving on the board of directors of a listed U.S. firm. In several cases, the SEC was required to develop derivative regulations to help enforce the Act (Snell and Wilmer 2002).

Since the Act's passage in 2002, the U.S. stock exchanges have been submitting more restrictive corporate governance guidelines for SEC approval, to coincide with the tenets of Sarbanes-Oxley. After several cycles of proposals and public comment, the SEC approved the NYSE's Corporate Governance Listing Standards (NYSE 2004a, 2004b) and NASDAQ's very similar guidelines (NASDAQ 2003) in November 2003. The rules require that listed companies have a majority of independent directors on their boards (with very restrictive definitions of "independence"), that independent directors meet regularly without management present, and that listed companies adopt a code of ethics or conduct (NASDAQ 2003, 2004b). In addition, the NYSE requires firms to adopt and disclose corporate governance guidelines and to have both nominating and compensation committees composed entirely of independent directors (NYSE 2004b). NASDAQ requires listed firms to gain independent director approval of nominations and compensation, but does not require independent committees (NASDAQ 2003).

Sarbanes-Oxley and its follow-on regulations and guidelines have created an enormous bureaucratic burden for American corporations, both innocent and guilty. The legal and administrative costs associated with adopting the new rules average $1 million per company, according to the Business Roundtable, with total costs of complying with Sarbanes-Oxley alone expected to exceed $5.5 billion in 2004 (Iwata 2004). Executives tended to acquiesce or even embrace the new restrictions in the aftermath of Enron and related scandals, to avoid being painted with the same brush (Useem 2002). Now that they have been struggling—and paying—to comply with the maze of regulations for two years, however, they are speaking out (Iwata 2004; Thain 2004; *Wall Street Journal* 2004).

Many complain of the unnecessary complexity and inconsistencies of the Act, while others focus on the heavy costs of compliance. Some note that the details of such legislation—particularly such hastily passed legislation—tend to be "worked out in court," which frightens even good executives (Murphy 2003). Some small companies are delaying going public, and others who are already publicly traded are delisting their stock (Barker 2004; Murphy 2003). The president of the NYSE has also observed that the rigors of Sarbanes-Oxley, which includes provisions for foreign firms, have caused the number of new listings of foreign stocks to drop (Thain 2004). One *Wall Street Journal* editorial, however, claims that executives' current alarmism is merely a reaction to being subjected to appropriate market forces (*Wall Street Journal* 2004). Corporate officers' recent anti-Sarbanes-Oxley campaign may ultimately lead to revisions in the regulations.

Corporate Governance Structures

The United States is the quintessential "outsider system" (Nestor and Thompson 2000), embodying all of its features: dispersed ownership, increasing institutional holdings, the primacy of shareholders, strong shareholder protections, strict disclosure requirements, strong capital markets, and a reliance on equity financing. American corporations' defining characteristic is their very dispersed ownership, a rarity in international comparisons (La Porta et al. 1999).

La Porta and his colleagues' (1999) statistics are again helpful. Of United States's large, publicly traded firms, 80 percent are widely held, defined as having no single shareholder in control of 20 percent of the voting rights. The remaining 20 percent are controlled by families, with none of the American firms controlled by another widely held corporation. U.S. shareholders must own an average of 19.19 percent of a company's shares to achieve 20 percent voting control, suggesting that different classes of voting stock are not important to corporate control, and none of the U.S. firms is held in a pyramid structure of intermediate corporations. The U.S. family that controls a top 20 firm controls on average only that firm, and in 75 percent of the cases the controlling family has a family member on the board or in management. None of these controlling families shares control with another shareholder who holds at least 10 percent of the voting right.

Some may assume that this characteristic ownership dispersion leads to lack of managerial oversight and decreased profitability. However, in the United States, profitability actually declines with ownership concentration until it reaches 43 percent, at which point it begins to increase (Gedajlovic and Shapiro 1998). One reason for dispersion to not harm profitability may be that the external market for corporate control is a stronger curb on managerial discretion in the United States than internal controls placed on management by shareholders, according to many researchers. However, updated studies may find that over the last decade the escalating involvement of institutional shareholders in U.S. corporations has dramatically increased the amount of internal control executives now face.

The shareholder base of U.S. corporations has become increasingly consolidated with the rapid growth of institutional investing. More than

60 percent of U.S. equity is now held through institutional investors, including mutual funds and public and private pension funds (Securities Industry Association 2002). While not all fund managers choose to intervene with portfolio firms (Pozen 1994), those who do control a huge pool of equity.

The managers of these large funds—some of which hold 500 or more portfolio stocks—have begun to rely heavily on the counsel of third-party advisors when deciding on a firm's need for intervention or on how to vote beneficiaries' proxies (Baue 2003). An early, influential player in this field is the Investor Responsibility Research Center, which focuses primarily on social issues, but the current market leader is Institutional Shareholder Services (ISS). ISS was instrumental in swinging institutional investors' proxy votes on the contentious Hewlett Packard-Compaq merger (Burrows 2003), and more recently threw its considerable weight behind the no-confidence vote of CEO Michael Eisner at Disney (McCarthy 2004). These visible examples of ISS's advisory power, along with its recent questionable recommendation that investors vote against Warren Buffett's reelection to Coca-Cola's board of directors, have placed ISS in the spotlight (Iwata 2004). Many business leaders are now calling for SEC regulation of these third-party advisors.

In response to the changing regulations and investor pressure, in recent years U.S. boards have changed dramatically. They are now considerably smaller, and directors sit on fewer boards, so that they are able to devote the necessary time and attention to the boards where they do sit (Monks and Minow 2004). A recent Business Roundtable survey found that 70 percent of the directors on member boards are now fully independent (Iwata 2004), a number that far exceeds the "majority" listing requirements noted earlier. In addition, the emphasis on audit integrity has led boards of directors' audit committees to meet more often and for longer periods (Byrnes et al. 2003).

While not subjected to regulatory pressure, another issue that has received considerable press in the United States is the prevalence of CEO duality. The call for the splitting of the roles has not been heeded, as a rule (Sweeney 2004). Almost 80 percent of S&P 500 companies still has a joint CEO and chairman. In those cases in which they are separated, a company insider, such as the former CEO, serves as chairman. One study concludes that only 4 percent of S&P 500 firms have a truly independent chairman of the board.

Business Ethics

For some time, the vast majority of large U.S. corporations has had codes of ethics (Hood and Logsdon 2002). As noted above, codes of ethics are now required of all NYSE-listed companies (NYSE 2004b), and those listed on NASDAQ are required to have a code of ethics or conduct (NASDAQ 2003). However, these requirements have come to pass because of recent abuses in practice. Here we outline the country's corruption statistics, followed by four key examples of recent scandals, and the treatment of stakeholders in the United States.

Corruption

While business risk is relatively low in the United States, with a risk of expropriation rating of 9.98/10 and a contract risk score of 9/10, American business is perceived to be somewhat corrupt (La Porta et al. 1998). La Porta and his colleagues reported a corruption score for the United States of 8.63/10, and it ranked eighteenth out of 133 countries with a 7.5/10 on Transparency International's (2004) Corruption Perception Index. Both political corruption and the remaining influences of organized crime helped to put the Chamber of Commerce's 1997 estimate of bribery, kickbacks, and payoffs in the United States at $12.4 billion per year (Johnstone and Brown 2004).

Scandals

The numerous scandals that rocked the U.S. stock market beginning in 2001 have been well publicized around the world, and are not detailed here. Instead, we briefly outline four of the most egregious corporate governance failures from this period. The most notorious, Enron, was led by CEO Kenneth Lay and financial wunderkind Andrew Fastow, who built a paper empire on impenetrable "creative accounting" (Jennings 2003; Monks and Minow 2004). Ironically, Enron's corporate governance and corporate social responsibility structures met most "best practices" guidelines (Sonnenfeld 2003), including a "dream" board of directors (with the exception of $380,000 annual salaries) (Jennings 2003). However, its officers' behaviors left something to be desired: The Enron board is known to have specifically voted to suspend its conflict of interest policy and code of ethics on multiple occasions. Years after other corporate officers had faced indictment, Kenneth Lay was finally arrested for fraud in July 2004 (Hays 2004).

Tyco's CEO Dennis Kozlowski indiscriminately acquired 200 companies around the world over a decade before investors' perusal of financial statements caused the stock to plummet in 2002 (Jennings 2003). The Tyco scandal is best known for Kozlowski's lavish personal spending of corporate funds and financial statements that camouflaged the company's poor operating performance in a landslide of paper acquisition gains.

In a similar vein, the WorldCom tragedy was instigated by CEO Bernard Ebbers that led the telecommunications company in a series of massive acquisitions that left passive directors enriched and investors baffled by complex financial statements (Monks and Minow 2004). Key facets of the WorldCom scandal are the directors' approval of enormous personal loans to Ebbers, the largest one-time write-off any U.S. firm had taken to date ($80 billion), and the largest bankruptcy in U.S. history.

Before its downfall, the Rigas family ruled Adelphia like a personal fiefdom, with family members in control of the executive suite and five of the board's nine director seats (Monks and Minow 2004). The family used company money for exorbitant personal purchases, awarded Adelphia contracts to their own companies, and defrauded minority stockholders out of millions of dollars before the company went bankrupt and five corporate officers were arrested in 2002.

Many of these scandals arose from the 1980s conclusion that firms suffering from "agency problems" between management and shareholders would do well to make executives into shareholders themselves (Jensen and Meckling 1976), which led to a managerial focus on increasing the short-term share-price. The U.S. media's ability to garner international publicity of American businesses' indiscretions may further contribute to a tarnished global image.

Stakeholder Management

Executives' opinions concerning stakeholder management have been thoroughly surveyed in the United States, and one consistent result emerges: Nonowner stakeholders are treated instrumentally, as a means to the corporate end of maximizing shareholder value (Agle, Mitchell, and Sonnenfeld 1999; Berman et al. 1999). Normative versions of stakeholder theory, in which managers place nonnegotiated stakeholder desires ahead of shareholders' right to residual profits, are not supported by respondents. These results align with Gedajlovic and Shapiro's (1998) argument, discussed earlier, that the United States has weak internal constraints, defined as those emanating from the firm's stakeholders.

This focus on shareholder value is likely to be supported by the U.S. populace, however, perhaps partly because equity investment is so widespread. In a large stakeholder survey of U.S. customers, the respondents, not surprisingly, ranked their own interests as most important, followed by investors' and the community's, and finally, by employees' (Maignan and Ferrell 2003). This result is in contrast to the perspectives of customers in France and Germany, in which investors were placed last by customer samples. Maignan and Ferrell conclude that this result supports the individualistic

U.S. perspective that businesses are expected to strive for their own economic well-being.

Some social issues researchers have studied the impact of instrumental stakeholder management on profit in the United States. Including shareholders, employees, customers, community, and the natural environment as stakeholders, Hillman and Keim (2001) found that instrumental stakeholder management has a positive impact on shareholder wealth creation. More specifically, Berman and his colleagues (1999) found that building relationships with customers and employees can significantly enhance financial performance, while increased effort related to the community, diversity, and the natural environment do not.

The primary way that stakeholders affect U.S. firms, then, is as shareholder stakeholders. As discussed earlier, institutional investors have an increasing impact on corporate affairs, and some are promoting social agendas: One third of the record 1,100 shareholder proxy proposals filed in 2004 related to social issues (Iwata 2004). Indeed, given the high percentage of employee ownership in the United States, due to Employee Stock Ownership Plans and stock options, employees' main governance benefits derive from their role as owners (Nestor and Thompson 2000).

Canada

Canada is less visible on the global economic stage than is the United States in part because its corporate governance and business ethics problems are fewer. This section examines first the country's changing corporate governance practices, then the current state of its business ethics.

Corporate Governance

Corporate governance reform is also underway in Canada. Recent problems in the United States led to "fluctuating" investor confidence among its northern neighbors, and encouraged leaders to develop their own reforms (Sarra 2003). In the process, they concluded that Canada's most critical corporate governance issue was the lack of protection of minority shareholders.

Economy

Canada's economy, while approximately the same size as Mexico's in terms of its 2002 GDP of $940 billion, comes closer to the United States in per capita terms, at $22,800 (OECD 2004a). The productivity gap between the Canada and the United States is attributed to Canada's extensive social programs that allow high levels of unemployment despite the country's well-educated labor force.

Legal

Canada is considered to be a mature legal state with a rule of law rating of 10/10 (La Porta et al. 1998). The efficiency of the judiciary system is slightly less robust, with a rating of 9.25/10. Like Mexico, Canada tends toward a more mixed state/business economy than the United States (Hood and Logsdon 2002) and takes a more socialistic approach to social programs than either neighbor. Canada's decentralized government allows for strong provincial autonomy, with relatively few restrictions at the federal level.

Economic regulation

Canada's economic regulations are considered to be very business-friendly, although its decentralized system of government allows business regulations to vary across provinces (OECD 2004a). In addition, Canada continues to impose limits on foreign ownership, reducing the potential influx of capital to support innovation.

Regulators are embroiled in two ongoing issues that reduce the attractiveness of Canadian stocks: provincial discord concerning the content and enforcement of corporate governance rules, and lack of protection for minority shareholders. These difficulties may contribute to regulators' need to compel Canadian investors to keep their investment dollars at home; 70 percent of Canadians' individual retirement savings plans and pension plans must be invested in Canadian companies to avoid adverse tax consequences (Rosen 2004).

The first distinctive feature of Canada's economic regulation is its decentralization, and the resulting jockeying among provinces. Ontario is home to the country's leading Toronto Stock Exchange (TSX), accounting for 90 percent of the nation's stock trading (Sarra 2002), although others, such as the Vancouver Stock Exchange in British Columbia, compete for listings. Notably, each province also houses its own exchange commission, so the Ontario Securities Commission (OSC) governs the Toronto Stock Exchange, the British Columbia Securities Commission (BCSC) regulates the Vancouver Stock Exchange, etc.

The 13 provincial exchange commissions do cooperate through the Canadian Securities Administrators (CSA) association, which has issued minimal corporate governance rules (Flavelle 2004). The rules include requirements for outside auditor certification by the Canadian Public Accountability Board, independent internal audit committees, and CEO/CFO certification of financial statements. All provinces are covered by the first requirement, while British Columbia is exempt from the second and third.

Traditionally, the Toronto Stock Exchange has established corporate governance rules for its listed firms and asked companies to "comply or disclose" (Burke 2002). Canadian regulators argue that they use disclosure instead of enforcement because they prefer to let the markets determine if an issuer's corporate governance practices are sufficient (McFarland 2004). Unlike the United States' periodic reporting, however, Canadian firms engage in a continuous disclosure regime, in which they must disclose material changes in corporate condition on an ongoing basis, including on a public website (Sarra 2003).

The Ontario Securities Commission's charter is to supervise the TSX and to intervene only when a broker or issuer behaves against the "public interest" (Burke 2002). This arm's length arrangement has led to ongoing tension between the OSC and TSX (Hansell 2003), tension that has been exacerbated recently by the TSX's inability to enforce corporate governance disclosure. Even after improvement in 2002, 37 percent of listed firms did not fully disclose their compliance (Graham 2003). As a result, the Ontario Securities Commission proposed corporate governance securities regulations in January 2004 that will supplant TSX's listing rules when approved (Colman 2004; Flavelle 2004; Hansell 2003).

The OSC's proposed regulations include guidelines for a majority of independent directors, an independent chair or lead director, a written corporate governance policy, job descriptions and assessment mechanisms for directors and the CEO, independent committee membership, and a written code of conduct and ethics (Colman 2004; Garrett 2004; McFarland 2004). While companies will still not be legally compelled to comply with the guidelines, under the OSC system they must "comply or disclose" or face a breach of securities law (Flavelle 2004; McFarland 2004).

Not all provinces agree about the benefits of nationwide uniformity (Sarra 2003). While 11 of the 13 securities commissions backed the OSC's proposed corporate governance guidelines (Flavelle 2004), Alberta ultimately withdrew its support and backed the more flexible version proposed by British Columbia and Quebec in April 2004 (BCSC 2004a; CNW 2004).

The disagreement resides primarily in the "principles versus rules" distinction discussed earlier. The OSC proposals would impose a more rules-based system on Canadian firms than they have faced in the past, while BCSC has been working to "streamline" its securities system, moving from a detailed code of conduct to a more flexible principles-based approach (BCSC 2004b; Garrett 2004; Sarra 2003). The British Columbia Securities Act passed in May 2004 focused on replacing rules with a new results-based system (BCSC 2004b). The ongoing discord between British

Columbia and much of the rest of Canada over the amount and type of disclosure and the source of enforcement promises only to escalate (Sarra 2003).

Still, all provinces are not created equal. While Canadian firms are able to incorporate under provincial or federal law, most Canadian companies choose to incorporate in Ontario (Burke 2002) and list on the TSX. Under recent amendments passed to the Ontario Securities Act, the OSC was granted increased enforcement power, approval of new offences, and the ability to impose increased penalties, including personal liability (Sarra 2003).

The second key issue in Canada's economic regulatory system is its lack of protection for minority shareholders. In recognition of that fact, a 1996 Supreme Court decision noted increased legislative support of shareholder participation in corporate governance, and, in 2001, major reforms to the Canada Business Corporations Act were enacted to further increase shareholder voice (Sarra 2003). Regardless of these initiatives, the prevalence of controlling shareholders in Canadian firms—and their de facto ability to veto minority shareholders' proposals—leaves minority shareholders little ability to affect their portfolio firms. It is not surprising, then, that Canada's shareholder proposal rights are seldom used. With fewer proposals come fewer lawsuits; fewer than 10 cases had been through the Canadian courts by 2003, so the country's shareholder case law is still underdeveloped (Burke 2002).

Instead of shareholder lawsuits, Canadian investors are more likely to invoke the "oppression remedy," which has broad powers and minimal procedural requirements (Burke 2002). This remedy protects minority shareholders against executive or director behavior "that is oppressive, unfairly prejudicial to, or unfairly disregards the interests of the complainant" (Sarra 2003, 408), and arose to compensate for what was considered to be weak protection of fiduciary duty.

Reforms are now also underway to allow shareholders to file civil liability suits against their portfolio firms (McClearn 2003). Business leaders consider the possibility to be overly onerous because of continuous disclosure: Shareholders could be allowed to file suit against corporate officers based on a "work in progress," without waiting to see an initiative's ultimate result. Notably, shareholders would still be unable to sue companies for violating corporate governance guidelines, because companies are required only to disclose, not to comply (Burke 2002). In the meantime, some Canadian investors are heading for U.S. courts. For example, disenchanted minority shareholders sued the Canadian company Biovail in New York after it cross-listed on the New York Stock Exchange (McClearn 2003).

Even without strong remedies, controlling shareholders' lack of fiduciary obligations to minority shareholders (Burke 2002), combined with the high potential for abuse, gives minority investors an incentive to monitor their portfolio firms (Sarra 2003).

Corporate Governance Structures

As discussed earlier, Mexico embodies an "insider" system of corporate governance, while the United States is an "outsider" system. Canada resides between the two in what Nestor and Thomson (2000) have characterized as a "hybrid" system. As in Mexico, corporations' voting rights are both concentrated and family-controlled, but, like the United States's, the Canadian system also features strong securities regulation, accounting transparency, increasing institutional ownership, and recognition of a minimal level of shareholder rights.

Again, La Porta and his colleagues' (1999) statistics are instructive. Forty percent of Canada's large publicly traded firms has a single shareholder in control of 20 percent of the voting stock, with the remaining 60 percent widely held. Twenty-five percent are controlled by a family, with 15 percent held by another nonfinancial corporation. To control 20 percent of the voting rights, the average Canadian shareholder must own 19.36 percent of the firm's stock, suggesting that voting shares are only slightly differentiated, and only 13 percent of Canadian firms are controlled through a pyramid structure. A given controlling family controls on average 1.25 of the top 20 firms, and 100 percent of Canada's family firms has at least one family member in management or on the board of directors. Twenty percent of family firms are controlled through a pyramid structure, and no families share control with a separate shareholder who controls at least 10 percent of the votes.

More qualitative Canadian analyses assert that in fact 70 percent (Sarra 2003) or even 75 percent (Burke 2002) of Canada's major corporations are actually under the control of a single or a handful of shareholders. An earlier study claimed that 382 of Canada's 400 largest companies were controlled by a single shareholder (Gedajlovic and Shapiro 1998).

While institutional holdings have not yet reached U.S. levels, institutional investors now hold 31 percent of all Canadian-based corporations on the TSX (Sarra 2003). They are a mature presence in corporate governance and have relied primarily on private negotiations and "collaborative intervention" over the last decade, but are demonstrating an increasing willingness to employ the media and the courts to achieve remedies (Burke 2002; Sarra 2003).

Similar to the U.S. Council for Institutional Investors, Canadian institutional investors have established the "Canadian Coalition for Good

Governance" (CCGG) to represent their interests (CCGG 2004). The Coalition promotes "best corporate governance practices," with an emphasis on shareholder protection, ethical management, independent committees, and performance-based compensation. The CCGG guidelines are very similar to those promulgated in the United States: no CEO/Chair duality, independent committees, a majority of independent directors, regular performance evaluations, and a relatively extreme requirement for director share ownership (CCGG 2004). This level of cooperation among Canada's institutional investors is not surprising. Unlike their more geographically dispersed counterparts in the United States, institutional investors in Canada are all based in Toronto, allowing for significant informal contact and coordination (Burke 2002).

Unlike institutional investors, who are beginning to make inroads in corporate governance, small investors in Canada are assumed to have diversified portfolios and use an "exit" strategy if unhappy with corporate performance, thereby reducing their need for regulatory protection (Sarra 2003).

Canada's boards of directors lie between the Anglo-American, shareholder oriented model and the Continental European, more stakeholder oriented models (Gedajlovic and Shapiro 1998). The boards exhibit little CEO duality, concentrated ownership guarantees large shareholders significant representation, and noninvestor stakeholders generally do not participate.

Among the countries in a recent study of internal and external corporate governance controls, Canada proved to be a unique case (Gedajlovic and Shapiro 1998). Canadian executives face both a strong external market for corporate control, facilitated by relaxed acquisition and takeover regulations, and strong internal constraints posed by vigilant controlling shareholders, leaving executives with virtually no managerial discretion. Thus, in Canada, interests are less likely to be misaligned between management and controlling investors than they are between controlling investors and minority shareholders, as is discussed shortly.

Business Ethics
Canadian business has demonstrated fewer ethical lapses than either of its southern neighbors. While it is a few years behind the United States in the adoption of corporate ethics programs and structures, it may not face as much public demand (Lindsay, Lindsay, and Irvine 1996). In a study of more than 150 major Canadian firms, 44 percent reported having ethical concepts in their corporate mission statements; the 20 largest companies in the study all had a code of ethics, while only 67 percent of the 19 smallest

did. This size effect may decrease over time, however. As discussed, the OSC proposal currently under consideration recommends that all TSX listed companies establish codes of conduct and ethics (Garrett 2004; McFarland 2004). In this section, we outline Canada's corruption levels, recent scandals, and approaches to stakeholder management.

Corruption

Canada is perceived to be one of the least corrupt countries in the world, with its rating of 8.7/10, placing it eleventh out of 133 countries in Transparency International's annual study (2004). La Porta and his colleagues (1998) rated corruption in Canada at 10/10, with a risk of expropriation of 9.67/10, and contract risk at 8.96. This lack of corruption may result from a combination of cultural norms and the lack of executive discretion noted earlier.

Scandals

While not in the same quantity or on the same scale as those in the United States, Canada has also been beset by corporate governance scandals, two of which are noted here. The founders and controlling shareholders of Livent Inc., a geographically diversified live theater company, defrauded investors and creditors out of C$500 million by falsifying financial statements for almost a decade (Flavelle 2004; Wam 2002). The company collapsed in 1998, and executives were indicted in both Canada and the United States on 19 counts of financial fraud (Wam 2002).

The YBM Magnex International scandal linked Canadian business with the Russian mob (Acharya and Yew 2002; Flavelle 2004). YBM founders, members of an organized Russian crime syndicate, defrauded investors of C$600M, C$100M of which was raised in a public offering as the company was being investigated by both the OSC and U.S. authorities. The OSC ultimately sanctioned five of the company's nine directors with directorship bans and costs, and the founding members remain wanted by the FBI. (Libin 2003). A previous Ontario premier who sat on the board was not sanctioned.

As mentioned, investor abuses in Canada appear to be more likely to be perpetrated by founding controlling shareholders of firms, taking advantage of poorly protected minority shareholders, in contrast with scandals in the United States that are more likely to be carried out by management against shareholders at large.

Stakeholders

Gedajlovic and Shapiro (1998) argue that, while stakeholders do not generally sit on Canadian boards, the boards are more stakeholder oriented than those in the United States. However, a study of ethics in corporate governance showed that among those Canadian firms that claimed to be implementing ethics programs, only 16 percent said that they used "ethics focused corporate governance" (Lindsay, Lindsay, and Irvine, 1996, 394). The term was defined as "a decision making process which includes representatives from as many constituencies of the organization as possible."

Indeed, Sarra (2003) has voiced concern over employee shareholders. As noted, Canadian regulators assume that small shareholders are diversified and will "exit" a stock if performance declines. Sarra notes that neither assumption holds in most cases of employee shareholders. They tend to hold large blocks of the stock, relative to their portfolio size, and to hold it regardless of fluctuations in share value. This loyalty, and lack of minority shareholder protection, hurt employees severely in the recent Canadian Airlines failure.

Apparently, the Canadian public would support a greater emphasis on stakeholder management. In a survey of 2006 Canadians, 74 percent support the contention that, in addition to profit, corporations should consider the effect of decisions on "employees, local communities, and the country" (Sarra 2003, 426). Notably, 36 percent of the respondents owned shares in Canadian corporations. A second survey of Canadians showed that 83 percent believe that corporations should "go beyond their traditional economic role," and 51 percent claim to have "punished" a firm over socially irresponsible behavior in the previous year (Macfarlane 2004, 45).

Conclusion

Corporate governance and business ethics in North America are clearly in a state of flux, with important transformations ongoing in all three countries. Mexico's increasing need of foreign capital and its current fight against a history of corruption, the United States's legalistic reaction to scandals that is now being fought by executives, and Canada's interprovincial debate over not only the content but also the style of guidelines demonstrate the fundamental nature of current reforms.

In the interests of contrasting this discussion with those of the remaining continental analyses in this volume, we summarize our findings in table 13.2. The dominant corporate model in Mexico and Canada is one of concentrated, family ownership and "insider" or "hybrid" control, in contrast with that in the United States, with dispersed, although increasingly concentrated, ownership and "outsider" control.

Stakeholder management in Mexico is minimal; although some paternalistic employee programs have existed, most are being phased out due to

Table 13.2 North American Characteristics for Cross-Continental Comparison

	Mexico	United States	Canada
Dominant corporate governance model	Concentrated; family ownership; insider control	Dispersed but concentrating ownership; outsider control	Concentrated; family ownership; "hybrid" control
Degree of stakeholder engagement	Minimal; some paternalism of employees	Instrumental; primary focus on shareholders	Moderate; reliant on social programs
Business ethics in corporate governance	Codes of ethics increasing; significant corruption	Codes of ethics required by law	Codes of conduct and ethics suggested in guidelines
Management and reporting of business ethics	Minimal; but increasing	Disclosure of waivers required by law	Comply or disclose; continuous disclosure regime
New developments in business ethics and corporate governance	Regulatory reforms; pressure from competition and foreign investors	Sarbanes-Oxley backlash; pressure from public and institutional investors	National guidelines emerging; increase in disclosure

competitive pressure. In the United States, instrumental stakeholder management is emphasized, with the intent of enhancing shareholder value. Canadian executives engage in a more mixed version of stakeholder management, but governmental social programs negate the need for significant stakeholder support.

Business ethics is evolving from differing starting points in the three countries. Mexico's history of rampant corruption will slow the pace of instituting business ethics in corporate governance, although codes of ethics are increasing. Management and reporting of business ethics infractions in Mexico is minimal, but increasing. The United States, while recovering from corruption and scandal, has the strictest legal controls of the three countries, and while it has for some time had the most prevalent ethics programs, codes of ethics are now required by law. The law requires any waivers to these codes to be disclosed to shareholders and the public. Canada's new corporate governance guidelines, when approved, are likely to retain the requirement for a code of conduct or ethics, although firms are required only to comply with the guideline or to disclose that they do not. Reporting of material business ethics infractions, however, would be subject to Canada's continuous disclosure regime.

New developments in business ethics and corporate governance are widespread in all three countries. Mexico's economy is undergoing fundamental regulatory reform, and pressure from competitors and foreign investors is compelling Mexican business to align itself more closely with global requirements for efficiency and transparency. In the United States, after two years of integrating Sarbanes-Oxley and exchange reforms, executives are striking back at the restrictive laws in an effort to reduce the resulting bureaucratic costs. At the same time, they feel extreme pressure for transparency and best practices in corporate governance from both the public and institutional investors. In Canada, some level of national agreement is emerging concerning corporate governance guidelines, and disclosure requirements are about to be enforced by law for the first time.

A final question to be addressed is whether these three systems of corporate governance are likely to converge. The opinions of international observers vary concerning general trends in international convergence. Garrett (2004) takes a strong stand that corporate governance systems will converge on rule-based systems, much like Sarbanes-Oxley. Similarly, Reed (2002) notes that reforms in developing countries are pushing them toward the Anglo/American model of (1) single-tiered board focused on shareholder interests, (2) dominant financial markets, (3) a weak role for banks, and (4) little industrial/government policy. He argues that developing countries are being encouraged toward convergence by shareholder-focused business interests and international financial bodies in search of governance that fits their norms.

Other observers take a more nuanced position. According to La Porta and his colleagues (2000), weak shareholder-protection countries would be wise to emulate strong protection countries, which embody robust financial markets, dispersed ownership, and efficient capital allocation. However, while such convergence is needed, particularly by weak shareholder-protection countries, it is likely to be resisted by powerful controlling shareholders. Nevertheless, although the researchers are skeptical about the likelihood of "legal convergence," they predict that weak shareholder-protection countries will experience some level of "functional convergence," such as that imposed by cross-listing in strong shareholder-protection countries. Similarly, Nestor and Thompson observe that, while some convergence is inevitable, "ownership and control arrangements . . . will remain to a considerable degree idiosyncratic" (Nestor and Thompson 2000, 23), due to the inertia of history and culture.

The argument for significant idiosyncrasies remaining seems particularly relevant to North American countries. The massive and influential U.S. economy has taken a position of strict legal enforcement of shareholder rights, so "convergence" implies movement in the direction of this newly redefined U.S. system. However, Mexico's strong Latino culture and long history of corruption and family control is not likely to give way to a legal system of robust minority shareholder rights. Similarly, the ongoing provincial debate between rules and principles in Canada is unlikely to conclude with the British Columbian bloc's acquiescence, and even the OSC's market-based guidelines approach is unlikely to be supplanted by strict legal rules.

These enduring national characteristics, however, are likely to be augmented by functional convergence, as Mexico and Canada become increasingly dependent on global equity markets (La Porta et al. 2000). However, as noted, some foreign listings on the NYSE may have already been deterred by the severity of Sarbanes-Oxley regulations (Thain 2004). The world's major exchanges may arrive at a slightly less restrictive set of listing guidelines to attract foreign firms, a trend that could leave the U.S. exchanges in an inferior position without additional reform.

Note

An earlier version of this chapter was published in *Business & Society* 44(1): 40–73. Permission to reprint this chapter was kindly granted by Sage Publishers.

References

Acharya, M. and T. Yew. 2002. Magnets and the Mob: YBM Debacle a Key Test for OSC. *Toronto Star* December 1: C3.

Agle, B.R., R.K. Mitchell, and J.A. Sonnenfeld. 1999. Who Matters to CEOs? An Investigation of Stakeholder Attributes and Salience, Corporate Performance, and CEO Values. *Academy of Management Review* 42: 507–525.

Barham, J. 2004. Latin Markets Hit Their Stride. *LatinFinance* February 2: 12–19.

Barker, R. 2004. When Companies "Go Dark," Investors Can Lose; Sarbanes-Oxley Is Raising the Cost of Being Public. *Business Week* May 24: 120.

Baue, W. 2003. Corporate Governance Ratings Take Different Approaches to Produce Similar Results [online]. (Accessed December 19, 2003) Available from World Wide Web <http://www.socialfunds.com/news/print.cgi? sfArticleId= 1201>.

BCSC. 2004a. Request for Comment Proposed Multilateral Instrument 50–104, British Columbia Securities Commission [online]. (Accessed May 17, 2004) Available from World Wide Web: <http://www.bcsc.bc.ca:8080/ comdoc.nsf/allbyunid/285bbb09caca382988256e7f0058de59?opendocument>.

———. 2004b. A New Way to Regulate, British Columbia Securities Commission [online]. (Accessed June 10, 2004). Available from World Wide Web: <http://www.bcsc.bc.ca./Policy/default.asp>.

Berman, S.L., A.C. Wicks, S. Kotha, and T.M. Jones. 1999. Does Stakeholder Orientation Matter? The Relationship between Stakeholder Management Models and Firm Financial Performance. *Academy of Management Review* 42: 488–506.

Burke, K.S. 2002. Regulating Corporate Governance through the Market: Comparing the Approaches of the United States, Canada and the United Kingdom. *Journal of Corporation Law* 27: 341–380.

Burrows, P. 2003. *Backfire: Carly Fiorina's High-Stakes Battle for the Soul of Hewlett-Packard.* Hoboken, NJ: J. Wiley & Sons.

Byrnes, N., D. Henry, E. Thornton, and P. Dwyer. 2003. Reform: Who's Making the Grade: A Performance Review for CEOs, Boards, Analysts, and Others. *Business Week* September 22: 80–83.

CCGG. 2004. Corporate Governance Guidelines for Building High Performance Boards, Canadian Coalition for Good Governance [online]. (Accessed May 17, 2004) Available from World Wide Web: <http://www.ccgg.ca/web/website.nsf/web/CCGG_Guidelines/$FILE/CCGG_Guidelines_v1_Jan04.pdf>.

CNW. 2004. Regulators Encouraging Debate on Corporate Governance Disclosure. *Canada NewsWire* April 23: 1.

Colman, R. 2004. Regulators Propose Corporate Governance Rules for Issues. *CMA Management* 78(1): 8.

Conger, L. 2004. Reforma School. *Institutional Investor* March: 1.

Creel, C. 2001. Mexico: Codified Rules, Not Case Law. *LatinFinance March*: 86–88.

Davis, G.F., and T.A. Thompson. 1994. A Social Movement Perspective on Corporate Control. *Administrative Science Quarterly* 39: 141–173.

Dorroh, J. 2003. Stay Out of the Shadows. *Business Mexico* 13(6): 42.

Economist. 2003. Finance and Economics: Looks Good on Paper; Latin American Stockmarkets. 368(8342): 101.

Estudillo, J. 2003. Law and Order. *Business Mexico*. May: 21.

Flavelle, D. 2004. New Securities Guidelines Would Be Voluntary. *Toronto Star* January 17: D4.

Garrett, A.D. 2004. Themes and Variations: The Convergence of Corporate Governance Practices in Major World Markets. *Denver Journal of International Law and Policy* 32: 147–174.

Gedajlovic, E.R., and D.M. Shapiro. 1998. Management and Ownership Effects: Evidence from Five Countries. *Strategic Management Journal* 19: 533–553.

Gips, M.A. 2003. Wheeling and Eealing. *Security Management* March: 110–112.

Graham, R. 2003. Still Lacking in Governance Disclosure, Investor Canada [online]. (Accessed May 17, 2004) Available from World Wide Web: <http://www.investorcanada.com/interview.php?contentID=1261>.

Grillo, I. 2003. Beating the Black Market. *Business Mexico* May: 51–52.

Hansell, C. 2003. The Road to GOOD Governance. *CA Magazine* December: 30.

Hays, K. 2004. Ex-Enron CEO Kenneth Lay Pleads Innocent, Associated Press [online]. (Accessed July 8, 2004). Available from World Wide

Web: <http://story.news.yahoo.com/news?tmpl=story&ncid=&e=3&u=/
ap/20040709/ap_on_bi_ge/enron_lay>.

Hillman, A.J., and G.D. Keim. 2001. Shareholder Value, Stakeholder
Management, and Social Issues: What's the Bottom Line? *Strategic Management
Journal* 22: 125–139.

Hood, J.N., and J.M. Logsdon. 2002. Business Ethics in the NAFTA Countries: A
Cross-Cultural Comparison. *Journal of Business Research* 55: 883–890.

Hummings, R. 2004. Dodgy Dealings of Salinas Pliego. *Business Mexico* March:
32–34.

Husted, B.W. and C. Serrano. 2002. Corporate Governance in Mexico. *Journal of
Business Ethics* 37: 337–348.

IFLR. 2003. Mexico Takes on Corporate Governance Challenge. *International
Financial Law Review* September 1: 62–64.

Iwata, E. 2004. Businesses Say Corporate Governance Can Go too Far. *USA Today*
June 24: B–1.

Jennings, M.M. 2003. Restoring Ethical Gumption in the Corporation:
A Federalist Paper on Corporate Governance—Restoration of Active Virtue in
the Corporate Structure to Curb the "Yeehaw" Culture in Organizations.
Wyoming Law Review 3: 387–511.

Jensen, M.C., and W.H. Meckling. 1976. Theory of the Firm: Managerial Behavior,
Agency Costs and Ownership Structure. *Journal of Financial Economics* 3: 305–360.

Johnstone, P., and G. Brown. 2004. International Controls of Corruption: Recent
Responses from the USA and the UK. *Journal of Financial Crime* 11: 217–248.

Kappaz, C. 2004. Building the Venture Capital Industry in Mexico. *Texas Business
Review* February: 1–5.

La Porta, R., F. Lopez-de-Silanes, and A. Shleifer. 1999. Corporate Ownership
around the World. *Journal of Finance* 51: 471–517.

La Porta, R., F. Lopez-De-Silanes, A. Shleifer, and R. Vishny. 1998. Law and
Finance. *Journal of Political Economy* 106: 1113–1155.

——. 2000. Investor Protection and Corporate Governance. *Journal of Financial
Economics* 58: 3–27.

Libin, K. 2003. When Enough Is Enough: The YBM Magnex Decision. *Canadian
Business* August 5–18: 13.

Lindsay, R.M., L.M. Lindsay, and V.B. Irvine. 1996. Instilling Ethical Behavior in
Organizations: A Survey of Canadian Companies. *Journal of Business Ethics* 15:
393–407.

Luhnow, D. 2004. New Static: A Mexican Media Billionaire Now Faces
Investigation in U.S. *Wall Street Journal* February 27: A1.

Luhnow, D., and P. Fritsch. 2002. Aggressive Audits: Mexico's Crusade to End
Corruption Stalls Government. *Wall Street Journal* September 25: A1.

Lyons, J. 2004a. Mexico Loosens Pension-fund Rules. *Wall Street Journal*
May 5: A–12.

——. 2004b. Personal Communication. June 16.

Macfarlane, D. 2004. Why Now? *The Globe and Mail* February 27: 45.

Maignan, I., and O. C. Ferrell. 2003. Nature of Corporate Responsibilities: Perspectives from American, French, and German Consumers. *Journal of Business Research* 56: 55–67.

McCarthy, M. 2004. Disney Strips Chairmanship from Eisner. *USA Today* March 4: B1–2.

McClearn, M. 2003. Full Disclosure: Proposed Civil Liability Provisions May Allow Shareholders to Sue for Losses. *Canadian Business Law Journal* November 24–December 7: 53–55. McFarland, J. 2004. Guidelines Urge Ethics Codes. *The Globe and Mail* January 16: B1.

Monks, R.A.G., and N. Minow. 2004. *Corporate Governance*. Cambridge, MA: Blackwell.

Murphy, C. 2003. Keeping Small Business Off the Street. *FSB: Fortune Small Business*. November: 18.

NASDAQ. 2003. SEC Approves NASDAQ Corporate Governance Rules [online]. (Accessed May 17, 2004). Available from World Wide Web: <http://www.nasdaq.com/about/NASDAQ%20Bulletin_110403.pdf>.

Nestor, S., and J. K. Thompson. 2000. Corporate Governance Patterns in OECD Economies: Is Convergence Under Way? [online]. (Accessed May 17, 2004) Organisation for Economic Co-operation and Development. Available from World Wide Web: <http://www.oecd.org/dataoecd/7/10/1931460.pdf>.

NYSE. 2004a. Corporate Governance, New York Stock Exchange [online]. (Accessed May 17, 2004). Available from World Wide Web: <http://www.nyse.com>.

———. 2004b. Final NYSE Corporate Governance Rules, New York Stock Exchange [online]. (Accessed May 17, 2004.] Available from World Wide Web: <http://www.nyse.com/pdfs/finalcorpgovrules.pdf>.

O'Boyle, M. 2003. On the Run. *Business Mexico* November: 38.

OECD. 2004a. Gross Domestic Product, 2002, Organisation for Economic Co-operation and Development [online]. (Accessed May 17, 2004). Available from World Wide Web: <http://www.oecd.org/dataoecd/49/61/15360253.pdf>.

———. 2004b. Economic Survey—United States 2004: Sustaining Strong Growth and Social Cohesion, Organisation for Economic Co-operation and Development [online]. (Accessed May 17, 2004) Available from World Wide Web: <http://www.oecd.org/document/27/0,2340,en_2649_201185_31457883_1_1_1_1,00.html>.

———. 2004c. Economic Survey of Canada, 2003, Policy Brief, Organisation for Economic Co-operation and Development [online]. (Accessed May 17, 2004.] Available from World Wide Web: <http://www.oecd.org/dataoecd/2/44/9226246.pdf>.

———. 2004d. Economic Survey of Mexico, 2003, Organisation for Economic Co-operation and Development [online]. (Accessed May 17, 2004.) Available from World Wide Web: <http://www.oecd.org/document/55/0,2340,en_2649_201185_19933623_70651_119663_1_1,00.html>.

———. 2004e. Economic Survey—United States, 2004: Product Market Competition, Organisation for Economic Co-operation and Development [online]. (Accessed May 17, 2004.) Available from World Wide Web: <http://www.oecd.org/document/61/0,2340,en_2649_201185_31460861_7 0867_119663_1_1,00.html>.

Pliego, R.S. 2001. The Brave New World of Corporate Governance. *LatinFinance* May: 61–62.

Pozen, R.C. 1994. Institutional Investors: The Reluctant Activists. *Harvard Business Review* 72(1): 140–149.

Reed, D. 2002. Corporate Governance Reforms in Developing Countries. *Journal of Business Ethics* 37: 223–247.

Ritch Grande Ampudia, J. E. 2002. Corporate Governance in Mexico. *International Financial Law Review* 21: 159–162.

Roe, M.J. 1994. *Strong Managers, Weak Owners*. Princeton, NJ: Princeton University Press.

Rosen, A. 2004. Taken for a Ride. *Canadian Business* April 12–25: 21.

Sarra, J. 2002. Rose-Colored Glasses, Opaque Financial Reporting, and Investor Blues: Enron as Con and the Vulnerability of Canadian Corporate Law. *St. John's Law Review* 76(4): 715–766.

——. 2003. The Corporation as Symphony: Are Shareholders First Violin or Second Fiddle? *University of British Columbia Law Review* 36: 403–441.

Schlesinger, M. 2002. Sarbanes-Oxley Act. *Business Entities* 2(6): 42–49.

Securities Industry Association. 2002. *Securities Industry Association Fact Book*. New York: Securities Industry Association.

Snell and Wilmer. 2002. A Guide to the Sarbanes-Oxley Act of 2002, and Recent SEC, NYSE and Nasdaq Rulemaking and Proposals, Snell & Wilmer L.L.P. [online]. (Accessed May 17, 2004.) Available from World Wide Web: <http://www.realcorporatelaw.com/pdfs/sw02.pdf>.

Sonnenfeld, J. A. 2003. Manager's Journal: Meet our Corporate Governance Watchdogs. *Wall Street Journal* March 11: B4.

Sweeney, P. 2004. Taking Off the Blinkers: Analysts Home in on Corporate Governance, Finding Plenty to Question. *The Investment Dealers' Digest* June 21: A1.

Thain, J. 2004. Sarbanes-Oxley: Is the Price too High? *Wall Street Journal* May 27: A20.

Transparency International. 2004. Transparency International Corruption Perceptions Index 2003 [online]. (Accessed May 17, 2004) Available from World Wide Web: <http://www.transparency.org/cpi/2003/cpi2003. en.html>.

Useem, J. 2002. In Corporate America, It's Cleanup Time. *Fortune* September 16: 62–72.

Wall Street Journal. 2003. U.N. Anticorruption Treaty Aims to Ease Retrieval of Dirty Money. December 9: A10.

——. 2004. Long and Short: Corporate Regulation Must be Working—There's a Backlash. June 16: C1.

Wam, K. 2002. Livent Chiefs on Fraud Charges. *Financial Times* October 23: 26.

Ward, R.D. 1997. *21st Century Corporate Board*. New York: John Wiley & Sons.